Ancient Rome's Worst Emperors

Ancient Rome's Worst Emperors

L.J. Trafford

First published in Great Britain in 2023 by
Pen & Sword History
An imprint of Pen & Sword Books Limited
Yorkshire – Philadelphia

Copyright © L.J. Trafford 2023

ISBN 978 1 39908 442 0

The right of L.J. Trafford to be identified as
Author of this Work has been asserted by him in accordance
with the Copyright, Designs and Patents Act 1988.

A CIP catalogue record for this book is
available from the British Library

All rights reserved. No part of this book may be reproduced or
transmitted in any form or by any means, electronic or mechanical
including photocopying, recording or by any information storage and
retrieval system, without permission from the Publisher in writing.

Typeset by Mac Style
Printed in the UK by CPI Group (UK) Ltd, Croydon, CR0 4YY.

Pen & Sword Books Limited incorporates the imprints of After
the Battle, Atlas, Archaeology, Aviation, Discovery, Family History,
Fiction, History, Maritime, Military, Military Classics, Politics,
Select, Transport, True Crime, Air World, Frontline Publishing, Leo
Cooper, Remember When, Seaforth Publishing, The Praetorian Press,
Wharncliffe Local History, Wharncliffe Transport, Wharncliffe True
Crime and White Owl.

For a complete list of Pen & Sword titles please contact

PEN & SWORD BOOKS LIMITED
47 Church Street, Barnsley, South Yorkshire, S70 2AS, England
E-mail: enquiries@pen-and-sword.co.uk
Website: www.pen-and-sword.co.uk
or
PEN AND SWORD BOOKS
1950 Lawrence Rd, Havertown, PA 19083, USA
E-mail: Uspen-and-sword@casematepublishers.com
Website: www.penandswordbooks.com

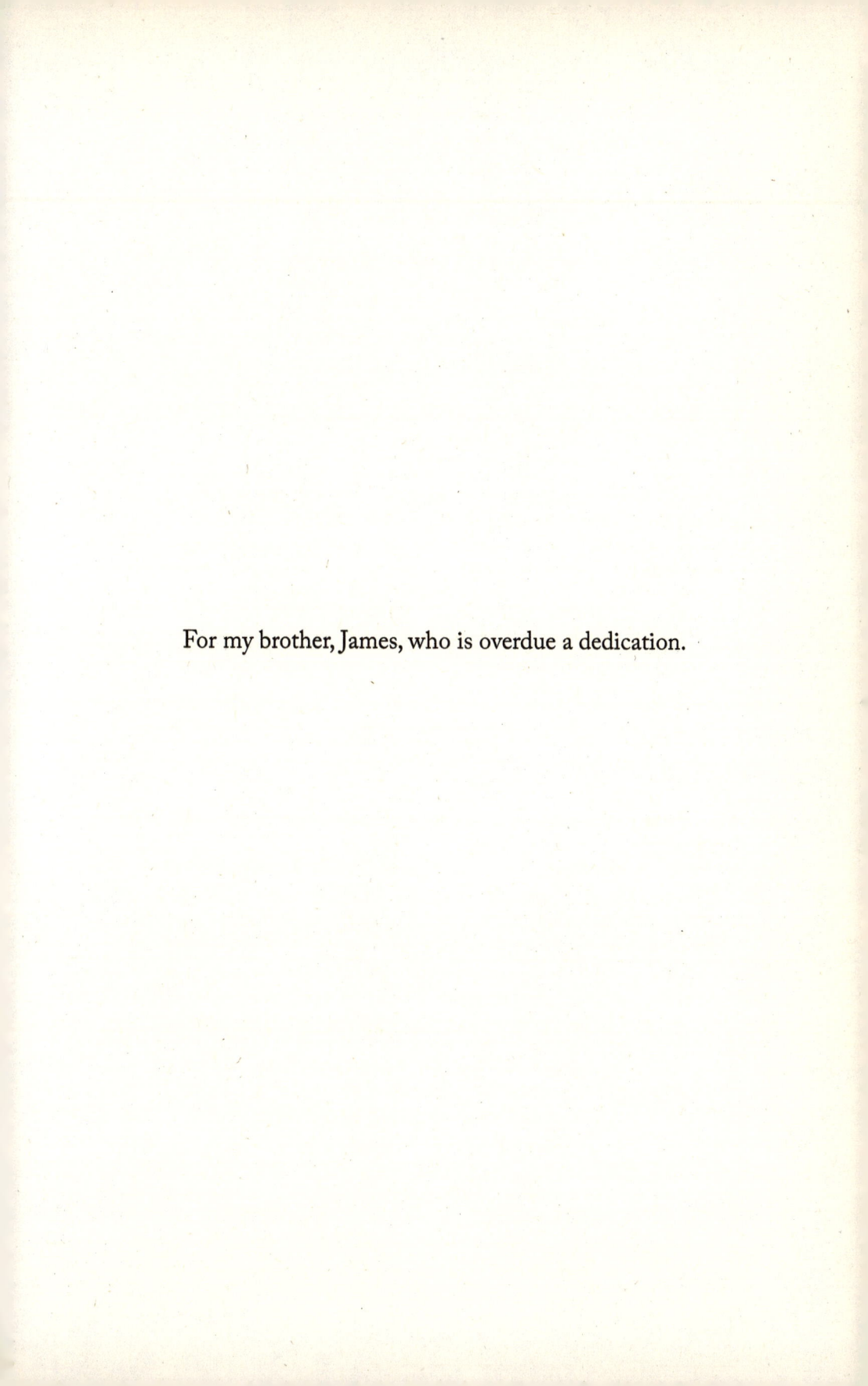

For my brother, James, who is overdue a dedication.

Contents

List of Illustrations ix
Introduction xi

Chapter 1   The Basics – What is an Emperor?   1

Part I: After Augustus. 14 CE–96 CE   17

Chapter 2   Caligula (37–41 CE) How Absolute is Absolute Power?   19

Chapter 3   Galba (68–69 CE) – The Man Who Should be King   43

Chapter 4   Vitellius (69 CE) – No Appetite for Power   50

Chapter 5   Domitian (81–96 CE) – A Swirling Paranoia   61

Part II: Welcome to the Golden Age, 96 CE–222 CE   85

Chapter 6   Nerva (96–98 CE) – The Hinge   87

Chapter 7   Lucius Aurelius Verus (161–169 CE) – Overshadowed   96

Chapter 8   Commodus (180–192 CE) – Monstrous Ego   99

Chapter 9   Didius Julianus (193 CE) – The Man who Brought an Empire   114

Chapter 10   Geta (211 CE) – For-Geta-ble   120

Chapter 11   Elagabalus (218–222 CE) – And Now for Someone Completely Different   128

Part III: The Third Century – Where Any Man Can be Emperor (briefly), 222 CE–284 CE   147

Chapter 12   Gordian I (238 CE) – He Came, He Did Not Conquer and Then He Went   151

viii Ancient Rome's Worst Emperors

| Chapter 13 | Silbannacus (253 CE) – The Phantom Emperor | 155 |
| Chapter 14 | Quintillus (270 CE) – Easy Come, Easy Go | 156 |

Part IV: Sorting It All Out – The Tetrarchy and Beyond, 284 CE–455 CE 159

| Chapter 15 | Valentinian II (375–392 CE) – The Boy Emperor | 164 |
| Chapter 16 | Petronius Maximus (455 CE) – Evil Genius | 171 |

Conclusion	178
Authors Note	179
Notes	180
Bibliography	196
Index	198

List of Illustrations

1. Marble Portrait of Augustus. (*Metropolitan Museum of Art*)
2. Rome: tomb of Augustus. Coloured engraving, c.1804–1811. (*Wellcome Collection*)
3. The Senate House. (*Scott Rowland*)
4. Temple of Mars Ultor in the Forum of Augustus. (*Scott Rowland*)
5. Bust of Caligula. (*Metropolitan Museum of Art*)
6. Bust of Germanicus. (*Digital image courtesy of Getty's Open Content Program*)
7. Bust of Agrippina the Younger. (*Digital image courtesy of Getty's Open Content Program*)
8. Ancient Greek statue of Emperor Galba in the Rotunda Hall at the Pio Clementino Museum in Vatican. (*Baudlin Alexei/Shutterstock*)
9. Speculum Romanae Magnificentiae: Galba, from The Twelve Caesarsca. Marcantonio Raimondi, 1500–1534. (*Metropolitan Museum of Art*)
10. Vitellius bust in red porphyry work of the sixteenth century, vintage engraved illustration. Magasin Pittoresque, 1880. (*Morphant Creation/Shutterstock*)
11. The Emperor Domitian. Claude, Buste Vatican, James Anderson, silver print. (*Digital image courtesy of Getty's Open Content Program*)
12. Garden in the palace of Domitian on the Palatine Hill. (*Scott Rowland*)
13. Stadium, Domitian's palace. (*Scott Rowland*)
14. Statue of a pouring satyr found at Domitian's Alban villa. (*Digital image courtesy of Getty's Open Content Program*)
15. Bust of Julia Titi c.90 AD from the Getty Museum. (*Digital image courtesy of Getty's Open Content Program*)
16. Forum of Nerva. (*Scott Rowland*)
17. Silver print of a Vatican statue of Nerva by James Anderson, 1813–1877. (*Digital image courtesy of Getty's Open Content Program*)
18. Statue of Trajan. (*Author's own*)
19. Marble portrait bust of Lucius Verus. (*Metropolitan Museum of Art*)
20. Equestrian Statue of Marcus Aurelius. Artist: Marco Dente (Italian, Ravenna, active by 1515; died 1527 Rome). (*Metropolitan Museum of Art*)

21. Marble Portrait bust of Faustina the younger. (*Metropolitan Museum of Art*)
22. Bust of Commodus. (*Digital image courtesy of Getty's Open Content Program*)
23. The Emperor Commodus as Hercules. Hendrick Goltzius (Netherlandish, Mühlbracht ,1558–1617 Haarlem). (*Metropolitan Museum of Art*)
24. The wrestler and gladiator Narcissus strangling the Emperor Commodus. Engraving by G. Mochetti after B. Pinelli. (*Wellcome Collection*)
25. Coin of Didius Julianus. (*Wikicomms/Numismatica Ars Classica NAC AG*)
26. Lucius Septimius Severus with his wife, Empress Julia Domna, and sons, Caracalla and Geta, whose face has been removed. Contemporary Roman painting. (*Granger, NYC/Alamy Stock Photo*)
27. Marble portrait bust of Caracalla. (*Metropolitan Museum of Art*)
28. Beryl intaglio with portrait of Julia Domna. (*Metropolitan Museum of Art*)
29. Rome. Italy. Portrait bust of Roman Emperor Elagabalus (203–222 AD), Capitoline Museum. Musei Capitolini. (*Adam Eastland / Alamy Stock Photo*)
30. The Roses of Heliogabalus. (*Heritage Image Partnership Ltd / Alamy Stock Photo*)
31. Marble bust of Alexander Severus. (*Metropolitan Museum of Art*)
32. Bas-relief with the image of the emperor who made a speech to the army. Fragment of an arch of Constantine. Rome. Italy. (*zebra0209/Shutterstock*)
33. Coin of Gordian I. (*Wikicomms/Classical Numismatic Group*)
34. Silver coin. Radiate and cuirassed bust of Silbannacus. (*The Trustees of the British Museum*)
35. Coin of Quintillus (c.270 AD). (*PJRStudio / Alamy Stock Photo*)
36. Fragment of a Togate Statue of Diocletian. (*Digital image courtesy of Getty's Open Content Program*)
37. The Tetrarchs – a Porphyry Sculpture of four Roman Emperors, Sacked from the Byzantine Palace in 1204. Now located on San Marco Square in Venice, Italy. (*ansharphoto/shutterstock*)
38. Statue of the Emperor Valentianus II (371 – 392 AD), Istanbul Archaeological Museum, Turkey. (*Gokhan Dogan/Shutterstock*)
39. Genseric sacking Rome 455 The Sack of Rome, Karl Briullov, 1833–1836. (*Yogi Black / Alamy Stock Photo*)
40. Coin of Petronius Maximus. (*Classical Numismatic Group/Wikicom*)

Introduction

The words 'Roman Emperor' conjure up a variety of images, likely ones of grandeur, excess and the power of life and death dispensed with a thumb pointed downwards in the arena[1]. The eighty-four emperors[2] that ruled Rome between the years 27 BCE and 476 CE ruled over an empire that stretched across continents and encompassed tens of millions of subjects. This was no easy job, to be an emperor was to face a daily inbox brimming with problems that desperately required solutions; barbarian incursions, military mutinies, revolting provinces, troublesome new religions, failed harvests, plague, inflation, riots – not to mention your own officials plotting behind your back to replace you. Being an emperor is hard.

Still, some of the eighty-four men who called themselves emperor proved to be rather good at it: introducing fair laws and sensible reforms, building roads and aqueducts, winning battles and extending Rome's dominion. They left an empire in their successor's hands that was happier, wealthier, and just better. A round of applause to them all.

This book is not concerned with such competence and success, where's the fun in that? Instead, we are going to shine a light on Ancient Rome's worst emperors in a glorious tour of 500 years' worth of terrible bosses. Along the way we shall stumble across the mad, the bad and the criminally ineffectual, taking in the most famous of Rome's rulers and some you've probably never heard of (because they achieved so little that was worth recording for posterity). This is the story of what happens when you hand over unlimited power to someone who is not up to the job. But before we tackle the very worst of Rome's emperors, we need to first answer some basic questions that will help steer our tour through five centuries of truly terrible leaders.

Chapter 1

The Basics – What is an Emperor?

Every history book will tell you that Rome's first emperor was Augustus. However, Augustus himself never referred to himself as emperor and neither did anyone else within his own lifetime. In fact, Augustus took great pains to stress just how much of a non-emperor he was. Writing in his seventy-sixth year, long into what every history book will tell you was his reign, the man himself writes, 'I possessed no more official power than others who were my colleagues'.[1] Up to the moment of his death in 14 CE, Augustus claimed that he had restored the Republican system of government. He hadn't. He'd instituted a monarchy in all but name, and how he did that is quite an extraordinary story.

Augustus wasn't the first man to obtain sole power in Rome, the city had been flirting with single man rule for a long time before it fully committed to it, bought the ring, and booked the venue. The Roman Republic had been founded after the overthrow of Rome's founding monarchy whose seventh king, Tarquinius Superbus, had turned out to be a despotic tyrant. The man who had done the overthrowing was Lucius Junius Brutus, who yes, was the ancestor of that other Brutus fellow who was also big on murdering despots.[2]

This Brutus makes a very stirring speech, 'I swear that with sword and fire, and whatever else can lend strength to my arm, I will pursue Lucius Tarquinius the Proud, his wicked wife, and all his children, and never again will I let them or any other man be King in Rome'.[3] The Republic was a system born out of this sworn intention that Rome would never be ruled by kings again and it wasn't, technically. It was, instead, later to find itself ruled by a series of men who had all the powers of a king, acted like a king, and handed their power onto their offspring, just like a king. They may have called themselves emperors, but kings were what they were.

The Republican system that preceded the age of the emperors had been devised to prevent that exact circumstance, stopping any one man becoming too powerful. In the Republic the top position of consul was shared between two men who were eligible to be consul once in their lifetime and for a single year only. The consuls were supported by a 600 strong body of Rome's greatest citizens (who in an odd coincidence all happened to be men from the same elite and wealthy patrician class) known as the Senate.

This worked terrifically well for close on four hundred years (with the odd blip) as Rome went about conquering a large slice of Europe. However, by the first century BCE this ideal of a perfectly balanced system where no one man could become too powerful was dangerously unbalanced, weighted down by a series of charismatic men who managed, for a short time at least, to achieve what should have been impossible.

How they did this was due to a factor that Brutus the Liberator couldn't have foreseen, Rome's huge standing army. That single year position of consul devised to stop any man becoming too powerful looked great on paper, but in practice it meant there was no continuity of government and long-standing issues did not get resolved.[4] It also created a stratum of ambitious men who having been consul, had achieved all they could politically in Rome. However, out on the fringes of the empire there still lay opportunities for them to obtain further glory by conquering new territory for Rome.

A consul may have only held the post for a single year, but Roman generals served for much longer,[5] time to build quite a rapport with their troops, especially if you were the sort of general who won battles. Anything nabbed from the enemy in the process of achieving glory for Rome fell directly into the money chests of the conquering general and his legionaries. What use was some far-off government with annually interchangeable figures to those legionaries? The answer was very little, their loyalty was to the commander who had enriched them.

A series of such men came to prominence in the first century BCE; Marius, Sulla, Pompey the Great and Julius Caesar being the most famous of these. These charismatic men used the reputations they'd gained from military victories to twist the Republican system to meet their needs. Marius held the consulship a record breaking seven times, something that should have been impossible, but rules were being bent and stretched and broken all over the place. Sulla marched an army into Rome and forced the Senate to grant him the position of dictator, ruling solo for three years. On the streets of Rome itself, disgruntled citizens could be whipped up into a mob by the right man and used to both intimidate rivals and get legislation passed, leading to increasing lawlessness.[6]

Pompey and Caesar teamed up with the richest man in Rome, Marcus Crassus, to form the first triumvirate. This was a secret pact sworn between the three of them to game the Republican system and get the officials they wanted elected, along with plush roles for themselves. Out of this alliance Caesar became governor of Gaul and was so wildly successful in his conquering efforts that Pompey and the Senate feared he would turn his Gaul-conquering army on Rome and seize power like Sulla had. They asked him to hand over that army, instead he marched them across the Rubicon[7] and so began a civil war, one of many in this era, between Caesar and Pompey the Great.

Caesar was the winner of this civil war, and he used the prominence gained from this victory to outdo Sulla by having himself declared dictator for life in February 44 BCE. Caesar could now sit back and relish being sole ruler of Rome. That relishing lasted but a month because in March 44 BCE Julius Caesar was hacked to death outside the theatre named after his rival, Pompey. Which is apt and something that Pompey the Great probably would have liked, had he not been decapitated four years previously.

The killers of Caesar were not shy about their motivations for stabbing their friend in the back – literally. They produced coins commemorating that day in March with the declaration *liberates*, meaning liberty. They believed passionately that by killing Caesar they had saved the Republic from one man rule, and they had… for a short time.

Julius Caesar's attempt at being the sole ruler of Rome had been a short and failed experiment. The next man to try the same would have to be much cleverer about how he went about it to avoid a similar fate to Caesar. He was, as we shall shortly see.

Enter Octavius

In 44 BCE Rome was collapsing. Politically the Republican system of government hadn't worked as it was devised to for decades. The way to get laws passed now was not by making a damn good speech and convincing your fellow senators of your wisdom, it was by hiring your own mob and intimidating them into seeing that wisdom.

A civil war that the city could ill afford so soon after the Pompey/Caesar bunfight was brewing between Caesar's murderers and Caesar's friend and would be avenger, Mark Antony. It was not looking good. Or it wasn't until into this maelstrom of mess walked an 18-year-old boy. His name was Gaius Octavius Thurinius and he was intent on claiming his inheritance as Julius Caesar's heir.[8] Twenty years later a grateful Senate would gift Octavius the name he is far better known by; Augustus.

Octavius/Augustus is the guy who sorts everything out. He does this by using some familiar tactics from the preceding century: getting your army to force the Senate to grant you extraordinary powers that don't fit with the Republican ethos, getting rid of your political enemies, and fighting your former allies to become top dog.

With Brutus and Cassius defeated at the Battle of Philippi in 42 BCE and former friend Mark Antony defeated at the Battle of Actium in 31 BCE, Octavius was the last man standing. He was 31 years old, still young enough to make the rest of us question our life choices and feel distinctly inadequate in comparison. Returning to Rome, Octavius stood before the Senate as the victor of two civil wars and handed back all the powers he'd forced them to give him over the preceding fifteen years.

'In my sixth and seventh consulships [28–27 BC], after I had extinguished civil wars, and at a time when with universal consent I was in complete control of affairs, I transferred the republic from my power to the dominion of the senate and people of Rome.'[9]

In return for receiving these powers back, and for the saving the Republic from the jaws of those charismatic men who sought to dominate it, the Senate reward their benefactor with a shiny new name, Augustus. It means majestic and certainly slips off the tongue much easier than Gaius Octavius Thurinius. We are told that Romulus was suggested, but our boy wonder passed on that one. Romulus had been a king; the newly named Augustus would distance himself from all references to monarchy. It was one of many canny moves.

Let us re-cap, Rome has been embroiled in decades of brutal civil wars and violence which have now ended with the Republic being restored and the Senate taking control of the political system once again. Augustus, the man who has successfully concluded these wars has handed back all the special powers granted to him during this tumultuous period and now goes home, has the Roman equivalent of a nice cup of tea and puts his feet up. Right? Wrong! Of course he bloody doesn't. Because that is not how you get a month named after you.

Setting the bar high – Rome's first emperor

It's called the Augustan Settlement, the mere mention of which is enough to make any ancient history undergraduate groan. The Augustan Settlement, this handing back of power to the Senate, is an extraordinary sleight of hand pulled off by a top-class magician.

'After this time I excelled all in influence [*auctoritas*], although I possessed no more official power [*potestas*] than others who were my colleagues in the several magistracies.'[10]

This is the trick Augustus introduced, to seemingly have no power but yet to exercise power. He called himself *Princeps*, meaning first citizen and for all his protestations of ordinariness he was nothing of the sort. Augustus ran Rome, he ran the Empire whilst all the time protesting that he was not doing so. Two questions naturally occur, how did he do this? And how the hell did he get away with it?

The answer to the first question is that in 27 BCE in that great historic moment when Augustus stood up having ended the civil wars that had plagued Rome for decades and handed back his powers to the Senate, he basically didn't. Or rather he handed some back and then the Senate gave him some extra special other powers that allowed him to do what he wanted to for the next forty years.

One of these powers was, and I'm afraid I'm going to throw some Latin at you, I promise it won't hurt, the *tribunician potestas* – the power of the tribune of the plebs. The tribune of the plebs was a position open to only those of non-patrician background, traditionally. Non-traditionally it was not unknown for the ambitious patrician to downgrade their status so they could be elected to the role. This was exactly what the patrician born Publius Clodius Pulcher did in 59 BCE. That Clodius' new plebeian father was younger than him signposted that this was a purely venal move on the ambitious Clodius' side.[10]

Patricians were supposed to be excluded from the post because the chief role of the tribune of the plebs was to represent the vast non-patrician, non-posh bulk of the Roman population and in effect act as a counterbalance to the oligarchic rule of Rome by the few wealthy families that dominated the Senate.

It was a role born out of violent clashes in the 5th century BCE, the like of which were a permanent mode of expressing public disapproval in Rome. At the heart of the discord was the treatment of plebeians who had fallen into debt, but that was only one grievance amongst many, and those grievances were being fully expressed. The initial response of the authorities was to suppress it quickly (and by quickly we mean brutally) because this period in the Republic was a very busy one with wars going on left, right and centre; wars that couldn't be put on pause to sort out a domestic squabble. Except this squabble escalated into what could be termed full out war, with suspicion and discord and panic on both sides.

Many plebeians fled Rome and holed up on mass on top of the sacred mount. The historian, Livy captures the mood of the time. There was a great panic in the city, and mutual apprehension caused the suspension of all activities. The plebeians, having been abandoned by their friends, feared violence at the hands of the senators; the senators feared the plebeians who were left behind in Rome, being uncertain whether they had rather they stayed or went.'[11]

In this atmosphere of suspicion and fear, there was another concern, 'what would happen next if some foreign war should break out in the interim'?[12] This worry, that Rome wouldn't have enough men to form an army to protect it from the growing numbers of enemies the fledgling power was rapidly accumulating, was what spurred on a solution to the crisis.

'Steps were then taken towards harmony, and a compromise was effected on these terms: the plebeians were to have magistrates of their own, who should be inviolable, and in them should lie the right to aid the people against the consuls, nor should any senator be permitted to take this magistracy.'[13] This magistrate was the tribune of the plebs, a representative for the grievances of the plebeian population of Rome and one that came with some impressive powers.

For instance, it made the holder of the position 'inviolable' which meant to physically attack their body was to commit a terrible crime. Presumably this was introduced to stop the senatorial class simply bumping off any tribune whose policies conflicted with their interests. Not that this worked wholly, for there were tribunes who exactly that happened to, most notably the Gracchi brothers whose efforts to introduce land reform to the benefit of the plebs led to them both being hacked to death by posh boy senators. Literally. Livy tells us that the senators smashed up wooden chairs to provide makeshift weapons for killing Gaius Gracchus.

Symbolic this inviolability might have been, but symbols have power and this one did because it elevated Augustus above his peers in the Senate. However, there were other less symbolic and more practically useful powers that came with the *tribunicia potestas* such as the right to summon assemblies of the people and, crucially, the right to veto any legislation passed by the Senate.

Alongside the *tribunicia potestas* Augustus was granted the governorship of several provinces, including Spain, Gaul, Syria and Egypt. These happened to be the provinces that had Roman legions situated in them. And then as the cherry on the top of this ice cream of powers, the Senate granted Augustus *imperium*. This gave him all the powers of the top job in Rome, the consulship, whilst allowing him to also claim, 'the consulship was also offered to me, to be held each year for the rest of my life, and I refused it'.[14] This is the Augustan magic trick in action, having power whilst publicly denying that you have it.

The *tribunicia potestas* gives Augustus power to gather and address the people whenever he wants, to veto any law he does not like and neither the Senate nor anybody else can lay a finger on him or face dire consequences. The governorship of certain provinces gives Augustus access to more legions and men than the Roman state has. *Imperium* gives him the power of a consul to introduce legislation. Can you see how he does it now?

The Roman historian Tacitus lays out some of the other ways that Augustus consolidated those powers granted to him. 'The army was seduced with bonus, the civilians with cheap food and the senatorial elite by way of promotion both politically and financially if they toed the official line. Then he gradually pushed ahead and absorbed the functions of the Senate, the officials and even the law.'[15]

In Augustus' own words he tells us how he used that right to appoint magistrates he'd been granted, 'I increased the number of patricians on the instructions of the people and the Senate. I revised the roll of the Senate three times'.[16] Revised the Senate to include allies and those who would do what he said, is the unspoken line here. He also used his power to usher in his relatives to key political positions, often years before they were technically eligible. We find Augustus' stepsons, Tiberius and Drusus standing as quaestors and praetors five years before the minimum age. Tiberius was first consul aged 29, eleven years before the minimum age. Augustus' grandsons, Gaius and Lucius achieved positions even younger, becoming consuls at only 14 years old.

All these relatives were sent to the provinces in various capacities. Drusus was a skilled military commander achieving triumphs against the endlessly troublesome German tribes. Gaius was sent east to help smooth over a tricky accession to the Judaean throne. Tiberius had been sent on a diplomatic mission to Parthia to retrieve the standards lost by Marcus Crassus.[17] This further cemented Augustus and his family, and not the Senate, as the key power in Rome for those in the provinces. There, government by Senate and People was looked upon sceptically as a matter of sparring dignitaries and extortionate officials. The legal system had provided no remedy against this, since it was wholly incapacitated by violence, favouritisms and most of all bribery.'[18]

The provinces got onboard with the Augustan trick because it was an improvement on what had come before, and that sort of answers our second question, doesn't it? How did Augustus get away with it, get away with making himself a king in a city that despised kings? The answer is because, like the provinces found, it was better than what had come before. For Rome this, as Tacitus says, was, 'the enjoyable gift of peace'.

Peace not just from the brutal civil wars that Augustus had ended but also from the decades of political instability, violence and factions that had marred the Late Republican era. The two key factions of that era, the *optimates* and the *populares*[19] had been so busy blocking each other's laws and opposing each other's beliefs that nothing had got done. Augustus got things done. The man never bloody stopped, he was a whirlwind dynamo of reform, of building, of just doing stuff and doing it well. It is this 'stuff' that gives us a blueprint for what a good emperor should be doing.

What makes a good emperor? Part 1: Doing Stuff

We are extremely lucky in that we have a document written by Augustus himself; I've used quotes from it several times already in this chapter. It was known as the *Res Gestae Divi Augustus*, the deeds of the divine Augustus, and it is a list of all the achievements that Rome's first emperor wanted to be recorded for posterity. These were inscribed onto the bronze pillars which stood outside his final resting place in Rome, the mausoleum of Augustus. Copies of these divine deeds were made and distributed throughout the empire so that nobody missed out on all the wonderful stuff that their emperor had been up to. That so many copies were made is how the text has come down to us.

Reading the *Res Gestae* for the first time is an interesting experience, the boastful tone is at odds with our modern sensibilities where achievements must be downplayed, and we must act humble and grateful when rightfully rewarded. Watch any Oscar acceptance speech and you will hear actors who have been judged by their peers to be the absolute best in their job, crediting and thanking others for their success.[20]

Augustus credits no one else for his successes. He uses 'I' 122 times in a text that is only 3,861 words long, proving that he has no time for eating humble pie, as is made clear by his opening line: 'At the age of nineteen [44 BC] on my own responsibility and at my own expense I raised an army, with which I successfully championed the liberty of the republic when it was oppressed by the tyranny of a faction'.[21] A singular sentence that is capable of rendering every reader over twenty feeling instantly inadequate. But that's just his opener!

What then follows is thirty-five paragraphs of things that he, Augustus, has personally done. They range from waging war to winning peace, from epic building projects to land settlements for retired soldiers and an impossible to ignore list of all the times the Senate felt compelled to award him with some sort of honour. There are so many of these and they are all zingers, but this one sums up these honouring occasions most perfectly. 'The senate resolved that an altar of the Augustan Peace should be consecrated next to the Campus Martius in honour of my return and ordered that the magistrates and priests and Vestal virgins should perform an annual sacrifice there.'[22]

Augustus is just an ordinary guy with no more powers than anyone else and gosh yes, the Senate runs everything but hey bring on the animals because it's time for that sacrifice we perform every year to him alone. That'll be the annual sacrifice that runs alongside, 'all the citizens, individually and on behalf of their towns, have unanimously and continuously offered prayers at all the pulvinaria for my health'.[23]

The tone of the *Res Gestae* can be summarised as "I'm brilliant at everything. Marvel". But the thing is, Augustus really is and yes, you can't help but marvel at what he managed to get done during his forty years in power. It is impressive and it leaves us a blueprint, in fact a guide to what a good emperor should do and be (certainly not humble, that's for sure). So let us put all those cringy feelings behind us and dig into what Augustus did that was brilliant and marvel at it.

'Since the city was not adorned as the dignity of the empire demanded, and was exposed to flood and fire, he so beautified it that he could justly boast that he had found it built of brick and left it in marble.'[24] So says biographer of the Caesars, Suetonius, and he's not wrong. Augustus certainly took it upon himself to renovate Rome. In the *Res Gestae* he dedicates three whole paragraphs to his building projects; he builds a forum and temples, theatres and roads, there are repairs to aqueducts and a basilica began by Julius Caesar. All public buildings.

Another way Augustus endears himself to the public, the ordinary folk of Rome is by giving them wads of cash (from his own pocket, he claims). The *Res Gestae* is spotted with statements like this one. 'To each member of the Roman plebs I paid under my father's will 300 sesterces.'[25] Those 300 sesterces (which is no small amount of money) is just the starter, the people of Rome are repeatedly treated from Augustus' deep pockets. In his fourth consulship they all get 400 sesterces each (again no small amount of money) and again in his eleventh consulship and a further 400 sesterces are handed out another time with the aside from Mr Humble First Citizen: 'these largesses of mine never reached fewer than 250,000 persons'.[26]

You can work out the maths for yourself, but just in case you don't have a calculator handy I'll help you out, it's 100,000,000 sesterces. As you can tell by the number of zeros this is a HUGE amount of money, and he does this three times. But this is not the end of it, there are further sums of 260 sesterces handed out to 320,000 people, 1000 sesterces (a whole year's pay) handed out 120,000 soldiers and 60 denarii handed out to 200,000 people.

But Augustus is not just generous with hard cash, oh no, he also handed out food to the people. 'From the consulship of Gnaeus and Publius Lentulus [18 BC] onwards, whenever the taxes did not suffice, I made distributions of grain and money from my own granary and patrimony, sometimes to 100,000 persons, sometimes to many more.'[27]

The *Res Gestae* equates Augustus' generosity with grain as akin to all those sesterces he was dolling out and it was, grain was crucially important in ancient Rome. There was a grain dole, a state led programme that handed out free grain to the poorest citizens in the city, thought to number around

200,000 people. That is a large chunk of people reliant on a subsidised food programme, it's also a large chunk of people who might get terribly tetchy if they didn't receive their free grain. Actually, there's no might about it, they do get terribly tetchy, as the emperor Claudius discovered: 'when there was a scarcity of grain because of long-continued droughts, he was once stopped in the middle of the Forum by a mob and so pelted with abuse and at the same time with pieces of bread, that he was barely able to make his escape to the Palace by a back door; and after this experience he resorted to every possible means to bring grain to Rome, even in the winter season'.[28]

This is the bread, lets now talk about the circus – that other way to keep the Roman population happy. We know this to be an important function of a Roman ruler because Augustus dedicates two paragraphs of the *Res Gestae* listing all the Games he held and/or sponsored. 'I gave three gladiatorial games in my own name and five in that of my sons or grandsons; at these games some 10,000 men took part in combat'[29] he boasts before going onto mention the twenty-seven other times he put on shows. The bread and circuses provided by Mr Deep Pockets kept the populace happy.

Another group that had to be kept happy were the army, these were the men whose support had propelled Augustus to the position he was in. Having lived through the dying days of the Republican system Augustus could not fail to realise that this support was not unconditional, it was very much conditional and if he didn't buy it then it was very much open to someone else to do so. Hence, we find multiple references in the *Res Gestae* about rewarding the army. 'I settled rather more than 300,000 of these in colonies or sent them back to their hometowns after their period of service; to all these I assigned lands or gave money as rewards for their military service.'[30] As with the plebeian population of Rome, Augustus digs deep into his own (perhaps) pockets for the soldiers. 'In my fifth consulship I gave 1,000 sesterces out of booty to every one of the colonists drawn from my soldiers; about 120,000 men in the colonies received this largesse at the time of my triumph.'[31] Just as with the civilian population, this is just one of many passages listing how damn generous Augustus is.

But there was another way that the army could be kept happy – conquering. 'The Pannonian peoples, whom the army of the Roman people never approached before I was the leading citizen, were conquered.'[33] Elsewhere Augustus notes the Dacian army who were compelled 'to submit to the commands of the Roman people'. That he 'added Egypt to the empire of the Roman people'[45] and 'extended the territory of all those provinces of the Roman people on whose borders lay peoples not subject to our government'.[34]

The Basics – What is an Emperor? 11

He says he brought peace to the Gallic, Spanish and German provinces, let us assume by the usual Roman method of brutally subjugating the locals until they 'decide' to be peaceful. He takes the Roman army where the Roman army had never been before, deeper into Africa and what is now modern-day Sudan, and exploring further into the Arabia peninsular, getting as far as what is now Yemen.[35] Not content with spreading peace over land, Augustus tackles the big blue wavy thing in-between provinces. 'I made the sea peaceful and freed it of pirates.'[36] Which necessitates an ooh-arrr me hearties but was actually a deadly serious task and one of great benefit to the empire. It made sea travel safer which encouraged more of the trade that enriched Rome and kept the luxury goods flowing into the homes of the city's mega wealthy.

This busy peace (war) making had a point behind it, not only did the extension of provinces keep the soldiers busy, but it also brought in valuable hard cash and added to the reputation of Rome as an all-conquering power. An all-conquering power thanks to Augustus, as he is not shy of saying.

It's not all war though, alongside the enforced relations with the world outside Rome, the *Res Gestae* is keen to stress the unenforced, we might even say diplomatic relations forged under Augustus' rule. 'Embassies from kings in India were frequently sent to me never before had they been seen with any Roman commander. The Bastarnae, Scythians and the kings of the Sarmatians on either side of the river Don, and the kings of the Albanians and the Iberians and the Medes sent embassies to seek our friendship.'[37] These similarly add to Rome's reputation and the wealth that comes from opening new trade routes.

What makes a good emperor? Part 2: Character

We have looked at the sort of things that a good emperor should do; from grand building projects, to putting on fabulous games, achieving military glory, and onwards to the more practical ensuring the people have full stomachs. But as well as being a do-er there was something else less tangible that made a good emperor: his character. Although character is not the word, the word we are going to employ is a Latin one that does not easily translate: *virtus*. The word virtue comes from *virtus* but its meaning is far richer.

Virtus comes from *vir* meaning man and is a collection of attributes that Romans believed made the ideal man. There are rather a lot of them, fourteen in fact, as defined by the Emperor Marcus Aurelius. These were *Auctoritas* (Spiritual authority, knowing one's place), *Comitas* (humour), *Clementia* (mercy), *Dignitas* (dignity), *Firmitas* (tenacity), *Frugalitas* (frugalness), *Gravitas* (gravity), *Honestas* (respectability), *Humanitas* (humanity, kindness), *Industria* (industriousness), *Pietas* (dutifulness), *Prudentia* (prudence), *Salubritas* (wholesomeness), *Severitas* (sternness, discipline), and *Veritas* (truthfulness).

However, these fourteen are not the end of *virtus*, there were many other qualities that the Roman male should aspire to as well, such as *spes* (hope), *concordia* (harmony), *felicitas* (happiness), *fides* (confidence), *securitas* (safety), and *liberalitas* (generosity).

Virtus was of crucial importance, and some anxiety it must be said, for the Roman upper-class male. The second-century Roman doctor, Galen suggested that you have somebody follow you round to point out all the times you were failing miserably in your *virtus* quest. A move which even he admits will, in its early stages, be, 'difficult and will be accomplished only at the cost of much evident unhappiness'.[38] That a doctor, in between prescribing hot baths and making pigs squeal[40] takes the time to write about how to improve your *virtus* quota demonstrates how important *virtus* was, it was part of your body along with your soul, which Galen also writes extensively about.

Let us look back to the man who defines what an emperor should be, Augustus, but this time with our *virtus* glasses and note how he demonstrates *virtus* on the job.

Auctoritas (spiritual authority, knowing one's place): 'The senate and people of Rome agreed that I should be appointed supervisor of laws and morals without a colleague and with supreme power, but I would not accept any office inconsistent with the custom of our ancestors'.[40]

Comitas (humour): 'His friend Maecenas, whose "unguent-dripping curls», as he calls them, he loses no opportunity of belabouring and pokes fun at them by parody'.[41]

Clementia (mercy), 'When foreign peoples could safely be pardoned, I preferred to preserve rather than to exterminate them'.[42]

Iustitia (justice): 'I drove into exile the murderers of my father, avenging their crime through tribunals established by law'.[43]

Frugalitas (frugalness): The simplicity of his furniture and household goods may be seen from couches and tables still in existence, many of which are scarcely fine enough for a private citizen. They say that he always slept on a low and plainly furnished bed. Except on special occasions he wore common clothes for the house made by his sister, wife, daughter or granddaughter'.[44]

Industria (industriousness): I could quote the entire Res Gestae here for it is nothing but Augustus being industrious, but I shall limit myself to this paragraph of busyness, which leaves me exhausted just reading it, 'I restored the Capitol and the theatre of Pompey, both works at great expense without inscribing my own name on either. I restored the channels of the aqueducts, which in several places were falling into disrepair through age, and I brought water from a new spring into the aqueduct called Marcia, doubling the supply. I completed the Forum Julium and the basilica between the temples of Castor and Saturn, works begun and almost finished by my father, and when that same basilica was destroyed by fire [AD 12], I began to rebuild it on an enlarged site'.[45]

Severitas (sternness, discipline): 'I captured about 30,000 slaves who had escaped from their masters and taken up arms against the republic, and I handed them over to their masters for punishment'.[46]

Honestas (respectability): 'By new laws passed on my proposal I brought back into use many exemplary practices of our ancestors which were disappearing in our time, and in many ways I myself transmitted exemplary practices to posterity for their imitation'.[47]

The laws he is referring to here are the *Lex Julia* and *Poppaea* which were concerned with public morals, and which incentivised marriage and childbearing whilst getting properly tough on adultery.

We have looked at what makes a good emperor in terms of what he does and his character. However, there is one other thing you need to do to secure yourself a good emperor ranking, something that Augustus certainly ensured when he composed the *Res Gestae:* a good write up.

What makes a good emperor? Part 3: Leaving a legacy

Augustus wasn't leaving anything to chance when it came to making sure his deeds weren't forgotten, he had them chiselled in stone and distributed across the Empire. Having your name engraved in five-foot high letters on a temple is also a handy way of making sure that no-one forgets it was you and nobody else who forked out the cash to build it. You will find emperors names stamped on everything from amphitheatres, to temples, to aqueducts, to roads as one big cry of I DID THIS.

Within his own lifetime an emperor had tools at his disposal to present himself as a good emperor, from the temple stamping mentioned above, to flattering statues that showed him in heroic poses, to coins minted with the attributes he'd decided he possessed and onwards to commissioning poetry that listed all his achievements and how wonderful he was.[48] There's also those handy treason laws that can be deployed on anyone who says something mean about you.

However, once you are dead those tools are no longer in your possession, and here enters a category of men who are directly responsible for most of what we think we know about Roman emperors – historians. The historian can single-handedly demolish the good works of an emperor with one memorable anecdote. Mud sticks, entertaining mud more so.

If I asked you what you know about the Emperor Nero, I'm betting that the peace brokered with the Parthian Empire over the status of Armenia, the initiative to prevent forgery and the distribution of 400 sesterces to every citizen of the city won't feature. Mother shagging and fiddling during an inferno likely will – neither of which have any basis in fact. But that there is the power of the historian, they can make you believe the unbelievable and so taint the reputation of an emperor for all eternity.

Much like we are setting out to do in this book, Roman historians have a checklist of what makes a good emperor, and it includes many of the same things we have identified; military success, building projects, possessing a good character etc. But whether credit is given for these achievements is coloured by the historian's own biases. Roman historians come from one slice of society; they are all freeborn, they are all male and they are all members of either the equestrian or senatorial class, both of which you need a substantial fortune to enter.[49]

We've talked about how a good emperor needs to keep the army and the people happy, but we need to add one more group to this list: the senatorial class. Because they are the chaps who will be likely writing about you. Upset them and you may well find your name attached to all manner of falsehoods.

The legacy that Augustus left his successors did not make this task of keeping the Senate happy easy. As we have seen, Augustus held power without holding any official position. He proclaims again and again that he is equal to his senatorial colleagues, he's not, he knows it and they know it, but they are prepared to play along with this delusion for several reasons – the key one being they really don't have any choice in the matter.

However, Roman politics is nothing if not brutally good at cutting men down who get above their station (literally) and Augustus would have met Julius Caesar's fate long ago if it had not been for two things: (1) he's really very good at the job and offered a much better deal than what had gone before; and (2) he makes an enormous show of respecting the Senate and publicly acts as if they are still in charge of the Roman state, whilst privately making sure whatever laws they make and whatever they vote on is what he wants.

It's another Augustus magic trick. But it works. The Senate feels empowered even whilst knowing they have no power. Treating them with respect and deference and honour is enough to encourage them to play along with the delusion. It's a delicate balancing act the success of which depends entirely on the personality of the man in charge. Augustus possessed the necessary guile, cunning, brutality, intelligence and, crucially, charisma to pull this trick off. His successors were not all so blessed, some of them even refused to play the game at all, dropping the pretence that they were anything but a king and the Senate their supplicants. They will be featuring heavily in our list of worst emperors.

Aside from offering fake deference and respect there is another much simpler way of keeping the senatorial class on your side. It's so simple you'd think every emperor would easily remember to do it, but you'd be amazed how often it completely slips their mind: not to execute members of the Senate. Because this is the thing that upsets them the most and they get really cross about it in prose. You'll be hard pressed to find them getting upset about the execution of any other class of person, as the historian Brian W. Jones notes, 'the death penalty was regarded by senators as obnoxious only when it applied to them'.[50]

Aside from keeping the senatorial class happy enough to give you a top-notch review for posterity, there is another keyway to ensure you're bigged-up after your death: make sure you have a successor to sing your praises and, if you're lucky, make you into a god.[51] As we shall shortly see, the emperors with the very worst reputations are the ones that had nobody waiting to step into their sandals.

What makes a worst emperor?

We have explored what type of character a good emperor needed to possess, we've explored what a good emperor needed to do, and we've explored who a good emperor needed to keep on side. But this book is not called Ancient Rome's Best Emperors, it's Ancient Rome's Worst Emperors, so let's get onto them and ask: what makes a worst emperor?

Well clearly one in opposition to all that we've described above; the anti-*virtus*, the non-do-er if you will, the please yourself and nobody else fellow. An emperor whose lack of *virtus* leaves a legacy of scandalous stories rather than good works. An emperor who shows no respect towards the army, Senate and people of Rome. An emperor who arguably leaves Rome in a worst state than he found it.

There are manifold reasons why emperors fail at being good, sometimes the deck of cards they are presented with as emperor is so dire that not even Augustus could have got out of that mess with his reputation intact. It's a near impossible job to build that infrastructure, put on those crowd-pleasing games and demonstrate how much *clementia* you possess when the barbarians are literally at the gates and imminent destruction waggling its fingers in your face.

They might have accidentally stumbled (and by stumbled we mean done something nasty to the previous emperor involving his death) into the position with no real training on how to do the job. Couple that with a lack of any discernible talent or useful skill set and you have the makings of a worst emperor there.

Or they might just have been so distracted by the perks of being emperor, the endless banqueting, the palace entertainment on offer and the unimaginable wealth, that they forgot to do any of the do-ing that would have made their name. No doubt killer hangovers are behind a lot of building projects that didn't happen, games that didn't get staged and wars that didn't get fought. We've all been there.

At the far extreme we have the men who took to the role as an all-powerful monarch a little too well, the emperors who discarded the Augustan cloak of being Mr Ordinary and went full out on being an unipotent monarch who could do whatever they wanted to whoever they wanted whenever they wanted, their grip on reality slipping away like an eel escaping the cooking pot.

Now that we are fully armed with what an emperor is and how to spot both a good and bad one, let us leap in and find some examples of the very worst who held the position. But stop! Before we jump into the abyss of truly terrible leaders making awful decisions and ruining everything, a quick word on selecting our worst emperors.

Over the 500 years of its history the Roman Empire changes a great deal, as does the role of emperor. To compare an emperor who ruled in the first century CE with one that ruled in the fifth century CE is like comparing Margaret Thatcher's record as Prime Minister with that of Queen Elizabeth I's rule. There are no useful comparisons. Therefore, we shall not be making any. Instead, I have selected our worst emperors from across the sweep of Roman history, hopefully to provide a variety of ways in which an emperor can be categorised as worst, but also, to illuminate how the role and the man required to hold it changed over time. This may mean that your favourite psychotically unhinged emperor does not feature, because I've already covered a similar psychotically unhinged emperor. But as Rome's first emperor Augustus would have said (at home out of the ear shot of historians), 'Suck it up – I'm in charge'!

Part I

After Augustus. 14 CE–96 CE

We have seen that Augustus never claimed to be a king or an emperor or a ruler of any sort. What Augustus had created was not the position of emperor, it was a collection of powers granted to him by the Senate that used together allowed him to take charge of Rome and her empire. Technically Rome is still a Republic, with the Senate as the ruling body in charge of running everything, it just happens that their views on running everything happen to exactly coincide with Augustus' views on how things should be run.

Which is all very jolly and works brilliantly whilst the master magician is alive but there is lurking underneath this brilliant magic trick, a fundamental problem and one that is going to be at the heart of a lot of trauma Rome will suffer in the future – if there is no job of emperor how can you hand it over to a successor?

Taking over – the succession

This was the problem that faced Rome's second emperor. His name was Tiberius, and at 55 years old with decades of public service behind him and a series of military roles, he was better qualified than anyone to step into his stepfather, Augustus' sandals. Tiberius was the first test of whether this nebulous role of emperor that Augustus had created would outlive him. In a way Tiberius is more important to Augustus' legacy than anything the great man had ever done himself. The *Res Gestae* certainly wouldn't have stood proudly displaying his achievements for centuries if there hadn't been a Tiberius to protect it.

Tiberius succeeded Augustus as the first citizen of Rome, but he might not have, the whole edifice that Augustus had created could have crumbled at that point. But it doesn't crumble. Tiberius successfully inherited Augustus' position in the Roman state, nebulous as it was, and ruled for twenty-three years dying in 37 CE. He left an Empire with strong borders and a treasury plump with coinage, which is to his credit. Augustus could not have chosen a better successor to secure his legacy, the emperors that followed would not be so fortunate in their choice of successor and that included Tiberius himself.

Chapter 2

Caligula (37–41 CE)
How Absolute is Absolute Power?

You'll have been expecting to see this name, perhaps you even brought this book solely for it, because Caligula is what we all picture a worst emperor to be; a deranged, sadistic ruler who delights in torture and humiliation. An unhinged king convinced of his own divinity, to whose increasing bizarre tune all must dance to. Caligula raises an interesting ethical dilemma in all of us: what would you do? Would you play along with his madness to survive, or would you risk a horrible death by stepping up and saying what everyone knows to be true?

He is memorably played by John Hurt in I Claudius, is the inspiration behind nasty King Joffrey in Game of Thrones, gets a reference in a Smiths' song and stars as a murderous wax work in a Madame Tussauds-style attraction gone horribly awry in an episode of the sci-fi sitcom, Red Dwarf. He was even the subject of a truly awful soft porn movie, which you may be pleased to hear we will be covering in more detail later in this chapter. Caligula is the ultimate and undisputed poster boy of what a worst emperor is.

If Tiberius was the first emperor to test whether Augustus' magic trick could be passed on, in Rome's third emperor we find a ruler unwilling to play the magician at all. Caligula comprehensively yanked back the curtain to reveal what everyone knew to be true but did not say: this was a monarchy, and he was the king.

In the five short years that Caligula ruled as emperor he would repeatedly test what that word meant and more particularly what power it gave him and how far that power stretched. Were there any limits to what an emperor could do? Caligula was a man on a mission to find out. Along the way we will gather up stories of such depravity and seeming insanity that they defy belief and very nearly description. But I am a writer, so I have dug deep into my thesaurus and given it my best shot.

The Great Hope

Tiberius died unloved by the Roman people. A successful administrator, he was a morose, gloomy man who had lacked the charisma of his stepfather Augustus. He had left the treasury full and the borders of the empire strong but had won few friends during his time as emperor. The Senate had more than enough reason to be glad of Tiberius' death, his reign had been marred by an increasing tornado of treason trials that had seen many of their number accused of disloyalty and facing exile, sometimes even death.

The opportunity to get rid of a political rival, bathe in the warm glow of the emperor's appreciation for saving him from terrible danger and get rich in the process[1] was a chariot everyone wanted to leap upon. And leap they did. This is evident in how ridiculous treason accusations get, with everyone trying to get a slice of an emperor-pleasing pie that was only ever meant to feed three or maybe four people. Biographer, Suetonius neatly summarises how wafer-thin these slithers of pie got. 'Acts as these were regarded as capital crimes: to beat a slave near a statue of Augustus, or to change one's clothes there; to carry a ring or coin stamped with his image into a privy or a brothel, or to criticize any word or act of his. Finally, a man was put to death merely for allowing an honour to be voted to him in his native town on the same day that honours had previously been voted to Augustus.'[2]

As you can imagine this didn't make for a comfortable working atmosphere for the senators who lived in daily terror of causing accidental offence to the emperor, and presumably took to holding very bad dinner parties with terrible food and atrocious entertainment to demonstrate that a quarter of their wealth really wasn't worth the effort of a court case.

This oppressive atmosphere even affected the emperor, who decided he'd much rather be on the Island of Capri having fun[3] rather than be forced to listen to endless accounts of which of his loyal senators were plotting against him/hated him/had a wee whilst holding an image of his dead stepfather. It was all a bit much for Tiberius and he never returned to Rome from his island holiday home.

Having been absent for a whole decade it was hardly surprising the ordinary people of Rome did not mourn this emperor who had abandoned them. On hearing of his death, they sang to the Tiber with Tiberius. While others, more bitter, 'prayed to Mother Earth and the Manes to allow the dead man no abode except among the damned'.[4]

With his cryptic nature, his gloomy demeanour and, in later years, a disfiguring skin condition, Tiberius could not win, nor did he care to win the affection of the people he ruled. Any affection they might have once harboured for their emperor had been comprehensively lost by his persecution of Agrippina, Augustus' granddaughter, and her family. Agrippina had been implicated in a plot against Tiberius, as had her two sons Nero and Drusus. All three had been exiled and all three had died horribly on their island prisons, a crime the ordinary people of Rome would not forgive Tiberius for. Not least when it transpired the supposed plot Agrippina had been involved in was the invention of Tiberius' own aggressively ambitious Praetorian Prefect, Sejanus. She was not the only one to perish because of Sejanus' lies.[5] Tiberius died in 37 CE, aged 77 years. He had ruled for twenty-three years. Rome was ready and eager for new blood.

This new blood came in the shape of Agrippina's only surviving son, Gaius. In 37 CE he was only 24 years old and with none of the training Tiberius had brought to the role of emperor. But what he lacked in experience he made up for in his superior lineage through his mother Agrippina but also his father Germanicus, a military hero (and grandnephew to Augustus) who died in very mysterious circumstances during Tiberius' reign[6].

Agrippina was a woman of unassailable virtue according to the historian Tacitus and on Germanicus, Suetonius has this to say, 'it is the general opinion that Germanicus possessed all the highest qualities of body and mind, to a degree never equalled by anyone; a handsome person, unequalled valour, surpassing ability in the oratory and learning of Greece and Rome, unexampled kindliness, and a remarkable desire and capacity for winning men's regard and inspiring their affection'.[7] A glowing portrait only slightly tempered by Suetonius' next line, 'his legs were too slender for the rest of his body'. Which is reassuring for the rest of us less than perfect people.

This new emperor is referred to by our ancient sources always as Gaius, but we today know him by another name, Caligula. Caligula was a nickname given to him by the Rhine legions his father was commanding at the time of his birth. They treated the infant Gaius as somewhat of a mascot and made him a pair of miniature military sandals to wear. Caligula translates as something along the lines of Little Boots or Bootykins. We will stick with using Caligula even if the man himself never called himself that, because it's how he is referred to in our era and it saves confusion. But also, because it somehow makes the cruelty and malice he later displays all the more chilling when committed by a man named Bootykins.

This new emperor came from good blood, you might even say the best blood – that of the mighty Augustus. He followed an emperor who had lost the loyalty of the Senate and the love of his people, a rule that had been marred by treason trials and executions. Things could only get better, and for a time they were. 'He fulfilled the highest hopes of the Roman people, or I may say of all mankind, since he was the prince most earnestly desired by the great part of the provincials and soldiers, many of whom had known him in his infancy, as well as by the whole body of the city populace, because of the memory of his father Germanicus and pity for a family that was all but extinct.'[8] So says our Imperial biographer, Suetonius. On accompanying Tiberius' body back to Rome this new emperor was met 'by a dense and joyful throng, who called him besides other propitious names their 'star', their 'chick', their 'babe', and their 'nursling'.'[9] The gloomy Tiberius certainly never attracted such cutesy pet names!

One of Caligula's first acts as emperor was to retrieve the ashes of his cruelly abused mother and brothers and pay them the respect they should have had as the family of Augustus. 'He appointed funeral sacrifices, too, to be offered each year with due ceremony, as well as games in the Circus in honour of his mother, providing a carriage to carry her image in the procession.'[10] For his father he renamed September, Germanicus. His grandmother Antonia was given honours equivalent to those Augustus' wife, Livia had enjoyed.

His surviving family members, the ones who had escaped Sejanus' purge of the Imperial family, were his three sisters Julia Livillia, Drusilla and Agrippina the Younger. He had their names included in all oaths. 'And I will not hold myself and my children dearer than I do Gaius and his sisters' as well as in the propositions of the consuls 'favour and good fortune attend Gaius Caesar and his sisters'.[11] They also appear on coins depicted as Securitas, Concordia and Fortuna – the Goddesses of security/stability, agreement/harmony and fortune/luck. This was what Caligula intended to achieve for Rome as emperor and he soon got cracking on that emperor checklist left by his great grandfather, Augustus.

Suetonius provides us with quite the ample list of the good deeds undertaken by the new emperor. There are a series of measures designed to keep the senators happy; those who had been unfairly banished by Tiberius were recalled, power was handed back to magistrates to make decisions without needing to appeal to the emperor, and in a move that drew a clear line between his reign and the previous one he declared, 'that he had no ears for informers'.[12] Those senators must have felt giddy with relief and glee. The dark days were truly over.

As the Suetonius quote used to open this section showed, Caligula had won over the people before he even reached Rome from Capri merely by not being Tiberius and by being the son of Germanicus and Agrippina. Neither of which he had any personal hand in. But even though he was the recipient of instant adoration, Caligula strove to keep his people happy. He did this via some truly magnificent games, some of which lasted from early morning to late evening. There were stage plays 'of various kinds and in many different places, sometimes even by night, lighting up the whole city'[13] says Suetonius somewhat vaguely, possibly because Caligula put on so many plays that it was too much effort to chronicle them all, or he just doesn't care enough about the theatre to even try.

In between chariot races Caligula introduced a new sport – panther baiting. Which sounds truly horrific to our modern ears but was the sort of thing Romans got off on. And if horribly killing panthers wasn't entertaining enough for you, Caligula had more to give. 'Furthermore, to make a permanent addition to the public gaiety, he added a day to the Saturnalia, and called it Juvenalis.'[14] Would that our own leaders have such concern for the gaiety of their public!

Another popular move was expelling, 'the sexual perverts called spintriae',[15] as Suetonius puts it without explanation, so feel free to insert your own depravity here. But probably his most popular move with the ordinary people of Rome was his deep pockets, Suetonius tells us: 'He twice gave the people a largess of three hundred sesterces each'.[16] Historian, Cassius Dio has a slightly differing total. 'To the people he paid over the forty-five millions bequeathed to them, and, in addition, the two hundred and forty sesterces apiece which they had failed to receive on the occasion of his receiving the toga virilis, together with interest amount to sixty sesterces.'[17] But no matter this inconsistency, the point being made is the same, Caligula was bloody generous and not just to the people, he didn't forget the Praetorian Guard in this bonanza of coinage – they received 1000 sesterces each.

So that's the Senate happy, the people happy, the Praetorians happy. The new emperor was following Augustus' 'How to be an Emperor' playbook to the letter, and this included the bit about building stuff. 'He completed the public works which had been half finished under Tiberius, namely the temple of Augustus and the theatre of Pompey. He likewise began an aqueduct in the region near Tibur and an amphitheatre beside the Saepta'.[18]

It's all going marvellously, isn't it? Caligula has won round all the groups an emperor needs to. He is enormously popular due to his generosity both in hard coinage and in throwing lavish entertainments. He's introduced popular new measures to recall the unfairly punished and punished the irritatingly undefined perverts. He has drawn a line over the dark days of Tiberius' reign and ushered in the light.

Which is the point at which Suetonius throws a bucket of cold water over us all in this pithy and chilling one liner: 'so much for the emperor; the rest of history must deal with the monster'.[19]

The Monster

It's difficult to know where to start with the reign of the Monster, because there is just so much material on him. Caligula the good emperor doing the good deeds listed above is covered in eight chapters by Suetonius; Caligula the Monster gets thirty-eight chapters. And those thirty-eight chapters are quite something.

Caligula the great hope, follower of the Augustan model of emperorship, beloved of the people, respected by the Senate, mascot of the army, not terribly warmed to by panthers (for very good reasons), seems to have ruled Rome for two years. The emperor who rules after that is a very different creature, almost unrecognisable to the young man who first stepped up to the purple.

We are going to delve into the career of The Monster using our friendly biographer Suetonius. Firstly, because he has one of the fullest accounts of Caligula's reign available to us and secondly because it's very entertaining and will satisfy everyone reading this book solely because they want to know what weird stuff that mad emperor got up to. But there's another reason why I have chosen to use Suetonius' account of Caligula more than any other, which we shall delve into in the next section when we pose the question: how much should we believe our sources? But that's for later, right now we shall let Suetonius overpower us with anecdote and mindlessly believe every scandalous, depraved, perverted, sadistic detail as we explore the reign of the Monster.

The great hope of Rome, as Suetonius kindly documented for us, closely followed the Augustan blueprint of what an emperor should do, with entertaining games, building projects and generosity to all and sundry being the order of the day. The emperor depicted in the next thirty-eight chapters does no such thing. He has no time for the Augustan magic trick of pretending to have no power, whilst having all the power. Caligula refuses to put on the top hat and white gloves, he is no magician. '[He]came near assuming a crown at once and changing the semblance of a principate into the form of a monarchy.'[20]

He's apparently talked down from declaring himself a king[21] but still he's not going to pretend in any way that he's not. 'In his clothing, his shoes, and the rest of his attire he did not follow the usage of his country and his fellow-citizens; not always even that of his sex, or in fact, that of an ordinary mortal.'[22]

But Caligula does more than refusing to pretend he has no power; he tests this power to see exactly what it allows him to do. We see this very clearly in a story Suetonius repeats about Caligula's dinner parties, where the emperor takes a keen interest in his senator's wives. 'As they passed by the foot of his couch, he would inspect them critically and deliberately, as if buying slaves, even putting out his hand and lifting up the face of anyone who looked down in modesty; then as often as the fancy took him he would leave the room, sending for the one who pleased him best, and returning soon afterwards with evident signs of what had occurred, he would openly commend or criticise his partner, recounting her charms or defects and commenting on her conduct.'[23]

The hapless husbands watching the emperor disappear with their wives made no objections, how could they? He is the emperor; he can exile them, he can take their entire fortunes for his own, he can have them executed. These are men who have seen exactly that happen to close friends during Tiberius' reign, so unsurprisingly they say nothing. Caligula now knows that an emperor's power is such that he can have sex with whoever he likes, wherever he likes irrespective of what society deems acceptable.[24]

It's worth noting the deliberate and calculated cruelty of Caligula's actions here because it will be a feature of his reign. Not only does the emperor have sexual intercourse with these senatorial wives (because he can) he sits there at dinner and tells her husband all the details of that intercourse, with the added humiliation factor of listing her shortcomings as a sexual partner.

This cruelty, this toying with those who should be his closest aids is evident in this extraordinary anecdote: 'sometimes he danced even at night, and once he summoned three consulars to the Palace at the close of the second watch, and when they arrived in great and deathly fear, he seated them on a stage and then all of a sudden burst out with a great din of flutes and clogs, dressed in a cloak and a tunic reaching to his heels, and after dancing a number went off again'.[25]

Terror and cruelty for Caligula are all part of the job but he inflicts these with a certain swagger, an added humiliation that suggests that he enjoys what he is doing. There was the equestrian who loudly protested his innocence as he was thrown to the beasts, the emperor had him rescued from the snarling animals, cut off the unfortunate man's tongue and then had him thrown back in. Then there was the manager of a gladiator barracks who was beaten with chains for the emperor's amusement. We are told this went on for several days until the poor man's brain was purified. Only then did Caligula order his death and the reason he did this had nothing to do with that Imperial quality of clemency, no it was because the smell was upsetting him.

Elsewhere he inflicted terror by his very nonchalance towards those he executed and their surviving family members. 'He forced parents to attend the executions of their sons, sending a litter for one man who pleaded ill health, and inviting another to dinner immediately after witnessing the death, and trying to rouse him to gaiety and jesting by a great show of affability.'[26] This delight in death is a marked feature of his reign. He apparently used to openly complain that there had been no public disasters during his reign (although if anyone had dared, they might have jested that Caligula himself was that public disaster) and wished for a great military failure such as the massacre of Quintilius Varus and his three legions in Germania during the reign of Augustus.[27] Or else a famine or an earthquake would do, so the emperor decided.

Let them hate me, as long as they fear me, Caligula is reported to have said. He was certainly doing his best to live up to that motto. Another time he was said to have cried out 'I wish the Roman people had but a single neck'.[28] Because then he, as emperor, could kill them all at once. Caligula had power of life and death over men, and he used this to amuse himself.

Alongside his exercising of his senate decreed powers to their limits and beyond, Caligula was starting to drift into believing he had powers above that of a man. 'He began from that time on to lay claim to divine majesty.'[29] He built a temple dedicated to the worship of him, complete with a life-sized Caligula statue which was dressed in the emperor's actual clothes. He very nearly instigates a war in Judaea by demanding that a similar statue of himself be placed in the Temple of Jerusalem for worship and is only just talked down from this plan. He even plays dress up as a god, and sometimes a goddess which had to be interesting given Caligula is described as being so hairy as to earn the nickname goat.

So far, we have covered Caligula's cruelty, his use of humiliation, and a belief in his own divinity – where's the sex stuff those of you who have seen the 1979 movie Caligula cry? It's coming, as Suetonius drops in this first century CE version of click bait, 'he respected neither his own chastity nor that of anyone else'.[30]

Taboo smashing

Like with everything else he did, Caligula was onboard with testing the limits of what he could get away with in sex. Earlier we looked at the tale of the emperor having sex with the wives of his party guests, these wives being elite, freeborn, married women this was a whopping big taboo breaker, but it was only the first of many sexual taboos Caligula was to stomp on.

Homosexuality, that is a preference for one's own sex was not a concept that was understood in ancient Rome, there aren't the words in Latin for homosexual or heterosexual. This doesn't mean that sexual acts between two partners of the same sex were necessarily acceptable in Roman society, just that they look at homosexuality a different way to how we do today, and they attribute a different set of acceptable and unacceptable behaviours that can feel quite alien to our twenty-first century thinking.

Sex-wise the Roman thinking was that the elite Roman male should always be the penetrator not the penetrated. This logically lends itself to determining who could be the male sexual partner of an elite Roman man, certainly not another elite Roman man since that would mean one of them would have to be the penetrated which was taboo in Roman society. A taboo that is evident by just how often Roman politicians are accused of doing exactly that, it's a way of besmirching their reputation.[31] An acceptable sexual partner had to be lower in status to an elite Roman male, most likely a slave or a freedman (an ex-slave). Neither of whom had any say on this, as Seneca records, 'sexual passivity in a freeborn male is a crime, in a slave a necessity and for a freedman a duty'.[32]

Amongst Caligula's recorded same sex partners is the actor Mnester. Actors had a curious position in Roman society, being both venerated and swooned over by the public, but also despised and considered the lowest of the low. The public were so enamoured of actors that fights were known to break out between rival gangs of their supporters. When these got terribly out of hand both the gangs of supporters and the actors would find themselves banished from Rome. This happened during the reign of Nero, somewhat unfairly since Nero himself was apparently an active participant in this disorder. '[He] would watch the brawls of the pantomimic actors and egg them on; and when they came to blows and fought with stones and broken benches, he himself threw many missiles at the people and even broke a praetor's head.'[33]

Actors also attracted a dedicated female following, fangirls if you like. Juvenal has quite a bit to say on how they were affected by theatrical performances.

> *When sinuous Bathyllus dances his pantomime Leda,*
> *Tucia loses control of her bladder, and Apula yelps,*
> *As if she were making love, with sharp tedious cries*[3]

Mnester himself later attracts his very own fangirl in the shape of Empress Messalina, wife to Caligula's successor Claudius and one of the most notorious women in ancient Rome. She was so enamoured of him that she commissioned a bronze statue be made of him for her own private enjoyment.[35] When this private enjoyment wore off, she decided she wanted her own flesh and blood version and went about seducing him in a rather novel manner. 'For she was desperately enamoured of him, and when she found herself unable in any way either by making him promises or by frightening him to persuade him to have intercourse with her, she had a talk with her husband and asked him that the man should be compelled to obey her, pretending that she wanted his help for some different purpose.'[36] Yes, if you can't frighten a man into bed the next best thing is to ask your husband to order him to obey your every whim. Romantic it isn't.

Actors may have been popular with the public and certain members of the Imperial family, but they belonged to a class of people known as the *infames* who lurked at the very bottom of Roman society. The *infames* did not enjoy the rights of Roman citizenship, such as protection from corporal punishment, they could not hold public office and were barred from raising criminal cases or appearing as a witness in legal cases. No citizen could marry a member of the *infames* and for the senatorial class this extended to their children and grandchildren.

Infamia was not necessarily a permanent state, it could be used as a punishment and revoked when it was felt the convicted had suffered enough from being bottom of the heap. But mostly the people cursed with *infamia* status were there because of their profession; actors, gladiators and prostitutes were all classed as *infames*. To dally with a member of the *infames* was to break a sacred taboo and several laws if you weren't careful. A consequence of which was to add an extra gleam of naughty illicitness to fooling around with them, one that the likes of Mark Antony could not resist. He had a long-standing dalliance with a very famous actress called Cytheris. Juvenal has the tale of the well-born Eppia, who broke all the rules connected to her sex and ran off with a gladiator.

Caligula's dalliance with Mnester was treading a well-worn, familiar path, provided, of course, that he was the dominant, penetrating partner in their bedroom antics. Although public demonstrations of his affection and favouritism went down less well. 'He used to kiss Mnester, an actor of pantomimes, even in the theatre, and if anyone made even the slightest sound while his favourite was dancing, he had him dragged from his seat and scourged him with his own hand.'[37]

We are back to that Roman virtue of nothing in excess, the judgemental line that no good Roman male should cross. Have your fling with an actor, but don't be shown to be too fond of him lest you end up on the wrong side of that line. One suspects there is a bit of jealousy here too, the emperor is the bestower of position and rank and honour, everyone wants to be close to him to benefit from that largess. That an actor, a member of the *infames* had that privilege no doubt put a lot of aristocratic noses out of joint.

Caligula's relationship with Mnester was semi-acceptable but in one of his other same-sex partnerships the emperor takes a giant step across the line of what was considered appropriate behaviour in the bedroom. 'Catullus, a young man of a consular family, publicly proclaimed that he had violated the emperor and worn himself out.'[38] To be sodomised by another man was to label yourself a deviant, a sexual invert, effeminate and certainly not a good Roman male, let alone one who should be demonstrating the very best combinations of *virtus* for all to emulate.

Also, very much over the line of acceptable sexual behaviour was the incest he was said to have committed with all three of his sisters from childhood. We should throw in here the four wives he clocked up, none of whom he managed to reach a third anniversary with. His second wife, Livia Orestilla, he actually picked up on her wedding day to someone else. 'At the marriage of Livia Orestilla to Gaius Piso, he attended the ceremony himself, gave orders that the bride be taken to his own house, and within a few days divorced her.'[39] All of this made a mockery of Augustus' morality laws which sought to encourage the institution of marriage as a permanent state.

As well as being sexually incontinent, Caligula was similarly excessive in his love of luxury and spending. As we saw in our good things Caligula did section, the emperor had been very generous to the people of Rome, but he was also extremely generous to himself.

'In reckless extravagance he outdid the prodigals of all times in ingenuity, inventing a new sort of baths and unnatural varieties of food and feasts; for he would bathe in hot or cold perfumed oils, drink pearls of great price dissolved in vinegar, and set before his guests loaves and meats of gold.'[40]

We should pause a moment here to appreciate what Suetonius describes as Caligula's ingenuity, for I bet none of us whilst daydreaming about that big lottery win have ever incorporated gold bread as a must have. For the record, and just in case any of you happen to win the jackpot, pearls do not dissolve in vinegar. Fritter away your fortune on a ham sandwich made with that golden bread or a relaxingly pungent Channel No 5 bath instead.

These extravagances were just the tip of one massive iceberg of spending. Tiberius, the ever sensible and frugal administrator, had left the treasury bursting with 270,000,000 sesterces. Staggeringly, this was all gone within a single year. Caligula had finally discovered that at least one of the perks of being emperor had a limit.

But Caligula was a man who could think very much outside the box, whether that be in inventing novel new ways to humiliate the Senate or coming up scandalous new additions to his sex life, he was an emperor who had ideas and was not afraid to implement them. Now needing cash Caligula came up with some canny get rich quick schemes, such as this one. 'If any chief centurions since the beginning of Tiberius' reign had not named that emperor or himself among their heirs, he set aside their wills on the ground of ingratitude.'[41] And reclaimed that gratitude to his own benefit.

The hint was taken with the happy result that now everyone was so terrified that they altered their own wills to include the emperor as a beneficiary.. Nice as this was, Caligula was impatient to receive these beneficiaries, because he was clean out of golden Hovis loaves and he fancied a BLT something rotten, 'so he accused them of making game of him by continuing to live after such a declaration, and to many of them he sent poisoned dainties'.[42]

Having forced his subjects to write them into his wills and then killed them to get hold of his legacy quicker, sold much of the palace contents to raise funds and having levied as many new taxes as he could, Caligula hit upon another money-making scheme: he opened a brothel in his palace. Not just any brothel in the ruling seat of an empire though, this was a brothel whose prostitutes were Roman matrons and freeborn youths.

This was a new low for Caligula, Roman matrons and freeborn youths were protected under *stuprum* laws. *Stuprum* roughly translates as 'shameful act' and though we don't have a full list of what counted as a shameful act we can deduce that it likely included sexual assault, messing about with vestal virgins and undoubtedly forcing well-born Roman women and youths into offering up sexual services in a brothel you have set up in the palace of the Caesars. Caligula was making a mockery of Roman sensibilities on what was proper but also smashing straight through a multitude of laws too.

Caligula on Campaign

There is one anecdote in Suetonius' arsenal of mudslinging that outdoes all that has gone before. It is the story that most frequently gets pulled out as evidence that Caligula was not just sadistic and cruel, but mentally unsound. It is the tale of what happened when Caligula decided to do what all the best Romans had done from the very founding of the city, fight a war.

He headed to Germania at some speed to accomplish this. But this campaign was a farce from beginning to end, finding no one to fight with, 'he had a few Germans of his bodyguard taken across the river and concealed there, and word brought him after luncheon with great bustle and confusion that the enemy were close at hand'.[43]

Caligula raced off into the woods to 'capture' this enemy and return in triumph.

But Caligula was not done play fighting. He decided he was going to invade that cold, dismal and damp island, Britannia. Lining up his army facing the channel, Caligula stood and gave the order. Except it wasn't an order to jump onboard the boats and advance across the sea, rather it was an order for his soldiers to go about the beach and collect as many seashells as they could. Which they did. When a mass of shells had been collected, Caligula claimed victory and began to contemplate the magnificence of his triumph.

What on earth the soldiers thought about this we do not know. It likely dented their legionary pride to be forced to collect seashells like children, they likely did not find it amusing. Which means we can add the army to the list of people Caligula had well and truly pissed off.

Death of an Emperor

So that was Caligula, an emperor who delights in torture, who finds death amusing, who humiliates the Senate, who spends the entire contents of the treasury on grandeur for himself and who partakes in sexual excesses that are both taboo and illegal in Roman society. An emperor who believes he is not only a king but also a living god. It was not terribly surprising that the reign of Caligula ends with his brutal murder.

The surprising part of Caligula's assassination is the why because it's not the why you'd think. Caligula was not assassinated for the crimes we have gloriously covered in this chapter. Nor was he killed in pursuit of a noble cause with an incredibly brave individual taking the ultimate step to save Rome from the unhinged ruler who was destroying everything. No, Caligula was assassinated because he made fun of someone's voice.

The someone in question was a Praetorian tribune named Cassius Chaerea. '[Caligula] used to taunt him, a man already well on in years, with voluptuousness and effeminacy by every form of insult. When he asked for the watchword Gaius would give him 'Priapus' or 'Venus', and when Chaerea had occasion to thank him for anything, he would hold out his hand to kiss, forming and moving it in an obscene fashion.'[44]

In the grand scheme of things, it's kind of petty. But if you look at any assassination in Roman history behind the grandiose, nobly expressed sentiment there are usually more personal feelings involved. Brutus and Cassius may have proclaimed themselves liberators and restorers of the Republic when they hacked Julius Caesar to death but lurking behind it was a smarting resentment and humiliation at being publicly forgiven by Caesar for choosing Pompey over him in the civil war. Also, Caesar had nicked Cassius' lions. 'Cassius hated the ruler, and among other charges which he brought against him was that of taking away some lions which Cassius had provided when he was about to be aedile.'[45]

Caesar had also been banging Brutus' mother for decades. From such small acorns of lion-nicking and mother-shagging, big oak trees of hatred, jealously and resentment grow. Cassius Chaerea had a whopping big tree, and he could see only one way of felling it, by murdering the emperor.

As his tormentor made his way through a covered passageway in the palace on route to see a play, 'Chaerea came up behind, and gave him a deep cut in the neck, having first cried, "Take that"'.[46] Others joined in, and a blood bath ensued. '[They] dispatched him with thirty wounds; for the general signal was 'Strike again'. Some even thrust their swords through his privates. At the beginning of the disturbance his bearers ran to his aid with their poles, and presently the Germans of his bodyguard, and they slew several of his assassins, as well as some inoffensive senators.'[47] Our thoughts and prayers go out to the families of those inoffensive senators who were just going about their non-controversial business, upsetting no one and instead got caught up in a stab fest.

So that was the end of Emperor Gaius aka Caligula aka Bootykins, but before we all scuttle off to read about our next worst emperor with the preconception he surely can't be any worse than Caligula (he's not, it's Galba who is bad in a non-depraved way, which is nice because it gives us all a break from grotesque sexual antics) we should perhaps ask the question that everyone always poses about Caligula, was he mad, was he bad or was he something else entirely?

The Disclaimer

In 1976, filming began in Italy on a biopic on the life of Caligula. The 1980 Press notes for this film underline the meticulous attention to detail in recreating the ancient world the film makers insisted upon. 'Each costume, whether for noble or peasant, involves accessories or leg-tie sandals, belts, buckles, necklaces and intricate hairstyles and ornaments. All artifacts were made by hand.[48] There were a staggering 3492 different costumes used in the film, including 2000 pairs of military sandals. This attention to detail was also lavished on the sixty-four custom built sets that were used in the film, which included a 'gold-leafed boat, over 160 feet long and 30 feet high, decorated with more than 100 intricately designed statues and 120 oars'.[49]

A plethora of exceptional acting talent was assembled: Malcom McDowell, Helen Mirren, Sirs John Gielgud and Peter O'Toole. Not to mention the thousands of extras employed to fully depict the scale and grandeur of Imperial Rome. The script itself was by the writer Gore Vidal. *Caligula* The Movie was a magnet for talent. In all $17.5 million was pumped into the production of *Caligula*, it should have been fabulous, a fascinating exploration into the psyche of Rome's worst emperor, exploring concepts around authority, the corrupting influence of power and the rottenness of politics.

Caligula the movie is not fabulous, it is, in the words of film critic Roger Egbert: 'Sickening, utterly worthless, shameful trash'.[50] So bad is it that the director, the writer and the entire cast, excluding Sir John Gielgud, sought to distance themselves from the film. And presumably immediately sacked their agents. What had gone so horribly wrong with a project so blessed with talent?

The surprising answer is Penthouse magazine, for they were the ones who forked out that $17.5 million. Given final editing rights, Bob Guccione of Penthouse watched director Tito Brass' shot footage and decided it was lacking in one thing: sex. Handily, he had the means to add it in from his ready supply of Penthouse models. Only he didn't tell the director, nor the writer, nor the cast that he was doing this. Presumably because he rightly suspected they would spoil his fun. The resulting film is nine-tenths soft porn and one-tenth something to do with a Roman emperor, I think, I was too distracted by naked bums to know for sure.

Caligula was a flop of humongous proportions that got into all kinds of trouble with the obscenity laws of various countries. In Boston, USA, a sexologist and a noted academic of Renaissance Literature were both called as expert witnesses to argue in court that *Caligula* the Movie had artistic merit and therefore in legal terms could not be considered obscene.[51] The Judge in his summing up decided they were wrong, and that the film did not have any 'literary, artistic or scientific value'. Presumably because he'd been forced to watch it too and was feeling quite cross about it. However, he stopped short of declaring it legally obscene on the basis that there was somewhere, floating about amongst the graphic sex and violence, a political commentary of some sort, which legally was enough to save *Caligula* the film from an outright ban.[52]

In Britain it wasn't until 2008 that an uncut version of the film could be seen, not that anybody wanted to see those extra minutes. Some time capsules are best left undisturbed', as the Guardian film critic, Peter Bradshaw put it.[53]

On the upside Sir John Gielgud absolutely loved it, according to Malcolm McDowell, 'I vividly remember his first day on the set. He asked me if I had been out yet? I said no and he replied, "Oh my dear, it's absolutely marvellous. I've never seen so much cock in my life!"[54]

One can't help, when contemplating the porning-up of *Caligula* the film, thinking of Suetonius' account of that emperor's reign. It's similarly pumped up to the max with the type of sexual debauchery that upsets British censors and knights of the realm. The 1979 film is heavily in its debt and yes, they do recreate scenes straight from Suetonius' account, incest, and all. Is Suetonius the ancient equivalent of Bob Guccione? Did he look at the reign of Gaius and decided it needed more sex, more violence, just more? Did he, in fact, porn it up? There is some evidence that he might just have.

Our sources on Caligula's reign are rather limited. Aside from Suetonius who is writing his account over sixty years after that emperor's death, we have Cassius Dio who offers up a similarly full account but he's writing nearly two centuries later. These two are our most detailed accounts on Caligula's reign, tragically Tacitus' account is lost which is a real shame because given the passing references he makes to Caligula in his surviving work, I suspect it was a real humdinger.

Elsewhere in Roman literature we can find mention of Caligula in the works of the philosopher Seneca who was a contemporary of the emperor. The Jewish historian Josephus (who lived roughly 37 – 100 CE) dedicates some passages of his work, The Jewish War, on the troubled relationship between Rome and Judaea to Caligula's own difficult relationship with Judaea after Bootykins decided what was missing from their most holy of holy temples was a statue of himself. 'Gaius did not demonstrate his madness in offering injuries only to the Jews at Jerusalem, or to those that dwelt in the neighbourhood, but suffered it to extend itself through all the earth and sea, so far as was in subjection to the Romans: and filled it with ten thousand mischiefs.'[55] Ten thousand mischiefs is a rather wonderful way of describing Caligula's reign.

Another Jewish historian, Philo of Alexandria actually met Caligula when he came to Rome as part of a diplomatic envoy charged with sorting out that whole statue thing. Although we may have scant details on Caligula's reign to compare with Suetonius' account, some of those details come from men who had first-hand knowledge of the emperor, which will go some way in helping us answer the question; did Suetonius porn up his biography?

Let us start with the example of Caligula's incest with his three sisters, a story that first surfaces in Suetonius' account and is entirely missing from the accounts of Josephus, Seneca and Philo of Alexandria. Tacitus' account may be lost to us, but we can deduce that he does not mention this incest either in his chapters on Caligula's reign by the amount of page space he devotes to demolishing Agrippina the Younger's character without dropping in this H-bomb of a character-destroying story. This is particularly noteworthy because he has the absolute perfect opportunity to drop that bomb during his account of how Agrippina became Empress of Rome. 'Agrippina's seductiveness was a help. Visiting her uncle frequently – ostensibly as a close relative – she tempted him into giving her the preference and in treating her, in anticipation as his wife.'[56]

Yes, that's right Agrippina seduced and married her own uncle. Which would count as incest had not Uncle Claudius changed the law to allow marriages between uncle and niece, which I guess we can count as a somewhat icky perk of the job. This is Tacitus' perfect moment to mention Agrippina's history of sex with relatives, that he does not bring this up whilst describing Agrippina's seduction of her uncle I think proves beyond doubt that he doesn't mention it in his lost chapter on Caligula either.

Why does he not mention it? It's certainly not from any coyness or pretensions of being above such tittle-tattle given he presents all the gossipy details of Agrippina's predecessor as Empress, Messalina. 'By now the ease of adultery had cloyed on Messalina and she was drifting towards untried debaucheries.'[57] From which we might deduce that Tacitus does not mention the Agrippina/Caligula incest story because he had not heard it, because it was not a story then. Only later does Agrippina find herself accused of having sex with her brother. It's a later invention. That's not to accuse Suetonius of inventing it, but he certainly popularises it and helps install it as a 'fact' about Caligula.

Other Suetonius 'facts' are similarly shaky. Take the whole Caligula believing he was a god thing, you'd expect to find that referenced all over the place, after all, according to Suetonius, Caligula insisted upon people calling him God. Except it does not appear on coins from the era nor on any surviving inscriptions. Which it would if it were a thing, surely? Another invention? Or perhaps an exaggeration, after all emperor worship was an established and acceptable part of Roman religion. It had been a cause of some embarrassment to his predecessor Tiberius, who had refused permission for a temple dedicated to his worship to be built in Hispania. In response to a similar request from Greece, Tiberius responded, 'myself I am satisfied with more moderate honours such as belong to men'.[58]

Tiberius was uncomfortable at being worshipped as a god; his stepfather, Augustus had been less so but with an important distinction based on geography. For the Eastern provinces, 'he permitted the aliens, whom he styled Hellenes, to consecrate precincts to himself, the Asians to have theirs in Pergamum and the Bithynians theirs in Nicomedia'.[59] However, this sort of thing was to be kept well away from Rome because having whopping big temples dedicated to the enthusiastic veneration of yourself complete with a waiting queue of devotees somewhat exposed Augustus' Mr Ordinary First Citizen Brand as the wrapping that it was.

This is the world Caligula has stepped into, a world where emperors are worshipped as gods (whilst claiming they don't really want to be). In this context the building of a temple dedicated to himself isn't extraordinary at all, it's pretty standard, although not usual on Italian soil. Perhaps it is this act that gets exaggerated into these accounts of Caligula believing he was divine.

There are definite holes in Suetonius' account, but there is also the telling way he introduces some of his anecdotes using phrasing such as: 'now the belief was', and 'for some writers say that'. Also, 'others write that' and 'he is said to have had'. Hedging his bets on their truthfulness in other words. This is not to diss Suetonius as a biographer; appointed keeper of the palace archives under Hadrian he had access to the private papers of the emperors he writes about and he uses these, quoting extensively from the correspondence of Augustus to back up his arguments. However, sometime shortly after completing his biography of Tiberius, Suetonius was sacked by Hadrian for 'overfamiliarity with the empress Sabrina'. This is intriguingly mysterious, especially since the Praetorian Prefect Clarus was sacked alongside Suetonius for the same offence.[60]

Whereas Tacitus' Annals and Histories are an epic (and very quote worthy) triumph on the corrupting influence of power upon the Roman state and character, Suetonius' aim is no less lofty. His biographies are doing that very Roman thing of weighing up a man's *virtus* or lack of. Therefore, he doesn't arrange his stories chronologically but rather by theme, the perfect format for the reader to judge the emperors worth. It's also very handy when you happen to be writing a book called Ancient Rome's Worst Emperors that Suetonius collates all the emperors' worst bits together, which is one of many reasons why I love him.

The spirit of Roman elite politics was to sling as much mud at your opponent as possible in the hope that some of it would stick, however under despotic rulers you had to be very careful what you said lest you end up in a very messy public trial culminating in your exile or execution. Once that despotic emperor was gone it's not surprising that there might burst forth a whole avalanche of 'remember when he did that' stories and it would not be surprising if in recounting these tales the teller might exaggerate them a little in the standard manner of Roman politics, and that other people repeating that story might ham it up a bit too to outdo flashy Gemellus' story on the couch next to theirs.

Suetonius is the curator in chief of these stories, and we must thank him for it. Because although some of them are flaky on details they tell us so much about how the ancient Romans thought about Caligula. He had a reputation and even though that reputation got more extreme over time to the levels of 'barely believable' and 'probably rubbish', there's merit in unpicking it.

How he acquired such a reputation is down to two factors, firstly not everything is 'probably rubbish', there is agreement on some of Caligula's extreme behaviour from all our sources, including our eyewitness Philo of Alexandria. Secondly, the class of people these extreme acts were inflicted on was the same class who write history books, the senatorial class.

The Mad Emperor?

It's the question that every biography and TV documentary on Caligula wants to answer; was the emperor mentally unhinged? We'll ask the question too, although it's somewhat superfluous for us because Caligula has totted up enough stuff to be classed as a worst emperor irrespective of whether he was mentally unhinged or 100 percent sane.

As previously noted, the classes of people that Caligula inflicted his ten thousand mischiefs on, to use that wonderful Josephus quote again, were the senatorial and equestrian classes to which both the likes of Tacitus and Suetonius, and whatever sources they were consulting, belonged to. Keeping the upper classes sweet is all part of the Augustan *How to be a Good Emperor* guide, a chapter you should not skip if you want (a) a long and stab free existence, (b) a glorious legacy that lives on long after your extremely peaceful departure from the world, and (c) to become a god.

Caligula deliberately, repeatedly and it must be said, sadistically attacks the Senate and the equestrian order. If you'll recall from our summary of Suetonius' monster, Caligula slept with their wives, forced them to write him into their wills, visited humiliating punishments on them and later openly declared that his horse, Incitatus, would make a better senator. That Incitatus is never given the opportunity to prove this is one of the great what-ifs of history.

From the senatorial perspective this was Caligula's madness in action because who else would treat men of such illustrious standing and breeding with such contempt, as if they were of no more worth than a beggar on the streets? Who else would be so sadistically cruel to such a noble body but an emperor who had lost all sense of reality and how the world around them worked? 'Those poor, helpless, innocent victims' is the cry from our sources.

Let's whip this question round and stop asking *how* Caligula treated the elite classes and ask the more pertinent and revealing *why* he treated them that way. The why of this tale goes a long way to securing an answer to that question around Caligula's sanity, because his attacks on the Senate and the equestrian classes are not as mindlessly sadistic as our sources would have us believe. There's method in my madness, says Prince Hamlet in the Shakespeare play of the same name – there was method too in Caligula's madness.

Caligula's reign did not open with madness, it began with a great hope and a Senate in love with their new emperor. Remember how he said he had no time for informers, how he specifically didn't hold the consulship (the top position in Rome) continuously thus creating an opportunity for a member of the Senate to enjoy that illustrious position, how he brought back those senators who had been banished from the city? For the first two years of his reign relations were good and then suddenly they weren't. Why?

There are three points put forward as an explanation for this change from Caligula the 'Great Hope' to Caligula the Monster. The first occurred only seven months into his reign in October 37 CE when Caligula fell ill. There was an outpouring of public grief, prayers were said for the ailing emperor. Publius Afranius Potitus swore that he would gladly sacrifice his own life for that of the young ruler. Another citizen offered to fight as a gladiator if the emperor would only live. You can probably guess the punchline to this, yep when Caligula recovered, he made them do exactly that. 'Instead of the money which they hoped to receive from him in return for offering to give their lives in exchange for his, they were compelled to keep their promises, so as not to be guilty of perjury.'[61]

The Caligula that awoke from this unspecified malady was very different from the one that had ruled before, at least according to some of our sources. 'A severe disease attacked Gaius who had changed the manner of his living',[62] so says Philo of Alexandria. Robert Graves' fictional work *I Claudius* uses this same line as the point where everything goes wrong. Although Graves' Caligula is a monster from birth, responsible for his father's death, and committing incest with his sisters from childhood, this illness pushes him into a whole new dimension of madness. 'He's mad. He always was. But he's worse than mad now. He's possessed.'[63]

The death of Caligula's favourite sister, Drusilla in June 38 CE is another suggested moment for when the emperor's madness began to take hold. It is certainly true that Caligula was consumed with grief at his sister's death. She was given an elaborate public funeral and the rest of Rome was forced to mourn with the emperor. 'He appointed a season of public mourning, during which it was a capital offence to laugh, bathe, or dine in company with one's parents, wife, or children.'[64]

These two turning points, the unspecified brain illness, and the death of his beloved sister, form a neat explanation for Caligula's behaviour. Something external happened to him, that was not anybody else's fault. That something turned a previously sane and much-loved emperor into a sadistically cruel monster. Right, we've solved this mystery, on to the next emperor! Except there is something else that happens early on in Caligula's reign in the year 39 CE which offer a more satisfying and believable explanation of his subsequent actions.

The not so innocent victims?

Our accounts of Caligula's reign are of indiscriminate random acts of nastiness inflicted upon the senatorial class. Apart from those grovelling sycophants who publicly offered their lives in return for the emperors in the clear hope of profiteering, a not unreasonable hope given the senator, Livius Geminius received a million sesterces from Caligula for stating that he had seen the emperor's beloved late sister, Drusilla, 'ascending to heaven and holding converse with the gods'.[65] Cringy or what?

But this was what an emperor was faced with every day of his life, men of rank proclaiming their ultimate fidelity and love to you. If you want an insight into the kind of compliments an emperor was showered with, here's some choice sentiments from the poet Martial to the emperor Domitian. 'If two messengers were to invite me to dine in different heavens, the one in that of Caesar, the other in that of Jupiter, I should even if the stars were nearer, and the palace at the greater distance, return that answer: Seek some other who would prefer to be the guest of the Thunderer; my own Jupiter detains me upon earth.'[66] It's enough to bring your breakfast up.

This was the sort of flattery the young emperor enjoyed. How beloved Caligula must have felt in those early years and how devastated must he have been to discover that these honeyed words were just that, words. Words of praise and love that were as empty and meaningless as the promise of Publius Afranius Potitus to sacrifice his life if only the emperor would live. Because in 39 CE there were two attempts by members of the senatorial class to overthrow Caligula and one of these attempts involved Caligula's beloved sisters.

The first of these conspiracies is mysterious, it pops up abruptly and obliquely in Cassius Dio's account. 'During these and the following days many of the foremost men perished in fulfilment of sentences of condemnation and many others of less prominence in gladiatorial combats.'[67] In fact, continues Cassius Dio, there was nothing but slaughter – infuriatingly giving no explanation as to why. But the mention of 'sentences of condemnation' is telling because it suggests there was a legal process behind this slaughter. Which means there was a crime and what sort of crime would a group of foremost men get together to commit? Well, it's unlikely to be a bit of petty shoplifting. It's much more likely to be a plot, a conspiracy formed against the emperor. But that is all we can deduce because Cassius Dio never elaborates any further on it.

However, shortly after this mysterious whatever it was, Cassius Dio records a speech that Caligula delivers to the Senate that is very telling in its content. It's a speech about those treason trials under Tiberius and more particularly the role the senators themselves played in them. 'He took up separately the case of each man who had lost his life, and tried to show, as people thought at least, that the senators had been responsible for the death of most of them, and all by their votes of condemnation. The evidence of this, purporting to be derived from those very documents which he once declared he had burned, he caused to be read to them by the Imperial freedmen.'[68]

How those senators must have squirmed in their seats as the emperor reminded them of their past deeds and how they were active participants in actions they later denounced. He reminds them of how they treated the man who destroyed his own family, 'Sejanus also you first puffed up with conceit and spoiled, then put him to death'[69] adding, 'therefore I, too, ought not to expect any decent treatment from you.' Which is one massive hint that something big had gone down and that members of the Senate had been involved.

This speech reads very much like the wool has been lifted from Caligula's eyes, that he has suddenly realised that these men who claimed to love him are not his friends. They are the same men who signed the documents that condemned his mother and brothers to horrible deaths. And they were truly horrible deaths, Caligula's brother Drusus was starved to death, so desperate for food he ate the stuffing of his mattress. Agrippina, once the darling of Rome was so severely beaten by her guards that she lost an eye. These men Caligula stood in front of as their ruler had been instrumental in those deaths. Yes, they flattered him with cutesy nicknames and honours, but they had also bestowed such love on Sejanus and Tiberius, whom now they condemned in the harshest of language.

Whatever had happened, Caligula now saw things clearly; these men did not love their emperor, it was all words, nothing of it was true. Which is pretty much what he said in his speech to those senators. Their response? To heap a load of empty gestures on the emperor, thus spectacularly missing the point. 'Accordingly, they voted to offer annual sacrifices to his Clemency, both on the anniversary of the day on which he had read his address and on the days belonging to the palace; on these occasions a golden image of the emperor was to be carried up to the Capitol and hymns sung in its honour by the boys of the noblest birth.'[70]

Another conspiracy followed, one even more wounding to the young emperor for it involved his three sisters along with Marcus Aemilius Lepidus, the widower of his much-mourned sister Drusilla. Lepidus was executed, Agrippina, Livillia and Julia were sent into exile. Also involved undoubtedly would have been other members of the senatorial class.

In this context Caligula's singling out of the senatorial class makes a lot more sense. They aren't the entirely blameless sheep to the slaughter the historians of that same class would have us believe. They were active participants in plots to depose the emperor. Which will be a recurrent theme throughout our tour of worst emperors and why keeping the Senate happy should be on every emperors to do list.

Caligula took the other route of keeping the Senate in line, terrorising them. He'd been given the power of life and death over the very men who had destroyed his family – of course he was going to use it, of course he was going to get his revenge. In this context every action of Caligula's makes sense; condemning senators to work in the mines, forcing them to fight as gladiators, sending for them in the middle of the night in fear for their lives and then doing a little dance for them. He set out to terrorise and humiliate them and he succeeded. It still makes him a terrible emperor mind. One of the worst.

So, Suetonius likely porned up his account, the senators were overdue a humiliation and Caligula did not go suddenly demented on everyone's arse, but what about the seashells? The seashells thing is still a bit mad ruler-ish, isn't it? There's no denying that it is but still there could be a rational explanation, or perhaps not. I leave you to be the judge.

The tale, if you remember is that Caligula lined up his troops ready to invade Britannia and then instead of launching a full-on invasion, instead ordered his troops to collect seashells off the beach and then declared victory. Some historians have tried to make out that these bizarre actions were not bizarre at all but rather due to a simple misunderstanding/translation error. Caligula wasn't referring to seashells when he ordered his troops to collect *musculi* but rather the military huts used in sieges that were also referred to as *musculi*.[71] It's all those ancient historians' fault for not knowing proper military terminology! Which feels like a stretch so far as to tear a ligament.

Aloys Winterling in his biography of Caligula suggests that the collecting of the seashells was a deliberate attempt to humiliate the soldiers for refusing to cross the channel and fight[72]. There is no mention of Caligula's troops mutinying or refusing to fight which somewhat undermines this theory, in fact this whole explanation is based on the fact that under the Emperor Claudius some soldiers did exactly that and refused to cross the channel and take part in Claudius' successful invasion of Britannia. It is a neat explanation for Claudius ordering his troops to collect seashells had that happened, which it didn't.

Which leaves us with? I still don't think we need to jump on the mad-emperor wagon nor explain the incident away as a big chunk of nothingness, because it fits so very neatly with what we have learnt about Caligula in this chapter; he delighted in humiliation. The troops, just like many of the others who found themselves in Caligula's eyeline, didn't need to have done anything worthy of being humiliated. The emperor needed no reason, no excuse, no justification for any of his actions. He could do whatever he liked, to whomever he liked, whenever he liked. That was what being emperor was all about and always had been from the reign of Caligula's great granddaddy Augustus.

Augustus wielded his power behind a curtain, Caligula ripped open that curtain and let in the light. The other emperors that followed Caligula may have tried to tug the curtain shut, they may have hung up a pair of net curtains, but they couldn't fully block out that light. The secret was out. This was a monarchy and, in that monarch, lay absolute power.

After Bootykins

With Caligula's bloody corpse still twitching, the senators he'd so abused and humiliated decided they'd had enough of emperors. 'The senate was so unanimously in favour of re-establishing the republic that the consuls called the first meeting, not in the senate house.'[73] Unfortunately, they were as ever lagging behind events, because whilst they were debating political structures up at the palace, the Praetorian Guard had found Caligula's Uncle Claudius cowering behind a curtain and gone and made him emperor. The thought of those senators filled with glee and joy at taking back their ancestral rights stepping out onto the streets of the city ready to rule, only to discover there was a new emperor is too upsetting to think about. Their little disappointed faces!

Claudius was succeeded by his 17-year-old stepson Nero, a boy with even less credentials to rule than Caligula, but like Caligula he could claim descendance from Augustus. He was the last emperor that could, for with the death of Nero came the end of the Julio-Claudian dynasty. When Nero was overthrown in a coup in 68 CE the Senate had to look outside the palace for a new emperor. They found him in Spain.

Chapter 3

Galba (68–69 CE) – The Man Who Should be King

Servius Sulpicius Galba was possessed of everything that made a Roman great. To read of Galba's pre-emperor life is to be utterly exhausted by his *virtus* displaying. His family background is so rich on glory that even Mr ancestry.com Suetonius can't be bothered to put in the effort listing their accomplishments. 'It would be a long story to give in detail his illustrious ancestors and the honorary inscriptions of the entire race, but I shall give a brief account of his immediate family.'[1]

Galba was one of those Romans that was big on doing things the way they had always been done, a proper old school traditionalist. 'He persisted in keeping up an old and forgotten custom of his country, which survived only in his own household, of having his freedmen and slaves appear before him twice a day in a body, greeting him in the morning and bidding him farewell at evening, one by one.'[2] Given that wealthy Romans like Galba could own hundreds of slaves and freedmen. there was a sensible reason this tradition had been abandoned, people wanting to get to bed before the sun rose again.[3] Galba, however, was a man whose own comfort was of secondary concern to being a big old show off. How else to describe a man whose public career included running for twenty miles beside the emperor's chariot?

He was specially chosen to be proconsul of Africa to restore order to a province that had recently suffered a revolt, something he was supremely successful at. Suetonius puts this success down to, 'his insistence on strict discipline and his observance of justice even in trifling matters'.[4] This is a sentence worthy of underlining or raising a knowing eyebrow at. Remember it because it's going to become important later in this chapter.

For his achievements in sorting out Africa and also Germania, Galba received, 'triumphal regalia and three priesthoods, for he was chosen a member of the Fifteen, of the brotherhood of Titius, and of the priests of Augustus'.[5] A nice collection of positions to rub in the faces of his political rivals whilst retaining a dignified stance of restrained smugness.

Galba deserved to feel smug, he'd had quite the career, one that was so brilliant and gleaming that after the murder of Caligula, 'many urged Galba to take advantage of the opportunity'.[6] He sensibly declined the position on this occasion. In a similar Imperial vein, he sensibly declined a proposed marriage match with Caligula's sister Agrippina the younger.

Servius Sulpicius Galba, experienced politician and military general, distinguished above his peers for his impeccable service and even considered worthy of the Imperial family. Galba had it all. The full package. As Tacitus says: 'so long as he was a subject he seemed too great a man to be one and by common consent possessed the makings of a ruler'.[7] But the kicker is in the ending of that quote, Galba had the makings of a ruler, says Tacitus 'had he never ruled'. For as ruler, Galba messes it all up, royally, and, it has to be said, quickly. Named emperor in June 68 CE, Galba arrived in Rome in October of that year, and was decapitated in the Forum on 15 January 69 CE.

It took five years for Caligula's unhinged rule to unravel, fifteen for the mother murdering artiste Nero to fall from favour. Galba's time as emperor came to end after only seven months. Which you must admit is impressive, doubly so for a man who on paper had everything that was needed to be emperor. What went wrong so badly, so quickly?

Not being Nero

If forced to describe Galba in one word, that one word would undoubtedly be 'stern'. He is sternly stern. You can see this in a bust of him, it's a bust of dubious provenance and nobody can quite decide if it's Galba or Cato the Elder, but what we can say is that it's a bust of an undoubtedly stern man. Similarly, the coinage Galba issues during his short rule depict a hook-nosed man with a grim expression who looks like he would order your death the moment you displeased him in any way.

This sternness is evident throughout Galba's early career. There was the time he forbade his troops from clapping at a festival. The soldier caught selling rations who starved to death after Galba issued an order that no one was to assist him with food. The money lender whose hands he had cut off and nailed to his counter. Then there was the time he crucified a man whose Roman citizenship should have protected him from that fate.

Galba was an old school disciplinarian, which had worked wonders with getting the legions he commanded into shape and restoring order in the provinces he'd been parachuted into but was going to backfire spectacularly on him as emperor. This began from the very moment he arrived in Rome.

Galba (68–69 CE) – The Man Who Should be King

It should have been a time of celebration, the arrival of the new emperor in the city he now ruled, ready to take charge and make Rome greater than ever. There was quite a gathering at the Milvian Bridge, one of the key routes into the city, of people eager to catch a glimpse of this new emperor. Amidst the crowd of nosy citizens were a group of seamen who were using Galba's arrival as an opportunity to petition him with a not outrageous request. They had been haphazardly put together as a fighting force by Nero but now wanted to be recognised as a proper legion, with all the benefits that came with that. However, Galba was not in the mood to hear their petition and waved them away, telling them that he would listen to their demands at another time.

They had been waiting probably for hours for the arrival of the emperor's entourage, for this one golden opportunity to submit their request to the emperor face to face. Likely they would never get an opportunity this good again, likely Galba would get to the palace and forget all about their petition amongst the thousands of others an emperor received. 'They declared that the postponement was merely a way of refusing their demands, and were incensed, and followed along with unremitted shouts.'[8]

I think we can all agree that it is not a nice thing to be followed along the road by a group of sailors shouting at you. I think we'd also all agree that a group of incensed navy men probably weren't very polite in their shouting, I think we're all thinking that the new emperor found himself under a torrent of fruity language that was brutally blunt on their estimation of his abilities, personality and looks.

Galba, the man who starved to death a soldier for the crime of selling rations, was never going to let such a rabble of foulmouthed, disrespectful, undisciplined sailors get away with this behaviour. His career had been built on licking legions into shape, however this time he went too far and in full view of his new subjects. After some of the sailors drew their swords, Galba ordered his cavalry to charge into the crowd. Remember that this is a crowd that is made up of more than just those irritatingly shouty seamen. 'Not a man of them stood his ground, but some were done to death at once in the route, and others as they fled, nor was it a happy and auspicious omen that Galba should enter the city through so much slaughter and so many dead bodies.'[9] But the wholesale slaughter of the petitioners was not deemed enough by this new emperor, he ordered that the survivors of this unofficial legion be subject to decimation.

Decimation is one of those subjects that regularly gets pulled out, alongside gladiators and slavery, as proof of the ruthlessness and bloodthirstiness of the ancient Romans. Used exclusively in the army to quell rebellious spirits or punish cowardice, the legionaries would be split into groups of ten and within these groups they would draw lots. Whoever was unlucky enough to choose the white stone out of the bag would be beaten to death by the other nine black stone selecting soldiers. It's worth stressing that these nine men handed clubs and told to get to it were the comrades, even the friends of the poor unfortunate soul clutching that white pebble. Which is enough to make the hairs curl up on the back of your neck whilst wondering what is wrong with these people to devise such a cruel punishment? In 68 CE this was exactly the question that was asked of Galba.

Decimation was as archaically nasty to them as it is to us. It was a punishment that was used sparingly and to find examples of it in practice involves reading through hundreds of years of history. Prior to 68 CE, the last known use of decimation was by Mark Antony during his disastrous campaign against the Parthians in 36 BCE,[10] 105 years previously. To put this in context, the last person in Britain to be hanged was in 1964, a mere fifty-eight years ago. 105 years ago, women couldn't vote in the UK. Decimation was to the ancient Romans similarly antiquated, a relic very much of the past.

Galba's bloody entrance into Rome was a pattern of behaviour that had been present his entire career. The difference was that this disciplining, this strict adherence to the law without mercy was not being undertaken in some far-off province he was governing but rather in Rome right where everyone could see it. Where was the *clementia*, that grand gesture of mercy displayed by an emperor? Or the *liberalitis*, the giving freely to his people? In Galba it was nowhere to be seen. 'He condemned to death distinguished men of both orders on trivial suspicions without a trial. He rarely granted Roman citizenship, and the privileges of threefold paternity to hardly one or two, and even to those only for a fixed and limited time.'[11]

This is where it's worth remembering who came before Galba as emperor, because that is who the people on the ground are comparing him to, Nero. Nero who introduced two new festivals: the Juvenalia and Neronia for the entertainment of the people. Nero who on becoming emperor gave every citizen 400 sesterces and the praetorian guard a monthly donative of grain. Nero who rode chariots, read poetry and sung for the people. Colourful, generous, fun Nero. A handsome young emperor (despite his adherence to the gruesome neck beard and weight gain later in life) versus this miserly old man. 'His hands and feet were so distorted by gout that he could not endure a shoe for long, unroll a book, or even hold one. The flesh on his right side too had grown out and hung down to such an extent, that it could with difficulty be held in place by a bandage.'[12]

Galba had alienated the people with his harsh rule but where he really messed up was in alienating the soldiers, both those inside Rome, in the shape of the praetorian guard, and those posted in the provinces.

The Emperor Makers

Galba might have liked to believe he owed his position to those good men of the Senate. He didn't. The Senate only named him emperor after the praetorian guard had deserted Nero. Nero would not have fled the city and taken his own life had his guard not abandoned him. The praetorians were well aware of this, they'd cleared the way for Galba to be emperor and now they expected their reward. They expected this pay out because that was what their Prefect, Nymphidius Sabinus had promised them. '[He]persuaded the soldiery, as though Nero were no longer there but had already fled, to proclaim Galba emperor, and promise as largess seventy-five hundred drachmas apiece for the court, or praetorian guards as they were called, and twelve hundred and fifty drachmas for those in service outside of Rome.'[13]

Whilst Galba had been dallying in the provinces sorting stuff out before heading down to Italy, Nymphidius Sabinus had taken it upon himself to take care of matters in Rome. He may have started out believing he was merely supporting the new emperor, and what he imagined the new emperor wanted, but it didn't take long for Sabinus to acquire delusions of grandeur. This delusion hit a peak in the summer of 68 CE. 'He took to himself sole credit for the overthrow of Nero, and thinking himself insufficiently rewarded for this by the honours and wealth which he enjoyed, and by the company of Sporus, Nero's favourite (whom he had sent for at once, while Nero's body was yet burning on its pyre, and treated as his consort, and addressed by the name of Poppaea), he aspired to the succession of the empire.'[14]

Sabinus going further than his fellow Praetorian Prefect, Sejanus had ever dared, decided to proclaim himself emperor on the basis that his father could have been Caligula.

There was a chance this was true, Sabinus' mother, Nymphidia had been rather active in the palace, as Tacitus tactfully puts it, 'his mother was as attractive ex-slave who had hawked her charms among the slaves and freed slaves of the palace'.[15] She was a palace prostitute in other words, one who counted Caligula amongst her lovers and indeed, her son did bare a passing resemblance to that deceased emperor being described as tall and grim. However, even if it were true that Nymphidius was the son of Caligula, it gave him no claim on the throne. Without a named father, Sabinus took his status from his mother and she was an ex-slave. That the Senate, the army or even the people would rally behind an emperor of such lowly background was a ludicrous idea. Nymphidius' plan was madness. But that he thought it feasible tells you something about, (a) his state of mind at the time and (b) his absolute conviction that the support of his praetorian guard could make him emperor.

What had pushed Sabinus into concocting this plan to make himself emperor was news that Galba was less than pleased with his handling of Rome and as a result intended to replace him as Praetorian Prefect. This was too much for a man who had spent the summer being courted by senators and consuls alike. He couldn't step down into ordinary civilian life, he just couldn't. Fuelling this was the men he had at his disposal, the guards he'd promised Galba would be generous to.

However venal and self-serving the guard might have been it hadn't escaped their notice that removing two emperors within a few months of each other might not play well for their reputations, not least when they'd spent the past few weeks boasting about how they'd made Galba emperor. Plus, Nymphidius was hardly emperor material, not with his background, not with a mother like his.

When the Prefect came to the Praetorian camp to make his grand, 'I'm going to be emperor' speech he faced not his loyal troop of guards ready to support him all the way to the top, but a much more hostile audience. In the end Nymphidius didn't even get to make his speech, he was set upon by his own men and hacked to pieces. But there was a final, public humiliation for the Prefect who would be emperor. 'His dead body was dragged forth, surrounded with a paling, and exposed to public view all day.'[16]

You may be wondering what all this has got to do with Galba and him being a worst emperor. The answer is very little, since he was hundreds of miles away at the time. But the story of Nymphidius Sabinus is worth telling for some key reasons, firstly it's a fascinating tale of hubris and its destructive power, and secondly it shows just how Nero's lack of a successor opened up a can of wriggly worms that could never be re-sealed on who could be an emperor. Nymphidius really was ahead of his time, a lowly born soldier using the men he commanded to make him emperor is something that becomes a recurrent feature in the third century CE, and generally not to Rome's benefit. But mostly Nymphidius' story is important because it sets up the importance of the praetorian guard to Galba's rule, not only had they removed Nero for him, but they had also removed a hostile threat to his rule. Galba should be doubly grateful to them and, of course, they expected this gratitude to be expressed in coinage.

Galba's response pretty much sealed his fate. 'He declared more than once that it was his habit to levy troops, not buy them; and on this account he embittered the soldiers all over the empire.'[17] This was a catastrophic move, not only had he offended the soldiers that were present in Rome with some very pointy swords and a big grievance, he'd also, as Suetonius notes above, offended all the soldiers sitting in the provinces in huge numbers with similarly pointy swords. Those soldiers in the provinces looked at how Galba had been made emperor of Rome with only one legion under his command, and they got ideas.

Ideas were certainly brewing in Germania, where there were seven legions based under the command of Aulus Vitellius. If one legion could make a man emperor, seven certainly could and think what booty could be acquired along the way. When 1 January 69 CE came, the time when the troops across the empire would swear allegiance to the emperor for the coming year, the legions of Germania decided they'd rather not thanks. Instead, they declared Vitellius emperor and swore allegiance to him instead.

In Rome the Praetorian Guard were in a collective sulk, polishing their swords and feeling embittered. Enter Marcus Salvius Otho, a more plausible (but only just) candidate for their support than the man they had hacked to death some months before. Otho was in a sulk with Galba too since the emperor declined to make him his heir but never mind because Otho had a brilliant plan on how to succeed Galba as emperor that cut out the need for him to be the official heir. It was a plan he needed the Praetorians help with.

And so to bloody murder

We've banged on at some length on the importance of keeping the three groups of Roman society happy: the Senate, the people and the army. Galba is the perfect example of what happens when you don't do that. Galba's seven-month reign came to an end on 15 January 69 CE when Otho, with the kind assistance of the Praetorian Guard, overthrew him in a very bloody coup. Even if he hadn't, it was likely Galba's days were numbered anyhow, the Rhine legions were on the march down to Rome to make their man, Vitellius, emperor. Something Otho only discovered post-coup when he jogged up to the palace as the new emperor and was handed a pile of correspondence from Germania. Oops.

The death of Galba on the 15 January 69 CE was the kick off for what became known as the year of the four emperors. Galba makes our worst emperor list because had he not so comprehensively messed up at being emperor then the year of the four emperors would never have happened. 69 CE was a brutal year, as Tacitus, who was a teenager at the time explains. 'The history on which I am entering is that of a period rich in disasters, terrible with battles, torn by civil struggles, horrible even in peace. Four emperors fell by the sword; there were three civil wars, more foreign wars, and often both at the same time.'[18]

All of which could be lain at the feet of Galba, the man who everyone agreed would make the perfect ruler – had he never ruled.

Chapter 4

Vitellius (69 CE) – No Appetite for Power

'His besetting sins were luxury and cruelty. He divided his feasts into three, sometimes into four a day, breakfast, luncheon, dinner, and a drinking bout; and he was readily able to do justice to all of them through his habit of taking emetics.'[1]

'He delighted in inflicting death and torture on anyone whatsoever and for any cause whatever.'[2] He sounds like a real charmer, doesn't he? The subject of these two quotes is Aulus Vitellius. Vitellius was emperor number three in the year of the four emperors. He was succeeded or rather bloodily overthrown, as was rapidly becoming the norm in Rome at this time, by Vespasian. Vespasian ruled as emperor for ten years, proving rather good at it and started his own dynasty, the Flavians that lasted for nearly thirty years.

This is important to mention because any emperor who bloodily overthrows their predecessor needs to have a bloody good reason for their actions. One that paints them not as a man prepared to murder his way to the top job but rather as a man who has done Rome a colossal favour. The easiest way to do this is to ham up just how awful your predecessor was and how much better you are and isn't it so much better that you are emperor now and he's not? Vespasian had a whole decade to spin out this yarn.

So, all the terrible things I am about to tell you about the emperor Vitellius could be pure Flavian invention. If they are, they stuck amazingly well, for Vitellius has maintained his reputation as one of ancient Rome's worst emperors to this day. No smoke without fire, we might conclude, or rather no scandal without sin. Vitellius' alleged sins started early.

The Before Emperor Bit

Born in 15 CE the young Vitellius was sent by his father to make nice to Emperor Tiberius during those interesting Capri years. Doomed by association and rumoured to have helped his father's career at the expense of his chastity, Vitellus was given the nickname *spintria* meaning sex pervert; we are told this stuck with him his entire career. Which is the sort of thing Roman men did to each other all the time; Cicero was still making 'jokey' references to Julius

Caesar's alleged debauching by King Nicomedes thirty years after the alleged incident took place. Romans had long memories and an inability to let a good story die, especially when it painted your political rival as a sexual degenerate. Which is a sentiment I am thoroughly in line with, else I wouldn't be writing this book.

Suetonius continues his tale of Vitellius' career progression. 'Stained by every sort of baseness as he advanced in years, he held a prominent place at court, winning the intimacy of Gaius by his devotion to driving and of Claudius by his passion for dice.'[3]

Vitellius' career is nowhere near as energetic as Galba's but a talent for getting on with emperors and showing an interest in their hobbies is hardly a zinging insult. In fact, there's something to admire here in Vitellius' supreme talent of ingratiating himself with the tricky personality of an emperor, witness his handling of Nero's delicate artistic nature. 'Nero wished to compete among the lyre-players but did not venture to do so although there was a general demand for him and accordingly left the theatre. Vitellius called him back, alleging that he came as an envoy from the insistent people, and thus gave Nero a chance to yield to their entreaties.'[4] Masterful.

Suetonius is also grudgingly forced to admit Vitellius wasn't all that bad at the positions he'd been granted by those emperors he got on with so well. 'He afterwards governed Africa as proconsul and served as curator of public works, but with varying purpose and reputation.'[5] He even admits that Vitellius 'showed exceptional integrity'. And yet Vitellius as emperor has anything but integrity, in fact he bears no resemblance to this successful governor and courtier. Which leads to two possible conclusions, either all the stories of his utter baseness are entirely fictional or else Vitellius the man was undone by the role foisted upon him. Absolute power corrupts absolutely, as a wise man once said. I forget who.

The man who would be emperor (whether he wanted to or not)

The thing was that Vitellius didn't exactly seek power, rather it came to lay upon him with minimal effort required. In 68 CE when Nero took his final bow, Vitellius was in Lower Germania acting as governor. This was no star posting, the region was a difficult quarrelsome one, beset with war mongering local tribes who no doubt still felt the spur of Arminius[6] coursing through their blood and dreamed of committing a similar annihilation of the incomers. Also, the weather wasn't that great compared with Vitellius' contemporaries who were sunning themselves in gloriously clement Egypt or Spain whilst pretending to work.

The difficult nature of both Upper and Lower Germania had led to an increased number of troops based there; seven legions, totalling 70,000 legionaries. These weren't raw recruits freshly shipped out from Italy, these were seasoned fighters who'd seen multiple action facing off against those troublesome locals. Remember how Galba became emperor with only one legion? The German legions remembered it too. Galba's one legion were no doubt profiting from their association whereas, '[they] had put up with hard and unrewarding service in an uncongenial area and climate, under strict discipline'.[7]

Nothing likely would have come of this discontent, bar probably more strict discipline applied to the selected backs of the most vocal to crush such sentiments, had it not been for two men (neither of whom is Aulus Vitellius). Their names were Fabius Valens and Alienus Caecina and it was they who both instigated and carried out the plot to make Vitellius emperor. As well as commanding legions, winning battles, sorting out insurrections within their own cohorts and overall being damn dynamic. Something that cannot be said for Vitellius during this period, but we jump ahead of our story, let us go back to a miserable and cold Germania in January 69 CE.

Valens and Caecina had been working on Vitellius ever since word of Galba's elevation had reached their damp corner of the empire. They repeatedly presented strong irrefutable arguments as to why he should make a bid for emperor; the troops were keen on the idea, the British legions would be sure to follow their lead, and everybody always said nice things about him. Also, he had a distinguished background that was fitting for an emperor, so fitting that if he didn't become emperor then whoever did might see him as a threat. How could Vitellius fail to be persuaded by such reasoned arguments as he was quite posh and all his troops thought he'd be great at being emperor? 'Vitellius was a man of lazy temperament, but he wavered under the strong impact of these arguments. The result was an 'idle longing rather than real hope.'[9]

On the 1st January it was traditional for the legions across the provinces of the empire to take an oath of loyalty to the emperor. In Germania this did not happen as usual, 'here and there individuals in the front ranks spoke up audibly, but the rest of the troops did not open their mouths'.[8] The German legions had publicly declared they did not support Galba as emperor.

Whilst the energetic Valens and Caecina marched their huge armies down to Rome to depose Emperor Galba (although two weeks into their march they will discover that Galba has been killed and it was Emperor Otho they are heading off to fight) Vitellius stayed in Germania. Whether this is a canny move to distance himself from Valens and Caecina's actions should it all go wrong, or down to laziness is open to interpretation. But Vitellius certainly doesn't strike you as someone particularly eager to jump fully onboard this crazy adventure he's been thrust into.

Whilst Valens and Caecina take on the responsibility of marching two huge armies hundreds of miles across Europe to Rome, Vitellius gives us a first insight into what kind of emperor the two commanders were seeking to install. 'Quick to take advantage of the privileges of an emperor, he gave himself up to idle pleasures and sumptuous banquets.'[10] Okey-dokey.

On route to Rome Caecina manages to annoy a previously perfectly peaceful tribe, the Helvetii into open warfare by stealing their money. Meanwhile Valens is gaining notoriety by threatening to set fire to the towns on his route unless they pay him. Vitellius aside from being the name invoked by his two generals as they butcher their way across the empire, is somewhat missing from the story.

Meanwhile, in Rome Otho was busy preparing for the arrival of the Rhine legions. Intricately involved in planning the defence, he decides on his generals, he decides on the battle plan, and he goes with his army to face Vitellius' legions. Otho was a leader. In comparison Vitellius' leadership style was to leave Valens and Caecina to get on with it. The most energetic action coming from Vitellius during this time are the letters he writes to Otho suggesting he steps down. 'At first both wrote in genial tones, resorting to pretence which was at once foolish and unbecoming: later, as if engaged in a common brawl, they each charged the other with debaucheries and low practices, neither of them falsely.'[11]

After some surprising setbacks the inevitable becomes evitable and Otho's much smaller and less professional army[12] are destroyed by Valens and Caecina's superior Rhine legions. The defeated Otho committed suicide, leaving Vitellius the undisputed emperor.

Being Emperor – an exercise in pleasure.

'With every mile travelled towards Rome, the emperor's progress became more riotous. It was joined by actors and gangs of eunuchs and all the other idiosyncrasies of Nero's court.' [13] So Tacitus sets the tone for the reign of Vitellius. Although one must ask the question – where are these gangs of eunuchs popping up from? Was it common for eunuchs to herd together and wander the streets outside Rome hoping to find a parade to join in with? Sadly, Tacitus feels no need to explain that one further, he is too busy disapproving of Vitellius who he adds, attended Nero's recitals, 'not – like the better sort – under compulsion, but as the slave and hireling of pleasure and gluttony'.[14]

Vitellius' gluttony is a theme that is returned to again and again. On his journey to Rome, he and his enormous entourage stop at every town on route, the townspeople, 'were exhausted by the necessity of supplying the multitude with food: the very land-workers and the fields now ready for harvest were stripped bare, as if this were enemy soil'.[15]

Suetonius has the dinner Vitellius' brother threw to celebrate his arrival in Rome that included, 'two thousand of the choicest fishes and seven thousand birds'.[16] Which is quite a spread, eat your heart out Downton Abbey! There was also the dish Vitellius personally invented, the Shield of Minerva. 'The livers of pike, the brains of pheasants and peacocks, the tongues of flamingos and the milt of lampreys, brought by his captains and triremes from the whole empire, from Parthia to the Spanish strait.'[17] Our palates are much changed from the ancient Romans because the Shield of Minerva sounds less like an example of supreme luxurious living and more of an 'I'm a Celebrity Get me Out of Here' bushtucker trial. If you're wondering what the milt of lampreys is, it's sperm, eel sperm. Which neatly answers the question what could possibly be a worse ingredient for a meal than peacock brains and flamingo tongues? Eel spunk.

Elsewhere we find Vitellius attending three dinners in a single night, each of them, Suetonius tells us, costing no less than 400,000 sesterces. Which is an awful lot of money that even Caligula would have spent on more useful things, such as having the entire meal coated in gold. This would at least have lengthened the time the full spread was appreciated.

The vast expenditure and time Vitellius spent on banqueting is highlighted by all our ancient authors. It is clear evidence for them that he is not fit to be emperor, we are back to *virtus* and what makes a good Roman. Ancient authors are extremely concerned about the corrupting influence that money and the luxury that money can buy has on a society – most particularly their own which had seen an influx of coinage as they conquered more and more territory. Livy in the introduction to his great history of Rome has this sobering and somewhat depressing take on what had happened to Rome. 'Let him follow the decay of the national character, observing how at first it slowly sinks, then slips downward more and more rapidly, and finally begins to plunge into headlong ruin, until he reaches these days, in which we can bear neither our diseases nor their remedies.'[18]

It's worth noting that 'these days' that Livy is living in are under the Emperor Augustus, an era that our history books refer to as a golden age. The Greek historian Plutarch describes the era of the second Punic war as a time, 'when there were so many great and outstanding men of that glory and virtue were thick on the ground'.[19] Whereas Cato the Elder who lived through the second

Punic war, ran for the position of censor with a platform of, 'cauterising the hydra like diseases of luxury and effeminacy'.[20]

In short, there was no agreed period when this golden age of Rome existed, it's somewhere *waves vaguely* back there. This didn't stop them trying to recreate this non-existent age by forcing people into behaviours that were considered proper using the legal system. The laws that get the most attention are the morality laws brought in by the likes of Augustus and Domitian, laws that are aimed at promoting marriage and punishing adultery. But there are also laws passed that limit expenditure and luxurious living. To the Roman mind the two are interlinked. Too much luxury led to softness, which led to effeminacy, which led to all kinds of sexual shenanigans that need tutting at. This is the subtext behind all those stories of Vitellius gluttony; he is soft, he is corrupted, he is loose of morals, he is lazy, he is not an energetic go-conquer-an-empire sort, he is not what a Roman should be. He should not be emperor.

Alongside gluttony the other marked feature of Vitellius' reign is the indiscipline of the legions. Galba's method of dealing with those troublesome sailors may have been harsh to the extreme but you can't deny that his decimation tactic worked because we never hear of those sailors again. Of course, in the long run it majorly backfired on Galba with the legions throwing their support behind Vitellius, a man who wasn't going to decimate them on the flimsiest of excuses.

Possibly any leader would have had difficulty controlling the Rhine legions, they were so many in number, certain of their superiority over all the other legions of Rome and they were chomping at the bit to get their hands on the spoils they felt they were due. Certainly, Valens was a gifted commander but even he faced difficulty controlling his troops. There was the falling out between some Batavian auxiliaries and the rest of the men which, 'broke out almost into open battle, and in fact would have done so had not Valens, by the punishment of a few men, reminded the Batavians of the authority which they had forgotten'.[21] But worse was to come for Valens. 'Thereupon the troops attacked Valens himself, stoned him, and pursued him when he fled. Declaring that he was concealing the spoils of the Gallic provinces and the gold taken from the people of Vienne, the rewards of their own toil, they began to ransack his baggage and explore the walls of his quarters and even the ground with their spears and javelins. Valens, disguised in a slave's clothes, hid in the quarters of a cavalry officer.'[22]

Valens does manage to restore order but there's a telling line at the end of Tacitus' account of this insurrection. 'Valens showed a wise moderation: he did not demand the punishment of any man; at the same time, that an assumption of ignorance might not arouse suspicion, he blamed a few severely. He was well aware that in civil wars the soldiers have more liberty than the leaders.'[23] Valens had realised early what the key lesson was of 69 CE; the army had the power. It was they and not the Senate, who supposedly ruled Rome, who were directing events. The only action that this body of 600 men could take was to wait and see what the army did next. This was a dangerous realisation that was going to have a huge impact on Rome's future.

After they have achieved their aim of making Vitellius emperor the troops were no better behaved in Rome. 'Not being used to crowds, they did not bother about avoiding collisions and sometimes fell over because the road was slippery or someone had jostled them. When this happened, the answer was abuse, developing into fisticuffs and sword play.'[24] Fisticuffs and sword play makes the behaviour of Vitellius' soldiers sound almost like fun. In other translations it's described as the far more believable, 'blows and the use of their swords'.

This was the Saturday night kicking out of the pub fights on a huge scale. As Tacitus notes, 'the troops were everywhere'. Too many to be housed in any barracks they wandered about the streets partaking in 'pursuits too shocking to be described'.[25] This isn't my translator going all coy again, I've checked other translations and annoyingly they don't describe these shocking pursuits either.

Fully engaged with enjoying the shocking pursuits of the big city and with daily drills, sentry duty and the usual strict regime of the Roman army having been abandoned, the tough, weathered legionaries of the Rhine quickly went to seed, 'they ruined their physique by idleness and their morals by indulgence'[26] tuts Tacitus. But worse was to come for these soldiers of the Rhine. Setting up camp on mass in the Vatican district with their tents crammed close together in the heat a Roman summer caused an epidemic of disease. What disease is never expanded upon, but it was apparently nasty enough to wipe out a significant number of troops.

The rapid decline in the standards and numbers of these troops is important because they are shortly to become very important to Vitellius. It is during this hot summer that news reaches Rome that the Eastern legions have declared Vespasian emperor. There was going to be a battle between the forces of Vespasian and the flabby, lazy, sickly and morally ruined troops of Vitellius.

To be or not to be emperor

Vitellius was facing the exact same situation Otho had, a rival emperor heading in his direction with an army set on deposing him. Otho had risen to the occasion, and the dandy friend of Nero of whom nobody expected anything of, became a leader. So devoted were Otho's soldiers to their emperor that they

Vitellius (69 CE) –No Appetite for Power   57

would have continued fighting Vitellius' far superior numbers. It was Otho himself who said enough was enough, that he would not risk their lives any further for his cause. 'His look was calm, his words intrepid, and when his courtiers wept, he restrained their untimely emotion.'[27] How very Roman and how very unlike the youth who infiltrated Nero's court by feigning love for an influential Imperial freedwoman, 'although she was an old woman and almost decrepit'.[28] Under pressure, Otho had redeemed himself; would Vitellius, now facing the exact same scenario of a rival emperor, do the same? The answer is a resounding, no, he would not.

Vitellius' initial reaction to this news is to not believe it and punish those who spoke of it. 'Vitellius himself spoke to the soldiers: he attacked the Praetorians who had lately been discharged, blaming them for spreading false rumours, and declared that there was no occasion to fear civil war, keeping back Vespasian's name and sending soldiers round through the city to check the people's talk.'[29] That old tactic of pretending a problem doesn't exist in the hope that it will just go away never works in childhood and it certainly was not going to work for an emperor either. Eventually it became clear that something would have to be done and Caecina and Valens were sent off to defeat Vespasian's forces just as they defeated Otho's.

Whilst they are off doing battle, Vitellius is doing – well not a lot. 'He took no steps to provide weapons, he did not try to inspire his troops by addressing them or by having them drilled, nor did he appear before the people. He kept hidden in the shade of his gardens, like those lazy animals that lie inactive and never move so long as you give them abundant food. The past, the present, and the future alike he had dismissed completely from his mind.'[30] If facing up to an enemy had been the making of Otho, it was the undoing of Vitellius.

This is possibly evidence that Vitellius was the puppet of Caecina and Valens from the beginning, that he never wanted to be an emperor, that he'd been forced into accepting the role because now faced with a god-awful situation, he simply collapses. He will not and cannot accept what is happening and as a result he dooms himself, possibly un-necessarily as Tacitus believes. 'For if he had only acknowledged the truth and sought counsel, he had still some hope and resources left; but when, on the contrary, he pretended that all was well, he made his situation worse by his falsehoods. A strange silence concerning the war was observed in his presence; discussion in the city was forbidden, with the result that more people talked.'[31] Tacitus is right. Vitellius is sitting on a huge army still, despite some defections to the other side. All was not lost for Vitellius had Vitellius responded as emperor.

Valens was killed in battle defending the emperor he made. Caecina, seeing which way the wind was turning suddenly decided that he'd been wrong about everything; Vitellius should never have been emperor and Vespasian clearly should. He deftly defected to the other side. Without these two whispering sweet nothings of glory and victory in his ear what would Vitellius do? The answer is shocking in the extreme, Vitellius stood down as emperor.

If this sounds like a remarkably noble thing to do, there was something in it for Vitellius, 'his own life and a hundred million sesterces'[32] was the deal he struck with Vespasian's brother, Flavius Sabinus. Not bad for a few months' work. Vitellius, with very little effort on his part had been made emperor, thoroughly enjoyed all the trappings that came with the job (food, banquets, entertaining, a bit of being all powerful, more food) and could now step away from it all with a hundred million sesterces weighing down the numerous wagons it would take to transport such a huge sum of money.

It was a sweet deal alright, but there was a problem: Vitellius might be getting a hundred million sesterces but what was in it for his soldiers, those Rhine legions who'd been causing mayhem in Rome these last few months with their fisticuffs? It was up to their now ex-emperor to tell them and persuade them to switch their allegiance, as he had, to Vespasian. 'If Vitellius had found it easy to convert his followers as to give way himself, the army of Vespasian would have entered the capitol without bloodshed.'[33] From which you may gather that Vitellius was not nearly as persuasive in getting his troops to lay down their arms as his two generals had been in persuading them to pick them up. Something that became brutally apparent during the ceremony where Vitellius was to officially abdicate.

Walking down the steps of the palace dressed all in black and accompanied by his family, Vitellius addressed the people of Rome, urging them to remember him. Which they'd likely do anyhow, for he was an enormous blob of a man who collated herds of eunuchs, feasted on eel spunk, and filled the city full of soldiers who'd inconveniently died all over the place. These were things not easily forgotten.

Vitellius went to officially hand over the symbols of his power, 'the dagger which symbolized the power of life and death over his subjects',[34] and the insignia of empire he was to deposit in the Temple of Concordia. However, when Vitellius went to hand over his symbolic dagger to the consul, Caecilius Simplex, Simplex refused to accept it. The crowd surrounding Vitellius began to yell out that he should go back to the palace and when he tried to exit from his life as emperor, they physically barred his way. 'Thereupon not knowing what to do he returned to the palace.'[35] The transfer of power had not been completed.

Was he emperor or not? 'Vitellius himself was in no position either to command or to prohibit. Emperor no longer, he was merely the cause of the fighting'[36] is how Tacitus puts it. Certainly, Vitellius was dead against executing Vespasian's brother Flavius Sabinus, who had been captured by his soldiers, knowing that it would spell the end of any possibility of him getting his hands on those hundred million sesterces and any chance of negotiating for his life with Vespasian. His attempt to offer Imperial mercy, that *clementia* to Flavius Sabinus was shouted down and the emperor chased back into the palace. This was an emperor who had lost control of events, he was utterly insignificant and superfluous to what followed.

A bloody battle commenced on the streets of Rome with Vespasian's forces triumphant. Vitellius was found by these triumphant soldiers hiding in the palace. They tied his hands behind his back and dragged him through the streets of Rome in a truly horrifying scene. 'All along the Sacred Way he was greeted with mockery and abuse, his head held back by the hair, as is common with criminals, and even the point of a sword placed under his chin, so that he could not look down but must let his face be seen. Some pelted him with dung and ordure, others called him incendiary and glutton, and some of the mob even taunted him with his bodily defects.'[37]

You have to wonder whether this mob who pelted Vitellius with dung was the same mob who only days earlier had insisted Vitellius was emperor and forced him to abandon his abdication. Tacitus certain thinks so, 'the mob reviled him in death as viciously as they had flattered him while he lived'.[38] The bound Vitellius was marched through the streets suffering continual jeers and blows from his former subjects to the site of the Gemonian Steps. Here lay the body of Vespasian's brother, Flavius Sabinus, who Vitellius had tried and failed to save. Nobody would make any efforts to save Vitellius. 'When a tribune mocked him, he retorted "Whatever you say, I was your emperor", thereupon he fell lifeless beneath a rain of blows'.[39] Such was the really quite horrible end of Vitellius.

A legacy tarnished?

Vitellius is a shoe in for inclusion as a worst emperor even if we discount the tales of excessive excessiveness as Flavian propaganda, which they likely are, if only for Vitellius' ability to spend such (unbelievable) sums of money on food that isn't even decorated with jewels. It's possible to make the argument that Vitellius is an extremely clever man who puts enough distance between himself and those acting on his behalf to give him the wriggle room to back out at any point. Which even if accurate, which it's not, would still make him a worst emperor.

Vitellius tossed away the title and the responsibility bestowed upon him by the Senate and people of Rome for a hundred million sesterces. It's hard to imagine a more craven act than that for the public duty minded Romans (although skip ahead to the chapter on Didius Julianus and you'll find worse, an act of such despicability it'll make your toes curl). It probably doesn't help Vitellius' cause that only a few short months before another emperor, Otho, faced with similarly desperate and unwinnable circumstances took a very different route; sacrificing his own life to save the lives of others. In that context Vitellius' hundred million sesterces pay out looks even more despicable.

He should never have been emperor and the signs are all there that he didn't particularly want to be. For Valens, Caecina and others Vitellius was a means to an end; they used him to enrich themselves and the soldiers they, not Vitellius, commanded. When Vitellius is standing alone he is horribly exposed; exposed for not being able to control his own soldiers, exposed for the lack of respect they hold him in, exposed for his inability to act decisively against the threat of Vespasian and his own greedy nature is exposed as he publicly choses money over duty. Yep, he was a worst one alright. Bring on the next dynasty!

Chapter 5

Domitian (81–96 CE) – A Swirling Paranoia

Ultimately the lesson of 69 CE was a dangerous one, not only could emperors be made elsewhere than Rome but the army, the body that was responsible for Rome's wealth and power, could be turned against her. As we have seen with Augustus, holding power was a delicate balancing act of competing forces. What 69 CE did was lift the curtain and reveal a tantalising ankle of who was really wearing the trousers, and it certainly wasn't the Senate. This is a learning that is going to have a catastrophic effect on the empire, but not yet, because up next is the super competent Flavian dynasty.

Vespasian, the victor of the turmoil that was 68/69 CE, managed to consolidate his rule and hold onto his prize. Ruling for ten years he patched up a battered and bruised Rome. A canny ruler, Vespasian sought to distance himself from the extravagances of Nero's rule, constructing a reputation as a humble and non-flashy geezer whose job it was to get stuff sorted. 'He was unassuming and lenient from the very beginning of his reign until its end, never trying to conceal his former lowly condition, but often even parading it.'[1]

It's all tosh. Vespasian might not have been born into the Imperial family, but he was born into a family that sent two sons into the Senate, something that was only possible with a substantial fortune of at least two million sesterces. Vespasian has left us two very important monuments from his time as emperor, one is the Colosseum, Rome's first permanent stone amphitheatre whose construction was begun under his rule and is a must see on every tourist's itinerary. The second monument is housed in Rome's Capitoline Museum and walked past by thousands of tourists each year with barely a glance, which is a shame because it defines Vespasian's rule far more than the Colosseum. In fact it defines the rule of every emperor thereafter, for it lays out on bronze what the powers of an emperor are. 'That it be lawful [for him] to make a treaty with whomever he shall wish, just as it was lawful for the divine Augustus, Ti. Iulius Caesar Augustus, and Tiberius Claudius Caesar Augustus Germanicus; and that it be lawful for him to convene the Senate, to report business, to transmit (business), to pass decrees of the Senate by report and by division, just as it was lawful for the divine Augustus, Ti. Iulius Caesar Augustus, Ti. Claudius Caesar Augustus Germanicus; and that when the Senate shall be convened according to his wish or authority, by his order or mandate or in his presence, the law in all matters should be maintained and observed, as if the Senate had been summoned and was being convened according to statute.'

The white gloves and top hat had been removed, there were to be no more magic tricks. This was what an emperor was, and this is what he could do.

Vespasian left one other thing to Rome, his son, Titus. This is the first time in the history of the emperors that a father was succeeded by his biological son. It wouldn't happen again for another 100 years when Marcus Aurelius handed power over to his son, Commodus. Titus stepped up as the second member of what was now a de facto dynasty, the Flavians, at the age of thirty nine, the very prime of life. A seasoned and celebrated general, Titus had spent decades at his father's side learning all that was needed to know about being a successful, good emperor. He was ready, more than ready, to rule.

And he did rule. For a measly two years, a fever carrying him off in 81 CE. It was now the turn of Vespasian's younger son, Domitian, to try his hand at being emperor.

The Last of the Flavians

'It was our delight to dash those proud faces to the ground, to smite them with the sword and savage them with the axe as if blood and agony could follow from every blow. Our transports of joy – so long deferred – were unrestrained; all sought a form of vengeance in beholding those bodies mutilated, limbs hacked in pieces, and finally that baleful, fearsome visage cast into fire, to be melted down, so that from such menacing terror something for man's use and enjoyment should rise out of the flames.'[2] So says a rather surprising vandal, the lawyer and prolific letter writer, Pliny the Younger.

Who had inspired such wrath in this usually mild man of letters? It's the Emperor Domitian, who Pliny served under, and it must be pointed out, prospered under too. During Domitian's fifteen-year rule Pliny held the positions of quaestor, tribune of the plebs, praetor and prefect of the military treasury, all of which would have to have been approved by the emperor. He isn't in the least bit grateful.

Pliny refers to Domitian several times in his letters to friends and always in an uncomplimentary light, one he certainly didn't use when the emperor and his statues were still standing. 'Once Domitian was dead I decided on reflection that this was a truly splendid opportunity for attacking the guilty, avenging the injured and making myself known',[3] he says so himself, in a passage that almost casts him in superhero mode. Roman Justice Man! He attacks the guilty! He avenges the injured! But only when the emperor is safely dead....

Pliny's career success was down to knowing when to keep his head down and his mouth shut. Only standing up for the injured when it was personally safe for him to do so and would benefit him most. Hardly superhero material but very much human material and a valuable insight into how the senatorial class survived under a worst emperor.

Domitian is the last Caesar to feature in Suetonius' biographical work *The Twelve Caesars*, after Domitian I'm afraid we lose Suetonius' valuable insights and gleefully collected sauce on emperors. As Domitian is categorised by Suetonius as one of his bad emperors we might expect a heavy dolloping of slaughtering, sadism, sex and shenanigans of the highest jaw droppingly scandalous. But frankly the Domitian chapter is somewhat of a let-down compared with Suetonius' chapters on the likes of Caligula and Vitellius. Sex-wise all Suetonius can dredge up is that Domitian called the act 'bed wrestling' and that he used to remove the body hair from his mistresses personally. Which is not so much scandalous as a helpful service.

True, there is a story that involves a passionate affair with a very famous member of the acting profession which ends in death, exile, and disaster. But this passionate affair is between Domitian's wife, Domitia, and an actor named Paris. Suetonius struggling for filth hams up an alleged affair between Domitian and his niece, Julia. Which sounds suitably scandalous, but probably wasn't as scandalous as we today would find it given that Claudius had legalised marriage between uncles and nieces, and Domitian's own father, the 'good' emperor Vespasian had once put Julia forward as a potential bride for his younger son.[4]

All in all, you finish the chapter wondering where all the sexy bits are, had Suetonius finally run dry of sauce? However, the story of Domitian is a meaty one even if it lacks the sauce and intense flavour of those Julian Claudian emperors that preceded him. It's the tale of a man undone by his own demons, demons that came with the job of being emperor.

The Spare

Disclaimer up front, Domitian fell out with the Senate, big time. As we've discussed previously, the senators are the keepers of an emperor's legacy, piss them off at your peril because they will destroy you with their shiny styli and papyri! What is interesting with Domitian is that they don't half struggle to blacken his name on occasions. In a passage dedicated to how much Domitian hated his older brother Titus, Suetonius throws in this beauty of a line. 'And after his death he bestowed no honour upon him, save that of deification.'[5] Yes, Domitian hated his brother so much he 'only' made him a god. What a bastard!

Domitian was born on 24 October 51 CE, the very year his father served as consul elect, in a house on the charmingly named Pomegranate Street in Rome. He was the youngest of Vespasian's three children, his sister Domitillia was five years his senior and his brother Titus a good decade older.

His father Vespasian's public career had begun at a sluggish pace, and only really got going thanks to his mother, Domitian's grandmother, putting the boot in. 'She at length drove him to it, but rather by sarcasm than by entreaties or parental authority, since she constantly taunted him with being his brother's footman.'[6] Booted firmly up the arse, Vespasian went onto to take part in Claudius' invasion of Britain and distinguished himself as a general. However, at the time of Domitian's birth he'd fallen foul of court politics by falling out with Empress Agrippina. Vespasian announced his retirement aware that there was little chance of him continuing his public career with Agrippina gunning for him.

After Agrippina's death it was safe for Vespasian to un-retire and he was given the governorship of Africa in 63 CE. In 65 CE Vespasian was part of Nero's tour of Greece and in 66 CE he was sent to Judaea to suppress a revolt that had kicked off there. Thus, from the age of 12 onwards Domitian likely saw very little of his father. Nor likely much of his brother either, who from 57 CE onwards was pursuing his own public career serving his military tribuneship in Germania and later joining his father suppressing the revolt in Judaea.

Quite who was looking after the young Domitian in his father's absence we do not know, details are very scarce on his early life although Suetonius still manages to throw in his usual accusation of sodomy with an even less believable than usual tale of the teenage Domitian being debauched by the later emperor Nerva. If you skip ahead to the chapter on Nerva you'll see why that tale is highly improbable, Nerva is just not the sort of man to do anything nearly as interesting. From which we may deduce that Domitian's early years were so singularly uneventful that there wasn't enough to concoct an even semi-amusing/scurrilous story.

Domitian's curiously anecdote free existence was blown apart in spectacular fashion when he reached his late teens and suddenly found himself centre stage in the swirling tornado that was the Roman political scene in 69 CE.

The Year that made the Man

Domitian's father, Vespasian, had made the bold decision to challenge Vitellus for the title of emperor. This bold decision was made in the warm, sunny and, compared to everywhere else at the time, safe eastern provinces. Whilst in the western half of the empire Otho and Vitellius had been bashing it out, Vespasian out in the east had quietly been collecting legions and weaponry to support his move.

Hundreds of miles away with his elder son Titus by his side, surrounded by heavily armed soldiers who had proclaimed their undying loyalty to him, Vespasian had the resources to bide his time before launching his invasion of Italy. His plan was to blockade the grain ships that sailed from Egypt and fed Rome, and so weaken Vitellius' position in Rome by starving the city.[7]

You would hope at some point during this scheming to dislodge Vitellius by starvation that somebody remembered Domitian. Because Domitian was not in the east plotting with his father and brother, in 69 CE the 19-year-old Domitian was in Rome. It might seem like an obvious point, but communication takes time in the ancient world, the fastest route from Jerusalem to Rome took twenty-six days, from Syria thirty-one days. It is therefore quite feasible that Domitian had no idea that his father was intending to proclaim himself emperor until he heard it along with the rest of Rome. Vitellius' response was swift, Domitian was immediately placed under house arrest. Worse was to follow.

Domitian's uncle, Flavius Sabinus held the position of City Prefect and had been instrumental during the abdication negotiations with Vitellius. When Vitellius abruptly did not abdicate as agreed, Flavius Sabinus fled with some men and his young nephew to the Capitol Hill in Rome. Here they barricaded themselves in hoping to hold out until Vespasian's forces arrived.

The next morning Vitellian troops advanced through the Forum and up the Capitol Hill. Despite a plucky defence, Flavius Sabinus' small number of troops were not enough to withstand the onslaught. In the confusion of battle The Temple of Jupiter that stood on the hill was burned to the ground. Flavius Sabinus and many others were captured and taken to Vitellius. There on the steps of the palace the crowd demanded that Flavius Sabinus be punished, Vitellius' wobbling position was such that he could not stop the soldiers from inflicting that punishment. 'Then they ran Sabinus through, mutilated him, and cut off his head, after which they dragged his headless body to the Gemonian stairs.'[8]

This is what they had done to the emperor's brother, a man who held the post of Prefect of Rome, a man that Tacitus describes as being, 'far from being despicable'[9] (which is a huge compliment because Tacitus hates absolutely everyone). What might they do if they go their hands on the emperor's son? Nothing good, that was for sure.

But what of Domitian? Where was he when his uncle was carted off in chains to his death? He'd managed to escape the siege of the Capitol Hill, with a bit of help. 'Domitian was concealed in the lodging of a temple attendant when the assailants broke into the citadel; then through the cleverness of a freedman he was dressed in a linen robe and so was able to join a crowd of devotees without being recognized and to escape to the house of Cornelius Primus, one of his father's clients, near the Velabrum, where he remained in concealment.'[10]

This is the point at which we could speculate how damn scary this must have been for the teenage Domitian. At 19 years old he hadn't yet completed the military service all elite young Roman men undertook and here he was in the middle of a fierce battle, with a raging fire rapidly engulfing all around him, surrounded by enemies and now hiding in what he hoped was a safe place as Vitellius' troops searched for him. Nothing in Domitian's life had prepared him for this.

This is the point at which the pedants of you will be yelling, 'you don't know what Domitian felt at that exact moment. You speculate, madam, you speculate'. But ha! I do not! Because we have quite an insight into Domitian's feelings, which were he was bloody grateful to have survived the events of 69 CE and I can state this with absolute conviction and confidence. 'When his father came to power, Domitian tore down the lodging of the temple attendant and built a small chapel to Jupiter the Preserver with an altar on which his escape was represented in a marble relief. Later, when he had himself gained the Imperial throne, he dedicated a great temple of Jupiter the Guardian, with his own effigy in the lap of the god.'[11] This very public display of his gratitude to Jupiter for saving him underlines just how desperate his situation, and he himself, had been at that moment.

69 CE was a pivotal year for Domitian, it pushed him into the limelight for the first time in his life. With Vitellius brutally removed from being emperor and with his father and brother still out east, Domitian was the face of this new dynasty in Rome, a role he had no choice but to accept. So, how'd he do? Over to Tacitus. 'Domitian had accepted the name of Caesar and the Imperial residence, with no care as yet for his duties; but with debauchery and adulteries he played the part of an emperor's son.'[12] Well, you would, wouldn't you?

Tacitus is being somewhat unfair as usual, since apparently Domitian manages to escape all those naked women to address the Senate and makes such a good speech that Tacitus struggles to find a put down for it. Similarly, Domitian is again not covered in naked ladies when Tacitus reports, 'at the next meeting of the Senate, Caesar took the lead in recommending that the wrongs, the resentments, and the unavoidable necessities of the past be forgotten'.[13] In

Tacitus' own account Domitian is physically present whilst a lot of not terribly interesting senatorial business is being done, hardly neglecting his duties. Elsewhere it's noted that Domitian is taking to performing his duties a little too well. 'In a single day he assigned more than twenty positions in the city and abroad, which led Vespasian to say more than once that he was surprised that he did not appoint the emperor's successor with the rest.'[14]

A letter dobbing in Domitian is sent to his father. 'He heard an unfavourable report concerning Domitian, to the effect that he was transgressing the bounds set by his youth and what might be permissible in a son.'[15] Which no doubt Tacitus means to sound sinister, as if Domitian is trying to usurp his father, but it reads to me like a 19-year-old boy thrust onto the public stage with no experience playing a role how he imagines it should be done.

Vespasian reached Rome towards the end of 70 CE to claim his throne. The new emperor was in for a surprise, because not only had Domitian been dishing out the honours like peacock brains at a Vitellian feast, but he'd also got married. The bride was Domitia Longina, daughter of the celebrated general Corbulo who'd fallen foul of Nero, and a direct descendant of Augustus via one of those many Julias who peppered the family tree. Domitia was fabulously well connected, she was also married to Aelius Lamia when Domitian met her. But what impediment was a husband to the son of an emperor? None, they were hastily divorced.

This is quite a big deal; Roman marriages were arranged between families often to forge political ties. Now that the Flavians were Imperial any marriage into their ranks was an elevation. That Domitian had likely got married without even consulting his father is unusual in those elite circles and rather backs up our sources' claim that Domitian left as the face of the Flavians in Rome had overstepped the mark. Or as Suetonius puts it, 'he exercised all the tyranny of his high position so lawlessly, that it was even then apparent what sort of a man he was going to be'.[16]

It's quite likely that the boy left behind in Rome whilst his father and brother pursued military glory in the east relished the light being shone on him for a change and eagerly took the perks that came with this sudden elevation. But Daddy was back now, and Domitian was no longer the sole face of the Flavians.

One of Vespasian's first acts when he returned home was to insist Domitian move in with him, bringing to an end the banging social scene his younger son had set up for himself in the epicentre of the family's Alban Villa. That had to smart.

The Rival Princes

The period 69/70 CE was clearly an important one to Domitian personally, one that he later sought to commemorate. You can understand why it was so important to him, it was a moment where all eyes were on him, when he mattered. Once his father and war hero brother returned to Rome, Domitian did not matter so much anymore.

That's not to say that Domitian is shoved into a cupboard and the door locked firmly behind him. One of Vespasian's recommending qualities for being emperor was the fact he had two adult sons, a ready-made dynasty that did away with the tension and uncertainty that had permeated Nero's childless reign. This new emperor was keen to stress the security this represented for Rome on his coins.

A coin minted in 71 CE shows the craggy head of Vespasian on one side, with an image of Titus and Domitian on the reverse sitting on the curule chairs (the chair of elected magistrates) with the wording 'Titus and Domitian, Caesar both, leaders of the next generation'. Elsewhere they feature together on horses ready to spear the enemy and on a coin face-off where you fear an imminent Glasgow kiss. Domitian was repeatedly depicted alongside his father and brother, he was important to the Flavian Dynasty, a young prince. Elsewhere he is *Augusti Filius*, the son of Augustus.[17]

Important Domitian might have been, but not as important as big brother Titus. 'When they appeared in public he followed the emperor's chair and that of his brother in a litter, while he also attended their triumph over Judaea riding on a white horse. Moreover, of his six consulships only one was a regular one, and he obtained that only because his brother gave place to him and recommended his appointment.'[18] Ouch. Although what's with the white horse? Is that a similarly killer dig at Domitian? Because riding a white horse sounds kind of cool.

Our sources ramp up an enmity between the two brothers. Suetonius claims Domitian 'never ceased to plot against his brother secretly and openly'.[19] Which you would think would be the opener to a whole paragraph listing at least the open plots Domitian hatched against his brother – it's not and Suetonius moves quickly on to his next topic. The next topic being how much Domitian hated his brother, but Suetonius offers up no actual evidence for this claim.

Cassius Dio believes that Domitian showed his enormous hatred for big brother Titus by his ban on castration when he was emperor, 'since Titus also had shown a great fondness for eunuchs'.[20] Which is a piss poor revenge even before you factor in Titus had been long dead by this time.

Titus was ten years older than Domitian, that's quite a gap for the brothers to find they had much in common. Also, throughout Domitian's childhood his brother was pursuing his own public career, something that would take him overseas for long periods of time. Titus, therefore, did not feature much in Domitian's early life, it's hardly surprising if the brothers were not particularly close.

It is inevitable that the two princes, these sons of Augustus as they were styled, would be compared with each other. The age gap between them meant that Titus was always going to come out looking better. At 31 he'd had the time to build up a public career and win plaudits for his bravery in the ongoing Jewish war. These were things his father could use to booster the Flavian dynasty's right to rule, maybe they got a little bigged-up, exaggerated even, leaving Titus appearing to be Mr Wonder Man.

Domitian was only 19, he hadn't had time to build up anything illustrious his father could boast about. He wanted to though, he so very desperately wanted to. 'To acquire power and rank that would compare favourably with his brother Titus, Domitian planned a quite unnecessary expedition into Gaul and Germany, from which his fathers' friends managed to dissuade him. He earned a reprimand for this and was made to feel more conscious of his youth and unimportance.'[21] There is another similarly humiliating incident for Domitian later on in Vespasian's reign. 'When Vologaesus, king of the Parthians, had asked for auxiliaries against the Alani and for one of Vespasian's sons as their leader, Domitian used every effort to have himself sent rather than Titus; and because the affair came to nothing, he tried by gifts and promises to induce other eastern kings to make the same request.'[22]

The gifts and promises did not work, Domitian was left in Rome. We can't know for sure whether our sources are right in claiming a rivalry between the brothers. Although if Domitian did loathe Titus, I can quite understand why based on this assessment of his character by Suetonius alone. '[He] was the delight and darling of the human race; such surpassing ability had he, by nature, art, or good fortune, to win the affections of all men.'[23] Urgh. Don't you instantly hate him too now?

During his father's ten-year reign Domitian was hardly the forgotten son, he held a number of important positions, conducts public business and appears on coins and inscriptions. When Titus died unexpectedly in 81 CE, only two years into his reign, Rome was gifted something it hadn't had since Tiberius succeeded Augustus, an emperor who had been trained for the role.

A Capable Emperor

Domitian became emperor in 81 CE; he'd spent twelve years as a prince and it was now time to become king. He was 30 years old. He was ready. He was readier than any emperor since Tiberius. However, he had not one but two hard acts to follow. Daddy Vespasian had got Rome back on her feet after the brutal civil wars of 69 CE, brother Titus was the 'darling of the human race'. How would Domitian compare? Would he finally prove himself the equal of his father and brother?

Trawling through Suetonius' account of Domitian's reign you find sentences like these, 'he made many innovations also in common customs' and, 'he administered justice scrupulously and conscientiously'. 'He was equally free from any suspicion of love of gain or of avarice, both in private life and for some time after becoming emperor; on the contrary, he often gave strong proofs not merely of integrity, but even of liberality.'[24]

Suetonius tells us that Domitian restored many, 'splendid buildings which had been destroyed by fire, among them the Capitolium, which had again been burned, but in all cases with the inscription of his own name only, and with no mention of the original builder'.[25] That the military campaigns he undertook were 'partly without provocation and partly of necessity'.[26] There is mention of lavish entertainments, including a new contest installed in honour of Jupiter. He is generous to the people. 'He made a present to the people of three hundred sesterces each on three occasions, and in the course of one of his shows in celebration of the feast of the Seven Hills gave a plentiful banquet, distributing large baskets of victuals to the Senate and knights, and smaller one to the commons; and he himself was the first to begin to eat.'[27]

Domitian undertakes campaigns to stamp out corruption and improve the morality of the nation. The cruel act of castration is outright banned under Domitian, and the price of eunuchs frozen so that the slave traders could not profit from this new law. We are told that, 'he would not accept inheritances left him by those who had children'[28] which is in vast contrast to Caligula's use of inheritances to keep himself in fancy sandals and golden bread.

Overall Domitian does a lot of stuff, Augustus type stuff, the stuff that emperors should be doing. The court poets of the day make such lovely work of praising this stuff that we shall take a moment to admire their efforts. Statius writes a poem praising the construction of Via Domitiana, the road that ran from Rome to the important coastal towns on the bay of Naples. There's quite a skill in writing an epic poem on the distinctly un-epic subject of a road but Statius is fully up to the task of celebrating this stretch of cobbles and the slightly improved journey times it enables.

'Come then, all you peoples of the East,
Who owe allegiance to Rome's Emperor,
Flow along in your unimpeded journey,
Arrive more swiftly, you Oriental laurels!
Nothing obstructs your wish, no delays.
Let whoever leaves Tivoli at daybreak
Sail the Lucrine Lake in early evening'[29]

Statius' fellow court poet Martial has something even less impressive than a road to write about, street widening. 'You, Germanicus, bade the narrow streets grow wide; and what but just before was a pathway became a highway. No column is now girt at the bottom with chained wine-flagons nor is the Praetor compelled to walk in the midst of the mud. Nor, again, is the barber's razor drawn blindly in the middle of a crowd, nor does the smutty cookshop project over every street.'[30] A glorious battle with the emperor victorious it isn't, but these poems tell us much about Domitian as emperor. He was a man who delighted in the detail and enjoyed being praised for it.

We saw this attention to detail in Suetonius' account of his reign, that campaign to stamp out corruption for example and we also find it in his religious dealing, such as in the case of the secular games. The secular games took place over three days and three nights combining sacrifices and proper respect paid to the gods with theatrical performances. These games, a feature of Republican Rome, had ceased to be held until Augustus revived the tradition in 17 BCE.

The secular games were not an annual event, rather they were to be celebrated after a set number of years repeatedly, rather like the Olympic Games. Rather unlike the Olympic Games the set schedule for the secular games had them being held every 110 years. There is a reason for this, and it's not just to make them extra special and exciting (although that probably featured somewhere in the thinking), the purpose of the secular games was to mark the end of a *saeculum* – that is the lifetime of a person. The Romans, rather arbitrarily one suspects, had decided this was 110 years.

The secular games marked something of significance then, they were intrinsically linked to the gods, and the gods were intrinsically linked to the safety and survival of Rome and everyone who lived on her streets be they emperor or pauper. They were a once in a lifetime event, everyone's lifetime. Or they would have been had not the emperor Claudius held them in 47 CE to celebrate the 800th anniversary of the founding of Rome. The people were not immune to the irony of the 'once in a lifetime' games being staged before they were due. 'The herald's proclamation was greeted with laughter, when he invited the people in the usual formula to games 'which no one had ever seen or would ever see again'; for some were still living who had seen them before, and some actors who had appeared at the former performance appeared at that time as well.'[31]

Domitian ignores these Claudius held games and calculates the date properly from Augustus. Being a stickler for those details again, we are told that, 'to make it possible to finish a hundred races on the day of contests in the Circus, he diminished the number of laps from seven to five'.[32] Of all the multitude of tasks an emperor faces in his daily life it's astounding that Domitian uses his time on what ultimately is a fairly inconsequential matter – the number of chariot races that can be completed in a single day. But the secular games are a religious festival and religion is something that is very important to Domitian, something that the details need paying attention to. Domitian is a man who makes sure things are done properly.

How not to make friends and influence people

So where does it all go wrong I hear you cry? Because Domitian would hardly be included in this book if he continued to whack it in the back of the net. Surely Suetonius has one of those pithy one liners he is so fond of? Of course, he does, it lacks the brilliance of 'so much for Caligula the man, history must deal with the monster'. But it serves the same purpose as the hinge sentence between Domitian's good emperor acts and his bad. 'But he did not continue this course of mercy or integrity, although he turned to cruelty somewhat more speedily than to avarice.'[32]

But don't get too excited because the bad Domitian is covered in thirteen Suetonius chapters versus ten for the good Domitian. If you'll recall Caligula's record beating ratio was eight good versus thirty-eight bad, and Domitian reigned three times as long as Caligula!

The bad acts listed for Domitian don't come anywhere near the depths of Caligula either, he doesn't set up a brothel in the palace, he doesn't get through a rapid changeover of Empresses, staying married to only Domitia Longina throughout his life (despite that affair of hers with an actor) and he doesn't think he's a god. It's all a bit lesser, a bit of a let-down after the scandalous tales we've been showered with previously by our Imperial muckraker in chief, Suetonius.

Take this tale for instance, 'he erected so many and such huge vaulted passage-ways and arches in the various regions of the city, adorned with chariots and triumphal emblems, that on one of them someone wrote in Greek: 'It is enough".³³ I mean it's funny and all, but this is in the bad deeds of Domitian section and the gist of the bad deed is that Domitian built too much nice stuff.

There is repeated reference to his arrogance which is supposedly shown by his enjoyment at hearing the people yell 'Good Fortune attend our Lord and Mistress'. And there's an accompanying claim that Domitian, 'took vast pride in being called 'master' and 'god'. These titles were used not merely in speech but also in written documents'. ³⁴

It pops up in Suetonius too, 'he began as follows in issuing a circular letter in the name of his procurators, 'Our Master and our God bids that this be done'. And so the custom arose of henceforth addressing him in no other way even in writing or in conversation'. ³⁵

Domitian not only makes his brother a god but also his deceased sister and mother, his niece Julia and his son who had died as an infant. Augustus may have styled himself the son of a god when he defied his adoptive father Julius Caesar, but Domitian was the son, brother, uncle and father of a god. This merry Imperial throng of gods, which also included Dad, Vespasian, could all hang out together at the temple of the Flavians Domitian constructed on the Quirinal hill.

After a victory against the German tribe, the Chatti Domitian added Germanicus to his already pretty long title of *Imperator Caesar divi Vespasianus Filius Domitianus Augustus pontifex maximus tribunicia postetas II imperator II praetor patraie consul designates VIII* in which context it makes far more sense to use the much snappier Master and God. He also does that thing which let's face it we'd all do if granted unlimited power, he renames two months after himself; September and October were to be Germanicus and Domitianus. Obviously, that doesn't stick long term, though I rather wish it had. Thirty days has Germanicus....

Elsewhere he gets himself elected censor for life, 'being the first and only man, whether private citizen or emperor, to be given this latter honour; he also received the privilege of employing twenty-four lictors and of wearing the triumphal garb whenever he entered the senate-house'.³⁶ Add to this all those massive grand buildings he erects and slaps his name on, and we are building up a picture of a man in love with the exercising of his own power. Which never did Augustus any harm, but Augustus had the Senate on his side, Domitian did not.

Before we move onto Domitian's relationship with the Senate, which is a big, meaty topic, it's worth us spending a bit of time on the why. Why did Domitian take on this grandiose stance, this adherence to titles and roles?

Partly you suspect it's that whole attention to detail thing that Domitian has going on, he's clearly taken notes on everything an emperor should do:

make relative a god – tick, rename month after yourself – tick, sock it to your dead brother in a series of petty revenges that he will never know about – sort of tick. But there's perhaps something else lurking behind these actions, an insecurity born of Domitian's background and experiences.

Domitian may never have harboured the hatred towards his brother our sources would have us believe, but Titus was still a tough act both to follow and live up to. Is it any wonder the non-war hero, overshadowed second son Domitian went overboard on trying to prove himself worthy of the job? We might speculate, because it's my book and I say we can, that the roots of Domitian's adherence to titles and the proper way to do things stems from his experiences in 69 CE. He'd been on the front line of events in Rome watching as one emperor replaced another in quick succession; he'd seen power won and power lost.

As emperor Domitian was not going to lose his, he was not going to show weakness nor fear – because look what both of those had cost the likes of Otho and Vitellius. From this perspective Domitian's adherence to titles and respect make perfect sense, they are things to hide behind, to cling onto as protection. Act strong, be strong, pay the military well and build loads of things to thank the gods for saving your life.

But what about the Senate, those band of 600 men who worked in partnership with the emperor? The lesson of 69 CE for Domitian was there, those wise politicians who'd raised an emperor and then quickly switched sides the moment things went less well. The men who'd stood by as he'd been placed under house arrest and his uncle executed, the same men who'd then run to the side of his father as if nothing had ever happened. They were not to be trusted.

Domitian's relationship with the Senate is what every biographer of him concentrates on, which is exactly what those senators like. It puts them centre stage with all the importance they believe they are entitled to and imagine they possess. Domitian is depicted as a bad emperor in the books that they write because he doesn't believe they are entitled to that importance. This is evident in both the number of key roles, such as censor, that Domitian takes upon himself and the number of positions that are filled by members of the equestrian class. Domitian pays no heed to senatorial feelings of entitlement, which makes perfect sense when you consider what a details man he is; why employ the mediocre solely because of their name? But Domitian's senatorial snub goes deeper than this, much deeper.

The Roman Forum was at the heart of the city, it was a place where business was conducted, justice was seen to be done in open air public trials, the gods could be thanked and placated in any of the numerous temples and every man wanted to hang out with his huge entourage of clients to show off his importance. Here then was the business of government also conducted in the Senate House by the 600 learned and august members appointed to the Roman Senate. It was the ancient seat of Roman government – sort of, for the Senate House itself was brand spanking new, part of Domitian's ambitious building programme, its previous incarnation having been burnt to the ground in a terrible fire during Titus' reign.

The site of the Senate House, if not the actual building itself, had been the centre of some great and not so great political decisions during the proceeding centuries. With the coming of Augustus and the principate, the power it once held had been moved upwards but it had still been the centre of decision making, even if the emperor predetermined what those decisions would be. Again, it was playing the Augustus game of pretending that the Senate held the same role they always had in government, whilst that not being the case at all. Domitian abandoned this model and recognised what everyone knew to be true; the emperor was the centre of power and wherever he went that power went with him. In Domitian's case, this was his favourite home, a villa owned by the Flavian family, twenty kms outside Rome in the Alban Hills.

It was to this villa that the young Domitian, having unexpectedly found himself the son of an emperor in 69 CE, decided to use as a base to test out what being a prince meant for him. According to Tacitus, lots of parties and nubile, young ladies who suddenly found him very attractive. Domitian maintained an unsurprising fondness for this home and vastly expanded it to be more fitting to an emperor. Ironically enough it's still the home of the extremely important, the remains of the villa are now part of Castel Gandolfo, a Vatican owned property frequented by the pope.

There are various stories about what sort of activities Domitian got up to here that don't involve nubile young ladies. Hunting was a favourite pastime apparently. 'There are many who have more than once seen him slay a hundred wild beasts of different kinds on his Alban estate, and purposely kill some of them with two successive shots in such a way that the arrows gave the effect of horns.'[37]

He held his arts festival there. 'The god that he revered most was Minerva, in consequence of which he was wont to celebrate the Panathenaea on a magnificent scale; on those occasions he held contests of poets and orators and gladiators almost every year at his Alban Villa.'[38] Amongst the surviving archaeological remains is a theatre and also a Hippodrome. Which give you some idea of the scale of the property but also the intention, this was no emperor's play palace or holiday retreat, this was his residence every bit as much as his palace in Rome.

A summons from the emperor in Rome meant a short walk from the Senate House, up the Palatine Hill, easy to pretend this was a friendly consultation prior to an important vote. It was less easy to keep up this pretence when that summoning meant travelling twenty kms to see the emperor. This was a court, Domitian was the king and wherever the king went the court did follow.

Compare this with Tiberius' retirement to Capri, that emperor sent all his business to Rome to be dealt with, he did not move the entire Senate with him. Probably because part of the reason he went to Capri was to escape the senators in the first place. When Nero undertook his tour of Greece, he took some senators with him (notably Vespasian who got kicked off the tour for falling asleep during one of Nero's poetry recitals) but he officially handed over power to his freedman Helius during his absence from Rome. Both cases keeping up the pretence that the Senate was the one that was running the business of Rome. Domitian exploded this myth.

Domitian's relationship with the Senate was strained; with one side, the emperor, refusing to give the Senate and senators the respect that history and position dictated they should be showered with. It probably didn't help relations either when he started executing them.

Domitian's reign is one that gets stamped with the epithet of 'terror.' Remember the usually mild Pliny the Younger's reaction to the emperor's death. 'It was our delight to dash those proud faces to the ground, to smite them with the sword and savage them with axes as if blood and agony could follow from every blow.'[39] Domitian, like Caligula before him, was to suffer the fate of *Damnatio Memoraie*, his name erased from statues and buildings alike. Which given the amount of stuff that Domitian built during his reign was a hand aching amount of chiselling. What had he done that was so bad that warranted such a fate?

Cassius Dio hits us with it. 'It would be impossible to discover the total number of those who were executed by Domitian.'[40] Suetonius backs up Cassius Dios statement: 'he put to death many senators, among them several ex-consuls, including Civica Cerealis, at the very time when he was proconsul in Asia, Salvidienus Orfitus, Acilius Glabrio while he was in exile'.[41] Suetonius also throws in some other names: the emperor's cousin Flavius Sabinus, his wife's former husband Aelius Lamia, the nephew of one-time (and not for a long time) emperor Otho, Mettius Pompusianus, Junius Rusticus, Helvidius.

These are not stories of anonymous victims the like of which Suetonius frequently throws at the feet of emperors, there's no 'some say' here. These are real people that Domitian ordered to be killed. Which is not nice admittedly, but put into the context of the times, Domitian's reign of terror isn't really that terrifying. The academic Brian W Jones has taken a close look at the evidence available for Domitian's alleged purge of the Senate, identifying twelve consuls/ex-consuls who were executed by him and it's worth pointing out not always for spurious reasons. 'On the ground of plotting revolution'[42] is the perfectly valid reason Suetonius attributes to some of these deaths.

Compare this total to the 300 senators who were listed for death under the proscriptions enforced by Mark Antony and the later beloved of the Senate, at least to his face, Augustus. Or to that of the Emperor Claudius, who was actually made a god by the Senate after his death. 'He inflicted the death penalty on thirty-five senators and more than three hundred Roman equestrians.'[43]

An uncomfortable facet of being emperor involved putting people to death. On the evidence presented to us it doesn't appear that Domitian applied this on a huge scale against the elite classes. However, it's all very well for us sitting 2000 years later on our comfortable DFS sofa with a cup of tea in one hand and this book in the other to say, 'oh come on Domitian's reign of terror wasn't that terrifying, perspective folks, perspective.' It is a quite different matter if you are that senator serving under Domitian, perspective isn't going to be much of a comfort to you. As is made clear by the accounts of two men who were there on the ground face to face with the emperor Domitian: Tacitus and Pliny the Younger. They both had public careers under Domitian, they met him and they have plenty to say on him.

Here's Tacitus talking about those days, 'Rome of old explored the utmost limits of freedom, we have plumbed the depths of slavery, robbed as we are by informers even of the right to exchange ideas in conversation'.[44] Tacitus goes on to describe what it felt like to be faced with the emperor, and it is chilling. 'The worst of our torments under Domitian was to see him with his eyes fixed upon us. Every sigh was registered against us; and when we all turned pale, he did not scruple to make us marked men by a glance of his savage countenance.'[45]

As Tacitus' fellow survivor of Domitian's reign, Pliny the Younger, backs up in a throwaway line that opens a letter to a friend: 'have you ever seen anyone so abject and nervous as Regulus since Domitian's death'?[46] But Domitian could intimidate by more than just a look, Pliny makes various references to Domitian's temper. 'Domitian was beside himself with fury' he says, 'he was infuriated by the hatred he had incurred for his cruelty and injustice'.[47]

We know Domitian had little respect for the Senate or the senators, Tacitus and Pliny likely felt that scorn every time they were face to face with the emperor. It had to make an edgy atmosphere. An atmosphere Domitian made even edgier with a dinner party he hosted at the palace one evening to which he invited the foremost senators and equestrians. This is what the party guests arrived to find: 'he prepared a room that was pitch black on every side, ceiling, walls and floor, and had made ready bare couches of the same colour resting on the uncovered floor; then he invited in his guests alone at night without their attendants. And first he set beside each of them a slab shaped like a gravestone, bearing the guest's name and also a small lamp, such as hang in tombs. Next comely naked boys, likewise painted black, entered like phantoms, and after encircling the guests in an awe-inspiring dance took up their stations at their feet'.[48]

Having made it home alive after such a terrifying evening, the party guests must have thanked the gods profusely, at least until there came a knock at the door and a messenger from the emperor was announced. The messenger had come with a gift from the emperor, but his real mission was to further mess with their minds. No wonder those senators smashed Domitian's statues when he died.

A Monster of his own making

So far we have covered all the many good things Domitian did as emperor, concluded that his reign wasn't as terrible when placed in context, whilst noting that it probably still wasn't much fun being a senator during this time. None of which explains how Domitian came to be brutally murdered on the morning of the 18 September 96 CE. Domitian might have had a fraught relationship with the Senate, but it was not those terrorised senators who killed him; it was members of his own household. The plot was formulated by Domitian's personal chamberlain, a man named Parthenius.

Parthenius is an individual tantalisingly just out of reach. As an Imperial freedman he is absent from the historical record as most were, unless they got too rich or too powerful, enough to put the senatorial noses who write those histories out of joint.[49] However, Parthenius does feature in a number of Martial poems. Martial was keen to get his poems in front of the emperor and was pursuing Parthenius for patronage. 'And if by chance (but for this we must scarcely hope) he shall have a moment to spare, beg him to present with his own hands our verses to the emperor; and to recommend this little book, so humble and so small, with merely four words: "This your Rome reads".'[50]

To this end Martial writes a poem to mark the fifth birthday of Parthenius' son, Burrus, and dedicates two poems to a toga that the chamberlain gifted him, 'you surpass in whiteness the lily, the budding flower of the privet, and the ivory which glistens on the hill of Tivoli'[51] From which we can deduce that Parthenius was a man worth cultivating, a man close to the emperor. 'You know the times when our Jove is at ease, when he beams on us with his own benignant countenance, with which he is wont to refuse nothing to suppliants'[5], a man who benefited from that association in power and wealth.

The role of chamberlain was hugely important in the palace job structure, Parthenius had made it to the very top at the pinnacle of his career, a peak that had taken decades of hard work to reach. He had made it, courted by the likes of Martial and no doubt many others, trusted and rewarded by Domitian 'so highly honoured by the emperor as to be allowed to wear a sword'.[53] Then he instigates a plot to brutally murder his boss. Jarring doesn't cover it.

Also involved in this plot were his fellow chamberlain Sigurus, and Entellus who was the Head of Petitions. Both men who also feature in Martial poems (Entellus apparently has a garden of such beauty it's worthy of a verse); both men in very high positions at the palace. The question is why? Why did these men who had benefited from the emperor turn so brutally on him? And it was brutal, the emperor had fought hard for his life leading to this horrifying scene from Suetonius. 'Domitian trying now to wrest the dagger from his assailant's hands and now to gouge out his eyes with his lacerated fingers.'[54] What in the gods name has led them to this very bloody point?

We know from Tacitus and Pliny what it felt like to be a senator serving Domitian, we sadly don't have any accounts on what it felt like to be a freedman or Imperial slave serving Domitian. We can, however, assume it was pretty bloody dark and bleak by what it led them, and not the senators, to do. Behind all this is a very telling line from Suetonius. 'He used to say that the lot of princes was most unhappy, since when they discovered a conspiracy, no one believed them unless they had been killed.'[55]

Domitian's actions from a dislike and a distrust of the senatorial class. to open hostility and tormenting them came from an increasing paranoia. It was a paranoia that, at least at first, was grounded in reality; emperors face daily threats to their rule, and it is an emperors job to root out that disloyalty and downright treason and give it a thorough squishing in a way that puts others off going down the same path. Domitian was not alone in facing such threats and he dealt with them accordingly, you'll remember those senators justifiably executed for plotting revolution during the early part of his reign. But something happens to Domitian as his reign progresses, 'after his victory in the civil war he became even more cruel, and to discover any conspirators who were in hiding, tortured many of the opposite party by a new form of inquisition, inserting fire in their privates; and he cut off the hands of some of them'.[56]

The civil war in question here was a revolt in 89 CE organised by the governor of one of the German provinces, Lucius Antonius Saturinus. Although this revolt was quickly quashed it seems to have played on Domitian's mind and his behaviour becomes much darker from this point onwards. Philosophers are expelled on mass from Rome, Rome's Jewish population is cruelly targeted with a new tax, as Suetonius personally witnessed. 'I recall being present in my youth when the person of a man ninety years old was examined before the procurator and a very crowded court, to see whether he was circumcised.'[57] There was also a persecution of Christians that touched upon the emperor's own family, 'Flavia Domitilla, who was a niece of Flavius Clemens, one of the consuls of Rome that year, was with many others because of the testimony to Christ, taken to the island of Pontia as a punishment'.[58] Remember the name Flavia Domitilla for it will pop up again, a niece of the emperor via Domitian's deceased (and deified) sister Domitilla, Flavia was later made into a saint by the Catholic church. Probably. There is some dispute over whether this saint Flavia happens to share a name with the emperor's niece and is an entirely different martyred Christian lady.

We also have in 91 CE the execution of the chief Vestal Virgin, Cornelia, which in the context of Domitian's increasing paranoia makes sense. The Vestals had become intrinsically linked with the prosperity and safety of Rome. At key moments in history where Rome is really suffering, such as during the second Punic war against Hannibal, we find the tale of a Vestal losing her chastity and being put on trial – almost as if it is entirely their fault that Rome is losing at war, as opposed to say rotten tactics by the male generals. Pliny says that Domitian pushed for the execution, from an extravagant notion that exemplary severities of this kind conferred lustre upon his reign.[59]

But might there also be a slither of paranoia behind it too – a feeling that an act, that we certainly see as cruel and heinous, might neutralise the threats to his rule that Domitian sincerely felt were all around him? After all it had worked during the second Punic war and other occasions during Rome's bloody history, hadn't it?

Some of Domitian's executions at this time reek of paranoia too. There is a cousin, Flavius Sabinus who was executed 'because on the day of the consular elections the crier had inadvertently announced him to the people as emperor elect, instead of consul'.[60] That nephew of the very brief ruling emperor Otho who was executed for marking the occasion of his uncle's birthday. Domitia's ex-husband Lamia is suddenly disposed of for a joke he allegedly made a good fifteen years before regarding the circumstances of his divorce. 'When Titus urged him to marry again, he replied: "Are you too looking for a wife"?'[61] I mean it's a terrible joke and unworthy even of the slightest snigger, one to ignore and brush away. Which Domitian of old had successfully done. This new ultra-paranoid Domitian could not let it lie.

Such was his paranoia that 'he lined the walls of the colonnades in which he used to walk with phengite stone, to be able to see in its brilliant surface the reflection of all that went on behind his back'.[62] Domitian had never been an easy character, lacking the charm of his older brother Titus, he was a man who liked his own company. 'He gave numerous and generous banquets, but usually ended them early; in no case did he protract them beyond sunset or follow them by a drinking bout. In fact, he did nothing until the hour for retiring except walk alone in a retired place.'[63] This love of solitude was so inexplicable to the Roman mind set where a life was always lived in public that it gave rise to stories about what the emperor got up to on his own. 'He used to spend hours in seclusion every day, doing nothing but catch flies and stab them with a keenly sharpened stylus.' Consequently when someone once asked whether anyone was in there with Caesar, Vibius Crispus made the witty reply: "Not even a fly".[64]

It says something about Domitian that the worst anyone could come up with was fly genocide as opposed to a series of heinous sex crimes the likes of which are scatter gunned over other emperors (and entertainingly so, as we shall see later). Never an easy man to get along with, Domitian was now something else entirely, he was a man lost to an all-encompassing paranoia that was tearing him and all around him apart and those on the very front line of this were those closest to him, his own household.

We are specifically told what led to his senior staff clubbing together to murder their boss. It was two executions, the first was that of the emperor's cousin Flavius Clemens who was abruptly removed from serving as Domitian's co-consul that year and got rid of 'on a very slight suspicion'.[65] as Suetonius puts it. Demonstrating to the senators, Domitian imagined were always plotting against him, that none of them were safe, not even a serving consul, not even a member of the Imperial family, not even someone who there was absolutely no credible reason to execute.

The second death that pushed Domitian's two chamberlains, his head of petitions and numerous others into hacking him to death was one that was targeted at them: 'to convince his household that one must not venture to kill a patron even on good grounds, he condemned Epaphroditus to death, because it was believed that after Nero was abandoned the freedman's hand had aided him in taking his life'.[66]

Epaphroditus had been private secretary to Nero and had been one of only three people who had accompanied that emperor on his final flight from Rome. Surrounded by soldiers intent on humiliating the fallen emperor, Epaphroditus had aided his master one final time, '[Nero] drove a dagger into his throat, aided by Epaphroditus, his private secretary'.[67]

This was the epitome of the absolute servant: a man who had risked his own life to get the emperor out of Rome safely, a man who had stayed loyal while the emperor's friends fell away in droves, including both the Praetorian Prefects whose job it was to secure the safety of the emperor, a man who helped the emperor escape a truly humiliating end. Domitian did not see it that way; lost in a swirling vortex of darkness Epaphroditus' noble final act was not noble, he had failed to protect an emperor, he had with his own hands killed an emperor. No man should get away with such a heinous action, even if it had happened twenty-five years before hand. It is very much like what happened to Lamia for his fifteen-year-old bad joke. It's illustrative of just how far Domitian was falling away from reality that he felt so keenly that a long-retired Imperial freedman should be punished for an act that he alone saw as grotesque.

And so Epaphroditus, who was likely a very old man by now, was first exiled and then executed for his part in the death of a long dead emperor. Domitian must have sat back, arms crossed satisfied with his work – they would know now, all of them, what would happen should they fail to protect him from those senators who wished him dead, they would suffer the fate of Epaphroditus, all of them.

In his mind he probably thought that he had terrorised them into absolute obedience and endeavour. He hadn't. What he'd done was set them on the path to doing the exact opposite, he had set them on a path of assassination. Because the lesson the likes of Parthenius and Entellus and Sigurus took from the execution of both Epaphroditus and Flavius Clemens was that none of them were safe from the emperor's paranoia. Not even loyal chamberlains with nice gardens and poets for friends.

They don't do the deed themselves, sensibly because what do civil servants know about the mechanics of murder? Instead, they found a handy volunteer in the shape of Stefanus, a steward from the household of the exiled and martyred Flavia Domitillia, who after his mistress' death had found himself incorporated into the palatine household. Stefanus was a man with a grudge and a score to settle, but handily one who could follow instructions. 'He stabbed the emperor in the groin as he was reading a paper which the assassin handed him and stood in a state of amazement. As the wounded prince attempted to resist, he was slain with seven wounds by Clodianus, a subaltern, Maximus, a freedman of Parthenius, Satur, decurion of the chamberlains, and a gladiator from the Imperial school.'[68]

An Imperial Tragedy

Despite Domitian's many successful acts as emperor he has to make it into our worst list. The brutal manner of his death and the sheer number of people from his household who participated in it, including according to Cassius Dio, the Empress Domitia who knew of the plot but did nothing to stop it proceeding, shows just how dark life under Domitian's rule had got. Cassius Dio says of Domitia that 'she stood in terror of her life'. She was far from alone on that score.

The smashing up of Domitian's statues by Pliny and his pals makes a lot more sense now, the relief from that daily terror must have been exhilarating. A relief no doubt felt by the Imperial household too. Domitian may not have the same level of cruel tales attached to his name as say Caligula, but he had created such an atmosphere of dread and fear that it overshadowed his many good works as emperor. Arguably Domitian was the architect of his own doom, his spiralling paranoia leading him directly to that what he feared most; conspiracies against him. It was perhaps inevitable that one of these would eventually succeed.

1. The man who singlehandedly invented emperors, Augustus.

2. Augustus' final resting place, the mausoleum where his ashes were placed in 14 CE. A text of the Res Gestae bigging up his legacy was displayed outside.

3. The Senate House, where the men who have to be kept happy hang out pretending they are still important.

4. Temple of Mars Ultor in the Forum of Augustus, part of Augustus' extensive building programme.

5. Rome's third emperor, Gaius better known as Caligula.

6. Germanicus, the war hero father to Caligula who mysteriously died when Caligula was only seven.

7. The very well-connected Agrippina the Younger, beloved sister of Caligula (until she plotted against him), dutiful wife to Claudius (until she had him poisoned) and devoted mother to Nero (until her darling son had her executed).

8. The Emperor Galba looking characteristically stern and surprisingly ripped for a 72-year-old.

9. Galba's sternness on display in a portrait created 1500 years after his death.

10. The short-lived emperor Vitellius, third of the four emperors of 69 CE.

11. The Emperor Domitian who was ultimately undone by the paranoia of his position.

12. A prodigious builder, Domitian added to the palace on Rome's Palatine Hill with a luxurious palace of his own. The photograph depicts a garden area.

13. Stadium built as part of Domitian's upgrading of the emperor's Roman residence.

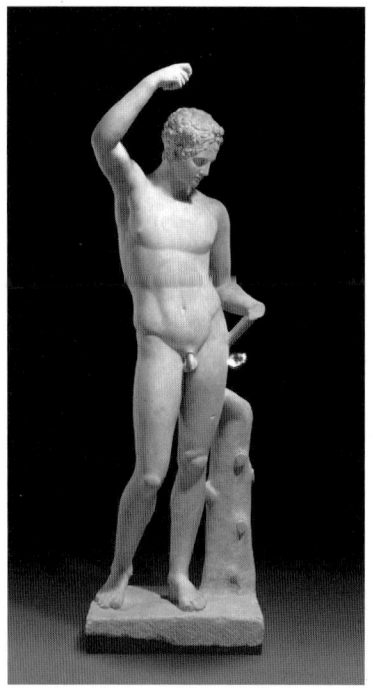

14. Statue of a pouring satyr found at Domitian's Alban villa which he much preferred to his Roman residence.

15. Domitian's niece Julia who he was rumoured to be having an affair with.

16. The Forum that Domitian built that Nerva very cleverly stamped his own name on.

17. The Emperor Nerva, another surprisingly ripped pensioner.

18. The 'best of emperors' Trajan, who may well have forced Nerva into making him his heir.

19. Lucius Verus, owner of the greatest beard in antiquity.

20. Marcus Aurelius, co-emperor with Lucius Verus and father of Commodus.

21. Faustina the younger, wife of Marcus Aurelius and mother to Commodus.

22. Commodus, being born to the purple gave him no advantage in the best emperor stakes.

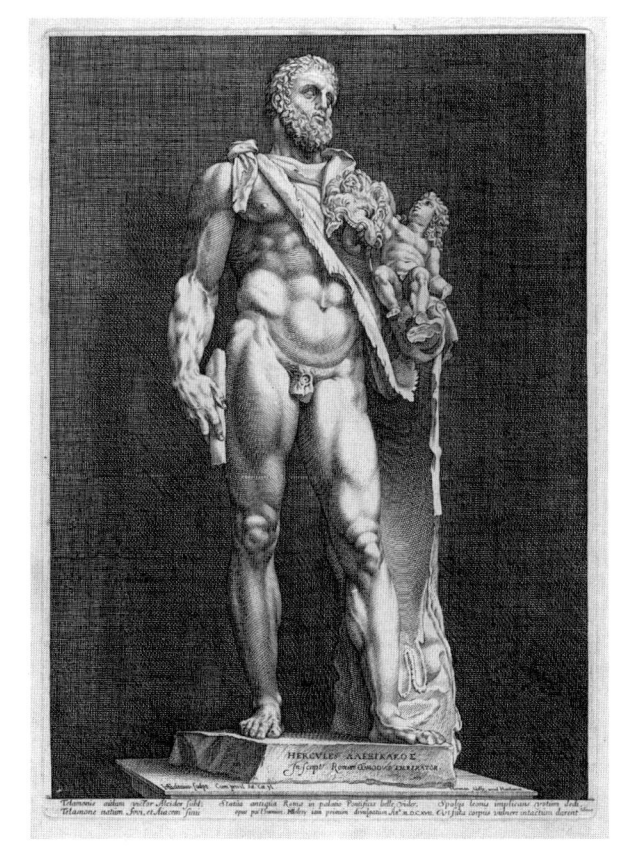

23. Commodus dressed up as his favourite god, Hercules.

24. The assassination of Commodus.

25. Didius Julianus, the man who brought an empire and immediately regretted it.

26. Happy families. Emperor Septimus Severus, Empress Julia Domna and their two lovely boys Caracalla and Geta. Geta's face has been scrubbed out.

27. The harshest glare of antiquity, big brother Caracalla.

28. Mother to Caracalla and Geta, Julia Domna.

29. Elagabalus, Rome's most eccentric emperor.

30. The Roses of Heliogabalus. Death by flowers! An improbable but entertaining story.

31. Elagabalus' cousin and successor, the much more sober and boring Alexander Severus.

32. An emperor with his army; his power base but also his likely murderers, particularly in the third century.

33. One of the first of the fleeting third-century emperors, Gordian I.

34. These coins are the only reason we know there ever was an Emperor Silbannacus.

35. A fleeting presence, the Emperor Quintillus.

36. The man who sorted out the chaos of the third century, Diocletian.

38. The terminally weak, Valentinian II.

37. The Tetrarchs having a group hug before all falling out.

39. The Vandals sacking Rome in 455 CE, something that can be fully placed at the feet of Petronius Maximus.

40. A coin of Petronius Maximus which rather ambitiously depicts Petronius holding a cross, his foot resting on a globe with the word victory inscribed.

Part II

Welcome to the Golden Age, 96 CE–222 CE

The dynasty that followed The Flavians you'll find referred to as the Antonine, but Edward Gibbon is his seminal, and indeed massive book, *Decline and Fall of the Roman Empire*, (which makes both a handy door stop and fly squasher the likes of which Domitian could have done with), bestowed upon them the far catchier 'Five Good Emperors'.

'If a man were called to fix the period in the history of the world, during which the condition of the human race was most happy and prosperous, he would, without hesitation, name that the Roman which elapsed from the death of Domitian to the accession of Commodus.'[1] Which is quite a claim. Although not quite as bold as the claim made by one of these five, Trajan, who called himself *Optimates Princeps* which translates as the Best of Emperors. But then as previously noted, emperors are not short of ego and clever branding is all part of the job.

Looking closer into these eighty-five years, which Gibbon proclaims the pinnacle of happiness and prosperity, unearths vast barbarian incursions into Roman territory, military insurrections, genocide, mass senatorial executions and as the icing on this particular cake of calamity, a devastating plague that wipes out thousands of Rome's citizens. So why does Gibbon single out this era as so golden?

There is one thing that makes this era stand out from all others in Roman history, none of these five good emperors get assassinated, when one dies, power is seamlessly handed to the next. Which is quite something when we look back over the story of emperors so far with seven out of the eleven previous emperors definitely meeting a violent end and three out of the remaining four rumoured to have been non-violently murdered.[2] Only Vespasian so far has been allowed to die of an uncomplicated, non-conspiratorial natural illness.

A smooth succession meant a stable empire without marauding legions fighting their way across farmers' cultivated fields and blocking those lucrative trades routes with their marching boots. It meant the system could run as Augustus envisaged it over 100 years before and run it did, with new provinces being conquered and added to the empire, and vast infrastructure projects completed. Gibbon is right to give the credit for these successes to those five good emperors; Nerva, Trajan, Hadrian, Antoninus Pius and Marcus Aurelius.

They faced many adversities, but they did so with competence which is refreshing and maybe if I'm honest, a little boring. Trajan might crown himself the best of emperors, but his megalomania does not extend further into a series of juicy and entertaining anecdotes à la Caligula or Vitellius for me to pepper this section of this book with. These five emperors gleam even brighter when compared with what comes after them, it's the same calamity cake but left in the hands of the very much incompetent Commodus. But more on Commodus and his one-man mission to destroy everything bequeathed him later – and it's worth tuning in for because it's a hell of a tale involving ostrich decapitation, poisoned beef and a haram of very lovely ladies. Appetite wetted let us return to the boringly competent – or are they?

You might think I'd be hard pressed to find any worst emperors amongst our five good men, but even on the most gleaming gold there can be found a smudge.

Chapter 6

Nerva (96–98 CE) – The Hinge

Nerva became emperor in the wake of Domitian's assassination. Because somebody had to, and it may as well have been Nerva. A sentiment the murderers of Domitian appear to have agreed with. 'Accordingly, they hastened the plot which they already were forming; yet they did not proceed to carry it out until they had determined who was to succeed to the Imperial office. They discussed the matter with various men, and when none of them would accept it (for all were afraid of them, believing that they were testing their loyalty), they betook themselves to Nerva.'[3]

Nerva was certainly not an obvious choice to be emperor. The exact how and the why he ended up as emperor in 96 CE are all a bit of a mystery. Cassius Dio, quoted above, believes Nerva was fully aware of the plot to kill Domitian. The speed at which he steps into Domitian's shoes and job, he's made emperor on the very same day as the assassination, suggests forward planning on somebody's part. But it doesn't necessarily follow that Nerva was in it from the start. Every member of the Senate faced with the bloody corpse of Domitian knew that a successor was needed and fast, because Rome had been in this position before and it had not gone well for anyone.

This was 96 CE, only twenty-five years after Nero had committed suicide leaving as Domitian had, no designated successor. This void had led to the chaos of 69 CE when the legions had pitched their own candidates against each other in one singularly brutal year. People had not forgotten 69 CE; people still feared another 69 CE. 96 CE could well be that year.

The Senate needed a new emperor quickly to fill the gaping power void before the news spread to the provinces and the governors based there fancied themselves a laurel leaf hat. Nerva was the Senate's choice, and it all works out fine, 96 is no 69 CE. The afeared civil war does not happen and as noted at the beginning of this chapter, Rome enters an eighty-five-year period of peace, prosperity and stability. None of which is down to Nerva, who ruled as emperor for a paltry sixteen months. Nerva is the hinge, not the door to this golden era and there are some very good reasons why he makes our worst emperors list.

The unlikely Emperor

The similarities between what Rome had faced in 68 CE with Nero's death and what it now faced with Domitian's corpse messing up the shiny palace floor are present. The void of Nero's death had been filled by Galba. Like Nerva, Galba had been the choice of the Senate. Galba and Nerva were also of mature years when they became emperor; Nerva was 66, Galba an even more advanced 72.

But here the similarities end because Nerva is no Galba. Certainly, nobody ever casually commented that Nerva had all the makings of a ruler, why would they? Because before 96 CE he barely even features in the historical record, his public career is so sketchy as to be almost non-existent. We know he was praetor in 65 CE, we know he held a consulship in 71 CE and another in 90 CE with the Emperor Domitian as his fellow consul. That is it.

We looked at Galba's background and achievements in an earlier chapter but it's worth revisiting in the context of Nerva's lack of achievements and because I forgot to mention the elephants before. Galba we are told, 'began his career of office before the legal age, and in celebrating the games of the Floralia in his praetorship he gave a new kind of exhibition, namely of elephants walking the rope'.[4]

If introducing tight rope walking elephants to Rome was not enough of a legacy (and by god it is!) Galba goes onto be governor of Aquitania, Africa, Upper Germany and Spain. All of which he distinguishes himself in. He's parachuted into provinces to sort out the legions which he naturally succeeds in achieving and he demonstrates amazing stamina and fitness. '[He] particularly distinguished himself, while directing the military manoeuvres shield in hand, by actually running for twenty miles close beside the emperor's chariot.'[5]

What a guy! No wonder the Senate made him emperor. I think we can all agree with Tacitus that Galba had all the stuff, all the experience that a ruler required.

In comparison to Galba's dynamism Nerva appears somewhat of a wimp, there's no mention of him ever being a provincial governor let alone him being appointed as the only man in possession of the attributes needed to successfully sort out disorderly legions, as Galba was. There's absolutely no mention of Nerva ever serving in any military position, something that was de-rigour for all Roman men of the elite classes. There's certainly no mention of Nerva introducing a new spectacle of wonder to Rome that would be considered worth recording by a biographer a hundred years later. He's also not in the best health, 'Nerva was so old and so feeble in health (he always, for instance, had to vomit up his food) that he was rather weak'.[6] What has Nerva got going for him? Well, apparently, he's quite the poet. That'll make up for his lack of military experience – not.

The question of course is, why the hell did they make him emperor? To answer that we first need to go back into that non-illustrious public career of Nerva's because there's some tantalising snippets that might help us solve this mystery.

Mysterious Favours

As we noted, Nerva was praetor in 65 CE, the year matters because it was in 65 CE that a whopping big conspiracy was hatched against the then emperor, Nero. Known as the Piso conspiracy this was a plot that had long fingers, as Tacitus puts it. 'Senators, equestrians, soldiers, and women themselves had vied in giving their names, not simply through hatred of Nero, but also through partiality for Gaius Piso.'[7] The Piso plot involved some big names, we know this because Tacitus lists most of them without feeling the need to say anything further about them – the name alone was enough for his audience.

Amongst those names were the poet Lucan and Nero's ex-tutor Seneca. Even worse was Faenius Rufus, who happened to be one of the Praetorian Prefects. We have seen the pivotal role the guard could play in emperor making and emperor removing, which underlines just how much danger Nero was in from these plotters. A single moment brings this chillingly to the fore. The Prefect, Faenius Rufus wasn't initially named as one of the plotters and he was present, undetected during the interrogation of some of the traitors. 'It was the same Rufus who, when Subrius Flavus at his side inquired by a motion if he should draw his sword and do the bloody deed during the actual inquiry, shook his head and checked the impulse which was already carrying his hand to his hilt.'[8]

Rufus was not only physically close to the emperor, he was also armed, and he could have at any moment struck down the emperor. Faenius Rufus did not escape detection for long, his fellow plotters were not happy to be so brutally interrogated by the very man who'd sat at the same table and talked treason with them. He was denounced and shared their fate. It was only fair.

This was then a credible plot, involving men close to the emperor who had the means to remove him. That they did not was down to those who raised the alarm, one of whom was Nerva. Quite what Nerva's role was in uncovering the Piso plot we do not know, his reward from Nero for this whatever it was is quite something. '[Nero] bestowed triumphal distinctions on the consular Petronius Turpilianus, the praetor designate Cocceius Nerva, and the Praetorian Prefect Tigellinus: Nerva and Tigellinus he exalted so far that, not content with triumphal statues in the Forum, he placed their effigies in the palace itself.'[9]

Emperors don't tend to allow ordinary folk to have statues of themselves in the forum and the palace, that's treading on the toes of the Imperial family. So whatever Nerva did it must have been crucially important to the dissolution of the plot. Or alternatively Nero, having realised how close he came to losing everything and how many of his so-called friends had been involved in wanting to murder him, was pathetically grateful to those that stayed loyal, which included Nerva. Although in that instance wouldn't the Forum be filled with statues of senators who weren't involved in the plot? We are back to Nerva having distinguished himself in a mysterious manner.

There's a similar mystery behind Nerva's next notable appearance in the historical record when he's made consul in 71 CE by Vespasian. The Flavian dynasty kept consulships very much in the family (Vespasian, Titus or Domitian held sixteen of the twenty ordinary consul posts during Vespasian's reign);[10] that a non-family member, Nerva receives one only two years into Vespasian's reign hints at some great favour that Nerva may have performed during Vespasian's battle to become emperor in 69 CE. Again, we have no idea what this is. But it's significant since Nerva was related to one of the other contenders in 69 CE; his sister was married to the brother of Otho (emperor two of four). An association that doesn't scar him from aligning with Vespasian, nor being exalted by that emperor.

That the Senate appoint him as emperor suggests that they at least had some knowledge of what these amazing feats of Nerva were and those amazing feats demonstrated some amazing abilities that aren't obvious anywhere else we meet Nerva. Or alternatively there were no amazing feats and Nerva is exactly as undistinguished as our sources portray him. But this very indistinguishableness (yes, it's a word and I'm using it) is likely what distinguished Nerva.

The saying goes in our society, behind every successful man there is a woman. In ancient Rome behind every successful man was a heap of lesser men hoping to gain his favour so that they might be similarly successful. Rome operated on a system of patrons and clients; a patron was someone of higher social standing with whom the client aligned themselves in the hope of benefiting from the friendship. Likewise, the patron hopes to benefit from the client in some way, which might be a vote in a forthcoming election or just to hang out with him in the Forum with the other clients to make him look very important and popular This made Rome a place of favours granted, and favours repaid, with debts on both sides.

An enormously successful and ambitious man, like say Galba, therefore is blessed with a team of clients ready to promote his interests at every given opportunity. These teams of supporters can very easily, at the higher end of politics, become factions. Within the Imperial family factions formed around anyone who might be a likely successor. In the precarious situation that was 96 CE, Nerva's very lack of impressive credentials and dynamism were perhaps what recommended him. An undynamic and sparse public career meant no gaggle of men vying behind him, eyeing up the Imperial throne. He'd never served with the army so there was no legion of soldiers bigging up their man, inspiring the jealousy and envy that would lead to other legions promoting their own contender. His close association with the Flavian dynasty meant he was acceptable to surviving supporters of the slain ruler. He was, in short, an uncontroversial choice unlikely to unsettle any scarcely buoyant seaworthy vessels.

Or perhaps Nerva's elevation had nothing to do with mysterious favours or a lack of distinction. Maybe Cassius Dio was perfectly correct in stating that Nerva became emperor because he was the only man Domitian's assassins found who would take on the job. For the Senate that appeared to be good enough. For the meantime.

The Perfect Emperor?

There might be an emperor in place but would the real power of Rome, the legions, accept him? And what about those troublesome power brokers in the city, the Praetorian Guard? Both groups who Domitian had amply rewarded and so might well be somewhat aggrieved at his brutal murder. Not to mention those conspirators who'd actively participated in Domitian's murder and who were still happily going about their business in the palace.

These were the bubbling problems that the new emperor now faced. How he dealt with them would determine whether Rome descended into civil war or not. This was the moment for the nonentity to prove himself. According to Cassius Dio, the emperor himself felt he'd more than proved himself worthy of the job. 'Nerva ruled so well that he once remarked: "I have done nothing that would prevent my laying down the Imperial office and returning to private life in safety".'[11]

Nerva's first moves were to undo the insidious nastiness of the last few, paranoid years of Domitian's reign. 'Nerva also released all who were on trial for treason and restored the exiles; moreover, he put to death all the slaves and the freedmen who had conspired against their masters and allowed that class of persons to lodge no complaint whatever against their masters; and no persons were permitted to accuse anybody of treason or of adopting the Jewish mode of life.'[12] There were to be no more treason trials, nor senators turning on each other to curry Imperial favour, this was to be a new era. The senators who had sworn in Nerva as emperor must have slapped themselves on the back as a job well done.

Those slaps probably got harder when Nerva returned property that had been confiscated by the state to its rightful owner. And they'd have been practically knocking each other off their feet with this one. 'In the senate he took oath that he would not slay any of the senators, and he kept his pledge in spite of plots against himself. Moreover, he did nothing without the advice of the foremost men.'[13] The senatorial class who had elevated him were very much in the forefront of Nerva's plans for Rome, but he didn't forget one of those other groups every emperor has to keep on side. 'To the very poor Romans he granted allotments of land worth 60,000,000 sesterces, putting some senators in charge of their purchase and distribution. When he ran short of funds, he sold much wearing apparel and many vessels of silver and gold, besides furniture, both his own and that which belonged to the Imperial residence, and many estates and houses — in fact, everything except what was indispensable'[14]

So that's keeping the people happy ticked off the list of things an emperor must do. There were also just laws introduced, 'Among his various laws were those prohibiting the castration of any man, and the marriage by any man of his own niece'.[15] And although his reign was too short for any great infrastructure projects, Nerva cleverly took the forum that Domitian had been building and slapped his name the hell all over it.

So, there we have it, Nerva worked successfully with the Senate. He took care of the poor. He introduced just laws. He had a forum. He displayed *virtus maximus* by dipping into his own pockets. Surely, I hear you cry, that is the very blueprint of a good emperor as determined by Augustus in the first chapter of this book, what gives? Why is Nerva a worst emperor?

Remember that murder of that emperor that was emperor before Mr Senate Pleasing Nerva? Remember what happened to the murderers? Of course you don't because the answer is nothing. Nothing happened to the murderers. They were still in post at the palace going about their business. This did not bother the Senate, removing Domitian had been very much in their favour. This did not bother the people particularly, they didn't hate Domitian like the Senate, they had no cause to, but he didn't possess the kind of personality that inspired their love either. Nerva dipping into his personal pockets to their benefit likely aided their collective forgetting of the emperor that had been.

But there was none of this collective forgetting by the army, nor the Praetorian Guard. They had not forgotten, and they were furious that Domitian's killers had yet to be punished for their crime. A bounty paid to them by Nerva did not make them un-remember this, not least because this new emperor had been foisted upon them. Bounty aside, the feeble and aged Nerva didn't look like what an emperor should be to them, he certainly didn't look like he possessed the energy to launch the types of military campaigns that soldiers profit from.

Domitian had undertaken and even accompanied his legions when they faced off against the Chatti and the Dacians, and although it was true that these were hardly glorious campaigns and sometimes even inglorious ones (Tacitus makes the claim that Domitian couldn't capture any Chatti for his triumph and so instead had some men dress up as Chatti tribe members instead), it was nonetheless proper fighting against a proper enemy, the sort of thing that legionaries like to do, as opposed to say building roads, practising their marching and hanging about in tents in some miserably cold province waiting for something exciting to kick off.

In short, and in the immortal words of Shania Twain (sort of), Nerva did not impress them much. This left them susceptible to the offers of any rival who could at a bare minimum eat a hearty meal without throwing it up again and stand up from a chair unaided. This is worth remembering whilst I recount what was happening with those soldiers who weren't shivering in tents far away from home but rather living it up in a nice cosy barracks on Rome's Viminal Hill, the Praetorian Guard.

Cassius Dio tells the tale extremely sparingly. 'Casperius Aelianus, who had become commander of the Praetorians under him as he had been under Domitian, incited the soldiers to mutiny against him, after having induced them to demand certain persons for execution.'[16] The certain persons the Praetorians were after were Parthenius, Entellus and Sigurus, the Imperial freedmen who had been the masterminds behind Domitian's assassination. That had been over a year ago, the question has to be posed; why were they so interested in punishing Domitian's murderers now?

There are two possibilities, the first is that Parthenius and his co-conspirators had been so successful at keeping the blood off their hands that nobody knew they were behind the plot. Which is very believable given that everybody who had played a physical role in the assassination, Stefanus for example, had been roundly hacked to death by the Praetorian Guard minutes after they had successfully hacked the emperor to death. There was no one left standing to dob them in, except clearly there was, even if the freedmen themselves were not aware of it. In 97 CE that someone, whoever it was, let the Praetorians in on the secret; the murderers of Domitian were very much still alive, unpunished and on the staff of this new emperor, Nerva. Their response was to storm the palace and insist that Nerva punish these evil doers.

This, according to Cassius Dio, is what happened next. 'Nerva resisted them stoutly, even to the point of baring his collar-bone and presenting to them his throat; but he accomplished nothing, and those whom Aelianus wished were put out of the way.'[17] Showing truly how little respect the Praetorian Guard had for Nerva and how toothless and powerless Nerva actually was. Never had an emperor been so humiliated. Although the humiliation Nerva suffered at the hands of the hands of the Praetorians was nothing compared to what happened to Parthenius, the chamberlain who'd once given a snow-white toga to an aspiring poet; he had his genital sliced off and put in his own mouth. No doubt to much amusement from the guards.

Perhaps it was this horrific end that led to Nerva running up to the Capitol hill where, '[he] said in a loud voice: "May good success attend the Roman Senate and people and myself. I hereby adopt Marcus Ulpius Nerva Trajan".'[18] Or perhaps not. Because it's all a bit pat, isn't it? That the Praetorian Guard should suddenly decide to avenge their dead emperor after a year of not doing anything about it and that the current emperor would respond by naming his successor in such a hurried and harassed manner. Pat. Staged. Orchestrated. Organised. By the man who was set to benefit, Marcus Ulpius Trajan. Perhaps.

Was this hurried declaration the result of terror, with Nerva rushing to name an heir who was popular with the army to protect himself from any further nastiness from his own Praetorian Guard? Or was Nerva forced at literal knife point to choose Trajan as his heir? Pliny the Younger in a speech suggests that the one being forced into doing something he didn't want to was not Nerva, but rather Trajan! 'But though you possessed the proper qualifications, Caesar, you were unwilling to become emperor. You had therefore to be forced. Yet you could not have been forced but for the danger that threatened our country; you would not have assumed the Imperial power were it not to save the empire. And I feel sure that the Praetorians revolted because great force and danger were necessary to overcome your modesty.'[19]

According to Pliny the Praetorians stormed the palace and threatened the emperor to persuade Trajan, who was hanging out in the provinces, that by the Gods above he was needed in Rome right now to stop them from storming the palace and threatening the emperor. I think I am not alone when I say, huh?

But Pliny sticks to his bafflingly uncredible theory, probably because Trajan is stood a few feet away from him as he's delivering this speech. He's dug himself that hole and there's no filling it back in again and stepping away whistling a jaunty tune. 'If only such calamity could induce you to assume the reins of government I should say that it was worth the price' he decides. Which could be read as a knowing wink to Trajan, a nod that everyone knows he was the one who told the Praetorians what to do and it all worked out for the best, didn't it? Or alternatively it could be read as just really rather callous towards the genuine life-threatening situation Nerva had faced. Sadly, Pliny the Younger isn't around to explain himself.

Gibbon's take on Nerva, one of his five good emperors, is not dissimilar to Pliny's take that Rome needed Trajan, 'his mild disposition was respected by the good, but the degenerate Romans required a more vigorous character, whose justice should strike terror into the guilty. Though he had several relations, he fixed his choice on a stranger'.[20]

Which completely shifts the blame from anything Nerva did or did not do and puts it firmly on the shoulders of the Roman people for being unashamedly degenerate. Although even Gibbon is conscious of the strangeness of Nerva choosing an absolute stranger over his own numerous relatives.

The truth of why Nerva made Trajan his heir can never be known, because Trajan does succeed Nerva and was in prime position to destroy any incriminating correspondence. But it would certainly be possible for someone working on Trajan's behalf to let slip the secret behind Domitian's death to the guard and reap the rewards from that action, whilst applying pressure on a beleaguered emperor.

Nerva died on 28 January 98 CE, three months after the Praetorian Guard had stormed the palace. He had ruled only sixteen months. In that short period, he had been humiliated and physically threatened in a way that no other emperor had ever. If you'll remember one of the powers an emperor held was that of tribune of the plebs which made their body inviolable, the emperor was untouchable, or rather he should have been. Nerva was not.

The Senate may have liked him for not executing them, but Nerva failed to charm any of the other sectors of society he needed to – most notably the Praetorian Guard and the army. It appears that throwing money at them was not enough anymore, the army were looking for that something extra in their rulers now, one that would over time change the nature of what emperors were.

The one success of his rule that Nerva is often credited with is preventing a civil war in the void of Domitian's death, but really his biggest contribution towards this was dying when he did. How long could he really have held onto Rome given what had happened on that day in October 97 CE? His credibility, his inviolability and all respect had been lost. Had he not died when he did, he most likely would have suffered a fate similar to that other stop gap emperor, Galba, or Vitellius, another emperor who lost control of the army.

The question therefore is not why have I included Nerva in our list of worst emperors, but why do Gibbon and others include Nerva as one of the five good emperors? The answer is that unlike our previous worst emperor Domitian, who I'm not even going to bother putting in the effort to argue was a much better emperor than Nerva – he just was, Nerva had a successor to big him up. It was in Trajan's best interests to tell the world how wise and capable the man who had chosen him (possibly at knife point) as his heir was.

Chapter 7

Lucius Aurelius Verus (161–169 CE) – Overshadowed

I have a poster on my wall that depicts a coin head of every Roman emperor that ruled from Augustus right up to Romulus Augustulus. I use it as a reference and as a means of depressing myself as to how many emperors I have left to cover in this book. Spoiler alert – it's more than a few. But there is an emperor missing from my poster and this isn't the only list of Roman emperors you will find him absent from either. For Lucius Aurelius Verus who legitimately ruled Rome as emperor from 161 to 169 CE somehow finds himself eternally skipped over, which is chronically unfair for a man who tried his hardest to be noticed by accentuating his blonde hair with gold dust.

We, however, shall not ignore Lucius Verus! Although we shall spend most of our time discussing why he is so forgettable that Gibbon on summarising the achievements of the Antonine dynasty fails to include him. He may as well as never existed.

Lucius Verus' nonentity-ness is jolly unfair because his life is littered with very repeatable anecdotes, mostly connected with what he did for funsies. These include that very odd pastime of Roman youths, going to taverns in disguise and getting yourself beaten up. Verus takes to this quite as well as the likes of Nero and Otho did before him, returning home 'his face was beaten black and blue'.[1] Then there was this equally baffling idea of fun. 'It was his wont also to hurl large coins into the cook-shops and therewith smash the cups.'[2]

Verus was fond of charioteers and of gladiators and of playing dice. He held many fine banquets, including one that allegedly cost six million sesterces, chiefly because Verus got insanely carried away with gifts for his guests. The lucky party goers were presented with Alexandrine crystal goblets, gold jewelled cups, golden vases with ointments in the shape of perfume boxes and 'the comely lads who did the serving were given as presents, one to each guest; carvers and platters, too, were presented to each, and also live animals either tame or wild, winged or quadruped, of whatever kind were the meats that were served'.[3]

There are not many dinner parties where you return home laden with gold and comely lads. Let's hope the party guests had enough space in their carriages to transport all those comely lads home safely. Oh wait, their host has thought of that, also gifting them 'carriages, together with mules and muleteers, and trappings of silver, wherewith they might return home from the banquet'.[4] Now you didn't get that level of thoughtfulness from the likes of Caligula, did you? You did not. Lucius Verus would annihilate all the competition in any given week of Come Dine with Me.

Portraits of Lucius Verus show him to be in possession of the best beard in antiquity (see image 19); a curly mass of luscious curls that the Historia Augusta describes thus, 'his beard was allowed to grow long, almost in the style of the barbarians'.[5] I like to believe that he sprinkled gold dust over this beautiful face fuzz alongside his yellow hair.

Elsewhere we find Lucius Verus owning a really big glass, which I believe merits repeating. 'Among other articles of extravagance he had a crystal goblet, named Volucer after that horse of which he had been very fond, that surpassed the capacity of any human draught.'[6] I hope you are, like me, now picturing a man with a gloriously curly beard struggling to lift an enormous goblet in his two hands to his lips.

Overall, the collator of these tales, a collection of Imperial biographies known as *The Historia Augusta*, portrays Lucius Verus as a man who knew how to have fun, who threw a good party and who liked to look nice and have nice things. It attempts to dig up some scandal. 'There was gossip to the effect that he had violated his mother-inlaw Faustina. And it is said that his mother-inlaw killed him treacherously by having poison sprinkled on his oysters, because he had betrayed to the daughter the amour he had had with the mother.'[7] But the authors don't really believe any of it and can't resist saying so 'however, there arose also that other story related in the Life of Marcus, one utterly inconsistent with the character of such a man'.[8] Lucius Verus has character and charm in abundance, two gifts that come in handy for a Roman emperor, just ask the morose, solitary Domitian.

You probably have some questions right now such as where you can buy an enormous glass just like Lucius Verus? What other beauty products he used to get his beard that glossy and also why the bejeebers have I never heard of this emperor? Two words: Marcus Aurelius.

That Other Emperor

When Lucius Verus was emperor between the years 161 and 169 CE, so was a certain young man named Marcus Aurelius, they were joint emperors. The

Historia Augusta account of Marcus Aurelius' life is one in direct contrast to that of Lucius Verus. Witness: 'Marcus Antoninus, devoted to philosophy as long as he lived and pre-eminent among emperors in purity of life'.[9]

Rather than donning a disguise and getting beaten up in taverns Marcus, 'adopted the dress and, a little later, the hardiness of a philosopher, pursuing his studies clad in a rough Greek cloak and sleeping on the ground; at his mother's solicitation, however, he reluctantly consented to sleep on a couch strewn with skins'.[10]

There are no stories of fun-sounding Imperial banquets in this life, rather we get tales like this: 'meantime Marcus was at all hours keeping watch over the workings of the state, and, though reluctantly and sorely against his will, but nevertheless with patience, was enduring the debauchery of his brother'.[11] Marcus Aurelius is the anti-Lucius Verus. His beard isn't nearly so glossy, and I warrant he never once gave a gift of a comely lad in his life, pah!

What Marcus Aurelius lacked in party spirit he made up for in longevity. Whereas Lucius Verus perished of possibly food poisoning, possibly smallpox, no scholar seems to care enough about poor Lucius Verus to definitively decide, in 169 CE, Marcus Aurelius kept battling on building a reputation for himself until 180 CE. Along the way he jotted down his private thoughts on philosophy and what it meant to be an emperor, thoughts that ended up being published and festooned across a variety of fridge magnets, tea towels and internet memes thus making sure that it is his name and not Lucius Verus' you remember.

Which is all jolly unfair on Lucius Verus who doesn't actually deserve to be included in a book entitled Ancient Rome's Worst Emperors since there is nothing during his rule that warrants that tag, as the *Historia Augusta* summarises: 'it is agreed that if he did not bristle with vices, no more did he abound in virtues'.[12] However, I include him because this is possibly the only damn history book where he'll get a chapter to himself and because you've never likely heard of him means his imprint as emperor was minimal. All the imprinting was being done by his more sober and distinctly less fun co-emperor. Marcus Aurelius is the one being emperor here, Lucius Verus may as well not exist. Which is not what you want from an emperor, or else what's the point of them?

Chapter 8

Commodus (180–192 CE) – Monstrous Ego

'For our history now descends from a kingdom of gold to one of iron and rust.' So begins Cassius Dio on the reign of Commodus or to give him the full titles he insisted on writing to the Senate using, *The Emperor Caesar Lucius Aelius Aurelius Commodus Augustus Pius Felix Sarmaticus Germanicus Maximus Britannicus, Pacifier of the Whole Earth, Invincible, the Roman Hercules, Pontifex Maximus, Holder of the Tribunician Authority for the eighteenth time, Imperator for the eighth time, Consul for the seventh time, Father of his Country, to consuls, praetors, tribunes, and the fortunate Commodian Senate, Greeting.*

Greetings straight back at you your Imperialness!

From which you might gather that the reign of Commodus is going to be an interesting one. This is also the chapter where Cassius Dio comes into his own because he was a senator during Commodus' reign and so was on the spot to witness all the mayhem and madness, and handily record it for us to enjoy. But before we get to those ostrich decapitations let us go back to the beginning, to a boy born to the purple.

To the Purple Born

Commodus was born on 31 August 161 CE to Emperor Marcus Aurelius and Empress Faustina, making him our very first emperor who was born into the job. This gave him a longer apprenticeship than any of our emperors so far, which you would think would afford him the training and preparation to become a truly excellent emperor, not least when you're learning at the feet of successful emperor and philosopher, Marcus Aurelius. I'm afraid it does not.

That Commodus is so very bad an emperor when Marcus Aurelius was so very good is something our ancient authors struggle with. The *Historia Augusta* puts several theories forward as to why this should be. If you're expecting some ruminations on the nature of parenting and preparing a child for a job that will bring them both riches and sorrows, or something on the psychology behind being heir to an empire and how that affects both yourself and how people treat you, downgrade those expectations. The *Historia Augusta* puts forward two suggestions as to why Commodus fails to live up to the accomplishments and general decency of his father:

- Marcus Aurelius was not Commodus' father (insert shocked emoji face). 'Many writers, however, state that Commodus was really begotten in adultery, since it is generally known that Faustina, while at Caieta, used to choose out lovers from among the sailors and gladiators.'[3]
- Commodus wasn't the product of adultery but something else entirely. One day the Empress Faustina was going about her daily empress business when a troop of gladiators happened to pass her by. Her gaze fell upon them, and she was struck by a sudden powerful lust for one particular gladiator, who we'll assume was proper sexy and not given to philosophical musings. This lust apparently made her extremely ill and her husband quite desperate. Eventually Faustina confessed her gladiator passion to her worried husband and being the man he was, he doesn't immediately divorce/exile/execute her, no he seeks advice as to how to help her. Which he may well have regretted doing, given this was this was the advice he received: Faustina should bathe in the blood of the object of her lust and then have sex with her husband. 'When this was done, the passion was indeed allayed, but their son Commodus was born a gladiator, not really a prince.'[4] So says the *Historia Augusta*, adding 'this story is considered plausible', trying to convince themselves of its veracity more than the reader I suspect.

There are a lot of questions here around the nature of Roman belief in magic, women's sexuality and how it was viewed by men, possibly around marriage and duty. But to my mind the bigger question is, how much blood did Faustina bathe in? Did they kill the gladiator Faustina fancied to fill her bath? And did she wash the blood off before having sex with her husband or after? Roman historians being what they are, infuriating, the *Historia Augusta* naturally pays no attention to important details such as these.

But let's crack on and leave the question of whether the fanciable gladiator was murdered, hanging (much like his corpse possibly was in some queer corner of the palace as they drained all the blood from it for Faustina's soak) and delve into what qualifies Commodus as a worst emperor. Absolutely everything! Commodus is full package of a worst emperor; a deranged playboy who neglects his public duties for his private pleasures, a blood thirsty ruler who turned on the noble and august senators, a megalomaniac who named not only every single month after himself but also Rome itself and demanded, 'that his age should be named the 'Golden Age', and that this should be recorded in all the records without exception'.[5] Commodus is everything a Roman emperor should not be. Which makes it all the more amazing that he manages to clock up a rule of twelve years before being murdered.

The reign of Commodus is rather neatly summarised by the man on the spot, Cassius Dio. 'Commodus was guilty of many unseemly deeds and killed a great many people.'[6] Bring on the unseemliness!

When Marcus Aurelius died he had been campaigning in the north against various tribes who'd taken to crossing over into Roman territory on mass. These were bigger incursions than had been faced before by previous emperors and ongoing. The forcible repelling of these tribes had kicked off in 166 CE; this was now 180 CE and the problem wasn't going away or being decisively ended. This kind of persistent threat was new to an empire that had always been crushingly superior and lacking enemies that could match it for military strength and tactics.

These tribes, the Macromanni, the Quadi, the Sarmatians and the Sarmatae were the front runners of a series of new threats the Roman Empire would face in the coming centuries – the *Pax Romana* Augustus had instituted was well and truly over. This is one big reason why Gibbon highlights the reign of his five good emperors as the peak of Roman civilisation, because from Marcus Aurelius onwards these threats are going to come thicker and faster and become more difficult to deal with, necessitating skilled leadership that wasn't always available.

Rome had been lucky with Marcus Aurelius, he had managed to hold things together despite being beset with problems; those troublesome northern tribes, an invasion of Spain by the moors, an insurrection in 175 CE by Avidius Cassius and to cap it all off, a devastating plague. Hanging over all of this was the ever-present issue of the Imperial finances. War was not cheap. Constant, ongoing war from multiple points in the empire, even more so – it burnt up a lot of coinage. This was the empire that Commodus inherited. It would have taxed the ingenuity of any emperor; it had certainly taxed his highly accomplished father. Commodus was 19 years old, and this was quite a burden for young shoulders to bear, even for one who had been born to the purple.

Commodus was with Marcus Aurelius on campaign at his death and one of his first acts as emperor was to make peace with some of those harassing tribes. To the Buri, 'he made peace with them, receiving hostages and getting back many captives from the Buri themselves as well as fifteen thousand from the others, and he compelled the others to take an oath that they would never dwell in nor use for pasturage a five-mile strip of their territory next to Dacia'.[7] The Macromani who had been suffering greatly at Roman hands, sent peace envoys to this new emperor. 'And, although Commodus might easily have destroyed them, yet he made terms with them.'[8]

Given the amount of time, effort and money that had been spent fighting these tribes this would seem like a good deal. However, our sources give no credit to Commodus for these peace settlements, they suspect him of ulterior motives. 'All the sycophants at his table, men who gauge their pleasure by their bellies and something a little lower, kept reminding him of the gay life at Rome, describing the delightful spectacles and musical shows and cataloguing the abundance of luxuries available there. They complained about wasting their time on the banks of the Danube, pointing out that the region was not productive in summer and that the fog and cold were unending.'[9]

As an inhabitant of Northern Europe, I can confirm it does indeed have an unending fog and can be quite cold, so I have some sympathy with those un-named sycophants. Cassius Dio has a similar explanation for Commodus having done something worthwhile and successful in securing those peace deals, 'for he hated all exertion and was eager for the comforts of the city'.[10]

And so probably the most successful thing Commodus ever does as emperor is written off as a mere desire to be warm. Again, as a Northern European I sympathise and fully understand that motivation. As did Commodus' army who rather fancied some comforts for a change, who can blame them? 'When the emperor's decision was announced, the army was in turmoil; all the soldiers wanted to leave with him, so that they might stop wasting their time in the war and enjoy the pleasures at Rome.'[11]

In their hefty and indeed, endless discussions about *virtus* the Romans are unanimous in their conclusion that city living is possibly the greatest threat to any man's *virtus*. Which is why the decent Roman brimming with *virtus* buys a small farm many miles away from the corrupting influence of the city and lives his days out ploughing the land and conversing with goats. Disclaimer – nobody ever does this ever; they just like to talk about it. It's the equivalent of that daydream you have about buying a derelict barn in Tuscany and renovating into a luxury villa despite not even knowing how to wire a plug.

Young people were the most at risk from their *virtus* being dented, as the poet Horace says on the young Roman male, 'he is soft as wax to be seduced into vice'.[12] Commodus was as malleable as the wax around a chunk of edam, as Cassius Dio notes, 'his great simplicity, however, together with his cowardice, made him the slave of his companions'.[13]

One of these men enslaving Commodus to pleasure was the Praetorian Prefect Perennis. 'Perennis indulged the emperor's youthful appetites, permitting him to spend his time in drinking and debauchery, and relieved him of Imperial cares and responsibilities.'[14] How very kind of Perennis to recognise that this new emperor was so very young to have such a burden of leadership placed upon his waxy shoulders and help lift some of that responsibility. No, of course that's not what he was doing. Perennis was the Praetorian Prefect, that guarantees that there was some ulterior dark motive floating about his scheming brain, and indeed there was. 'Perennis assumed full personal charge of the empire, driven by his insatiable lust for money, his contempt for what he had, and his greedy longing for what was not yet his.'[15]

Whilst Commodus was off having his youth corrupted and his *virtus* stripped off, Perennis was busy setting himself up nicely by using the emperor to eliminate anyone who irritated him. Strangely enough these irritants tended to be on the wealthy side and even stranger Perennis somehow ended up in possession of this wealth. Praetorian Prefects as a group had long lacked the ability to know when to say when. Perennis, like Sejanus and Nymphidius Sabinus before him was not satisfied to linger in a role that gave him extreme power and wealth beyond probably anyone else in the entire empire, he wanted more, he wanted to be Imperial.

'Commodus was persuaded to put the prefect's sons in command of the army of Illyricum, though they were still young men; the prefect himself amassed a huge sum of money for lavish gifts in order to incite the army to revolt. His sons quietly increased their forces, so that they might seize the empire after Perennis had disposed of Commodus.'[16] You do have to wonder why the role of Praetorian Prefect repeatedly leads to such treason. Perhaps their proximity to Imperial power led them to the same conclusion, that ruling an empire really wasn't that difficult and that they could do a much better job of it than the current holder of the post. It's always frustrating to play second fiddle to a first fiddle who, in the case of Commodus certainly, is only holding the bow by an accident of birth and probably the wrong way round.

Perennis was a man of experience (but not wisdom, as will be shortly become apparent) who had hit gold with Commodus. But like his fellow Prefects from history, who had trodden down this well-worn path of grandiose ambition, he had fatally underestimated the grudge level that resulted from bumping off members of the Senate for his own personal gain. 'The emperor's intimate friends, however, who had long been secretly hostile to Perennis (for the prefect was harsh and unbearable in his insolence and arrogance), believed that the time had come and began to bring charges against him.'[17] The army weren't best pleased about the Prefect's antics either.

The thing about being emperor is that the buck stops with you. You have in your hands the power to improve or ruin people's lives and they will and do hold you accountable for it. This might, in the case of the civilian population, involve shouting insults at the emperor across an amphitheatre or pelting him with turnips to fully express their annoyance with him. The army, when displeased with an emperor, didn't need to stock up on turnips, they'd been supplied with very pointy swords and trained how to use them. They could express their discontent far more effectively (though probably distinctly less satisfyingly than throwing vegetables at the emperor's head, by either (a) having a good mutiny or (b) having a crack at removing the emperor and putting someone they liked better in his place).

The soldiers in this situation had a third option open to them, they went to Rome to have a moan to the man who was officially emperor. 'Commodus met them and asked: "What is the meaning of this, soldiers? What is your purpose in coming?"'. They answered, "We are here because Perennis is plotting against you and plans to make his son emperor".[18] A message so blunt that even Commodus understood it and Perennis and sons were horribly executed.

He might have understood the message, but Commodus didn't learn the lesson behind Perennis' rise and fall from power (not to let any single man gain such influence again as to threaten his own rule) because Perennis' replacement as Prefect, Cleander, is even worse than his predecessor for grandiose ambition and taking the mick.

The mark of a good palace servant is to be entirely missing from the historical accounts. Remember Parthenius, the chamberlain who had Domitian killed? He only enters the written historical record at the point of committing this gruesome act. That Parthenius had risen to become a man of wealth and influence without any accompanying tales of being a duplicitous, greedy, grasping Imperial freedman indicates his smooth ability to get on with the senatorial class. Cleander was very much not this. 'And the Imperial freedmen, with Cleander at their head, after getting rid of this man [Perennis], refrained from no form of mischief, selling all privileges, and indulging in wantonness and debauchery.'[19]

Cleander's talented salesmanship in flogging off positions led to there being twenty-five appointed consuls in a single year. But it got worse than this. 'At his nod even freedmen were enrolled in the Senate and among the patricians.'[20] Ancient Rome was a very class-based society, rigidly so. Class controlled every aspect of a Roman man's life; what public roles he could hold, whether he could serve in the army, which laws protected him, whom he could marry, what width stripe he could have on his toga, down to where he was allowed to sit in the amphitheatre. Class mattered enormously in the ancient world.

The biggest class distinguisher in ancient Rome was between the freeborn and those born into slavery. The freeborn enjoyed rights that those born into slavery, even if later freed, did not. To underline this class distinction freedmen had not been allowed to stand for the public offices that were the traditional career route for any elite Roman male. The membership of the Senate had widened considerably since Republican days where it was dominated by a few old, established families, however, Cleander permitting ex-slaves to be senators was one that firmly stamped on the face of Roman sensibilities on how the world should work. The non-freeborn were lesser and needed to be kept so. Cleander's antics were also an attack on the senatorial class itself and the dignity and pride they held their lineage in; it demonstrated a total lack of respect for them.

The Senate wasn't the only body Cleander showed little respect for, in his pursuit of wealth he wasn't minded about the law either. 'He loaded with honours men who were recalled from exile; he rescinded decisions of the courts.'[21] He didn't have a lot of respect for the emperor either given he, 'had debauched certain of Commodus' concubines, and from them had begotten sons'.[22]

However, Cleander, despite wielding absolute power about the place with the incontinence of a man who's eaten a very bad oyster the night before, was still not content. It wasn't enough for him to completely undermine the dignity of a body that had ruled Rome for centuries, nor to become richer than any other Imperial freedman ever had, he wanted more. He wanted a legacy. Cleander's legacy was a public building campaign; he built a gymnasium and a public bath for the people, presumably stamping his name all over it. He then used some of the enormous wealth he had built up selling everything he could, to buy up the vast bulk of the public grain supply. Herodian has this as a calculated move. 'He hoped in this way to get control of the people and the army by making a generous distribution of grain at the first sign of a food shortage, anticipating that he would win the support of the people when they were suffering from a scarcity of food.'[23]

Cleander was getting very big for his boots. Surely you cry out, he is well overdue a nasty end. Yes, obviously he is and at least one of our sources attribute it to this purchase of the public grain supply. It turns out in a famine the people did not consider Cleander their benefactor, but rather held him responsible for the shortage in the first place. But what is interesting about how Cleander eventually falls is how like Perennis' end it is. If you remember a body of soldiers went to Commodus directly to complain about Perennis' power. With Cleander we get a similar tale of the emperor being approached. 'At first they attacked him bitterly when they thronged the theatres; later, however, they went in a body to Commodus, who was passing the time on his estate near the city, and there, raising a fearful din, they demanded Cleander for execution.'[24] This was a literal mob who would not be put off from their Cleander-removing mission by any soldiers sent in to disperse them. With neither the mob nor the soldiers willing to step down, a bloody battle followed.

Whilst all of this was going on, Commodus we are told, was in total ignorance and enjoying a pleasant stay at one of his many estates. Eventually the news of this Cleander-targeted unrest is brought to him. His response is pure panic. 'He was terrified by this pressing danger, which did not merely threaten but was already upon him.'[25] Cleander and all those associated with him were immediately executed.

What's interesting about the stories of both Perennis and Cleander is how ignorant Commodus appears at their antics. It takes a group of soldiers and a rioting mob to alert him to what is bleeding obvious to everyone else; these men have too much power. Cleander was stamping his name on buildings everywhere, you can't get more obvious than that! Yet Commodus hadn't noticed, more than happy to hand over the reins of government to them, without apparently considering it might come to threaten his own power; not once but twice.

There is a question lurking here, well several really, but let us start with the obvious one: whilst Cleander and Perennis were handing out government positions, commanding the legions and dealing with municipal matters, what the freaking hell was the emperor doing? And therein lies a story, quite a good one in fact. It's time to bring on those ostriches…

The thirteenth labour of Hercules

That Commodus was devoted to pleasures gets repeated mentions in our sources from the moment those sycophants accompanying the new emperor on campaign, 'kept reminding him of the gay life at Rome'.[26] This love of pleasures is what allows Perennis to manipulate him. 'For Perennis, being well acquainted with Commodus' character, discovered the way to make himself powerful, namely, by persuading Commodus to devote himself to pleasure.'[27] Cassius Dio mentions, 'Commodus, taking a respite from his amusements and sports',[28] to do his Imperial duty of executing important men.

But what were these pleasures, these amusements, these sports that so consumed the emperor? Well, there were the ladies. 'Commodus lived, rioting in the Palace amid banquets and in baths along with 300 concubines, gathered together for their beauty and chosen from both matrons and harlots.'[29]

There were the young men, 'he was not free from the disgrace of intimacy with young men, defiling every part of his body in dealings with persons of either sex'.[30] These men included one named Onon who possessed, 'a male member larger than that of most animals'.[31] What animals Onon's willy exceeded in size is another one of those essential questions that our historians infuriatingly brush past.

There were the practical jokes. 'It is claimed that he often mixed human excrement with the most expensive foods, and he did not refrain from tasting them, mocking the rest of the company, as he thought. He displayed two misshapen hunchbacks on a silver platter after smearing them with mustard, and then straightway advanced and enriched them. He pushed into a swimming-pool his Praetor Prefect Julianus.'[32]

There was the conning of the government out of funds for his own pleasure and amusement. 'He pretended once that he was going to Africa, so that he could get funds for the journey, then got them and spent them on banquets and gaming instead.'[33] He had a lot of baths. 'He used to bathe seven and eight times a day and was in the habit of eating while in the bath.'[34]

But mostly there was the dressing up as a gladiator and larking about in the arena. 'It is said that he engaged in gladiatorial bouts seven hundred and thirty-five times.'[35] Which is a weirdly precise figure that the *Historia Augusta* backs up by saying that Commodus insisted his every appearance was included in the public records. To give credit where credit is due, Commodus is actually very good at the sort of wholesale animal slaughter that ancient Romans get off on. Herodian is full to bursting with tales of horrific animal deaths at the hands of the emperor, of which this is by far the best. 'On one occasion he shot arrows with crescent-shaped heads at Moroccan ostriches, birds that move with great speed, both because of their swiftness afoot and the sail-like nature of their wings. He cut off their heads at the very top of the neck; so, after their heads had been severed by the edge of the arrow, they continued to run around as if they had not been injured.'[36]

Now decapitating ostriches on the move takes no little skill, and let's face it, is impressive. As is this tale too. 'Once when a leopard, with a lightning dash, seized a condemned criminal, he thwarted the leopard with his javelin as it was about to close its jaws; he killed the beast and rescued the man, the point of the javelin anticipating the points of the leopard's teeth.'[37]

That had to be quite a thing to witness as a spectator and near impossible to imagine any modern leader doing. Although I'm sure there are many of us who'd like to see our prime ministers face off with a leopard. Even Herodian grudgingly accepts it's kind of cool. 'As far as these activities are concerned, however, even if his conduct was hardly becoming for an emperor, he did win the approval of the mob for his courage and his marksmanship.'[38]

He is sniffier, though about Commodus' gladiatorial efforts. 'The people saw a disgraceful spectacle, a nobly born emperor of the Romans, whose fathers and forebears had won many victories, not taking the field against barbarians or opponents worthy of the Romans, but disgracing his high position by degrading and disgusting exhibitions.'[39] From which we may deduce there's less flashy tricks you can show off whilst despatching a human being compared to an animal. Also, you've lost the nail-biting tension that builds from wondering whether the ruler of the largest empire known to mankind is about to get his face bitten off by a lion. That's entertainment Roman style, folks!

This level of skill does not come naturally, it had to have taken a great deal of training and practice. Many, many hours of training and practice. Hours that should have been spent doing boring emperor things but hang on here's that friendly chap Perennis/Cleander who says he'll do all that boring stuff for me. You can see how it happened.

It takes a wise ruler to distinguish between a good advisor and a sycophant; it takes a strong ruler to openly hear and accept criticism. Commodus was neither wise nor strong. Which explains why he was so piss poor at selecting right hand men and why it took riots and mutinies before anyone dared to tell him just how deficient he was at judging character.

That the great simple Commodus, who had no interest in ticking off Augustus' check list of things good emperors do, and happily outsourced anything he didn't fancy doing to his latest best friend, manages to rule for twelve years is rather surprising. It certainly wasn't from want of trying to get rid of him, Commodus faced multiple plots against him and in that time honoured Imperial fashion a number came from within his own family.

An early plot, only two years into his reign, involved his sister Lucilla and is notable for being probably the worst assassination attempt in all of history. The assassin, one Quintianus, had Commodus within his sight and had his dagger drawn ready to strike. But before the stabbing could commence, and much in the manner of a James Bond villain, Quintianus decided that the emperor needed to know exactly why he was going to kill him. As Herodian dryly notes, 'Quintianus wasted time making his little speech and waving his dagger; as a result, he was seized by the emperor's bodyguards before he could strike and died for his stupidity in revealing the plot prematurely'.[40] Lucilla and her senatorial accomplices were rounded up and executed. 'This was the initial reason for the young emperor's hatred of the Senate',[41] we are told.

Like most of our worst emperors Commodus had a tricky relationship with the Senate. Commodus' promotion of Cleander, an ex-slave to prominence and Cleander's subsequent flogging of positions and ranks that were rightfully the provenance of those of senatorial rank, severely dented the pride of the Senate. It didn't make them like the emperor much because there was no benefit to them in doing so.

On the other side Commodus didn't much like the senators after some of their number had ganged up with his sister and tried to murder him. His reaction was akin to that of Domitian; act hard, act fast and terrify them into loyalty. Or else, as in the following example, act so fast that you catch the bastards before they have any treasonous thoughts. 'Commodus, likewise killed the two Quintilii, Condianus and Maximus; for they had a great reputation for learning, military skill, brotherly accord, and wealth, and their notable talents led to the suspicion that, even if they were not planning any rebellion, they were nevertheless displeased with existing conditions.'[42]

Which I guess could be described as a rare efficiency in the court of Commodus. Of course, such executions only encouraged more plotting by senators, which only encouraged more spurious making a point executions, which only encouraged more…. You get the idea.

Commodus' personal feelings on the Senate are no better demonstrated than by this tale. 'He erected statues of himself throughout the city, but opposite the senate house he set up a special statue representing the emperor as an archer poised to shoot, for he wished even his statues to inspire fear of him.'[43] Commodus was many things, but subtle was not one of them.

We are fortunate in having an eyewitness account of what it was like to be a senator when Commodus was emperor, our friendly historian Cassius Dio. From Cassius Dio we learn that Commodus insisted that the senatorial and equestrian class watch him play in the amphitheatre. The emperor would frequently command them to say: 'Thou art lord and thou art first, of all men most fortunate. Victor thou art, and victor thou shalt be; from everlasting, Amazonian, thou art victor'.[44] Except Claudius Pompeianus, who Cassius Dio tell us, 'preferred even to be killed for this rather than to behold the emperor, the son of Marcus, conducting himself in such a fashion'.[45]

The ordinary folk of Rome had similarly stayed away due to a rumour that the emperor wanted, 'to shoot a few of the spectators in imitation of Hercules and the Stymphalian birds'.[46] And even more horrifying than this was Commodus' love of audience participation. During one spectacular, Commodus rounded up every spectator, 'who had lost their feet as the result of disease or some accident, and then, after fastening about their knees some likenesses of serpents' bodies, and giving them sponges to throw instead of stones, had killed them with blows of a club, pretending that they were giants'.[47]

The people may have decided to stay at home with a bowl of roasted dormice and a full wineskin rather than find themselves the butt of Commodus' entertainment, however the senators had no choice but to put their bums on seats and be treated to such delights as this. 'Having killed an ostrich and cut off his head, he came up to where we were sitting, holding the head in his left hand and in his right hand raising aloft his bloody sword; and though he spoke not a word, yet he wagged his head with a grin, indicating that he would treat us in the same way.'[48]

Eek, is the word. As an attempt at intimidating the Senate into submission it failed, as Cassius Dio goes onto report. 'And many would indeed have perished by the sword on the spot, for laughing at him (for it was laughter rather than indignation that overcame us), if I had not some laurel leaves, which I got from my garland, myself, and persuaded the others who were sitting near me to do the same, so that in the steady movement of our armies we might conceal the fact that we were laughing.'[49]

Drunken madness

Commodus cut a ridiculous figure in the final years of his reign, Herodian says that, 'he fell into a state of drunken madness'.[50] The emperor ordered that he no longer be called Commodus but rather Hercules and he appeared in public either dressed as that demigod in a lion skin holding a club 'or a robe of pure purple with gold spangles'[51] which sounds stylish but was a bit too close to female attire for the Romans liking, even more so when he accessorised it with fine gems. Coins were issued describing Commodus as *Herculi Commodiano*, the incarnation of Hercules. He was entering that interesting phase of believing himself divine, something he got made official by the Senate. 'In truth, on the occasion when he laid before the senate his proposal to call Rome Commodiana, not only did the senate gleefully pass this resolution, but also took the name 'Commodian' to itself, at the same time giving Commodus the name Hercules, and calling him a god.'[52]

I doubt they 'gleefully' passed this resolution; more likely Commodus was present in the corner during proceedings waggling an ostrich head at them. How much further Commodus would have gone had he lived longer is difficult and fascinating to contemplate; after renaming himself, the months, the Senate, and Rome itself, what was left? Would he have insisted every legion of Rome be renamed after himself? Maybe every citizen would be forced to append their name with that of the emperor? Of all the emperors we have covered so far none have come close to Commodus for egomania.

We could speculate that all this naming things after himself is born of fear, a desire to elevate himself to the level of God to outrank those pesky senators that keep trying to kill him. We could argue that perhaps being born to the purple wasn't such a bonus after all, but rather a factor that led to an engrained belief of superiority over every man and beast. We could go along with Herodian and accept that Commodus was just steaming drunk for the last two years of his reign and never sobered up sufficiently to experience the horror of the 'oh god what did I do last night' moment that tends to refine most people's behaviour – at least until the next Friday big night out. Whereas

Caligula has been the subject of very many speculative TV documentaries and biographies, Commodus is relatively poorly served on this score, he does not attract the same interest which leaves the psychology behind his actions tantalisingly out of reach. The psychology that motivated his assassins is far easier to grasp; they'd had enough.

The plot, the one that succeeded (although barely just) was cooked up by the Praetorian Prefect Laetus, Commodus' most favourite concubine Marcia, and his chamberlain Ecletus. An inside job in other words, yet again the senatorial class proving themselves next to useless in removing unsuitable rulers, Julius Caesar was clearly just a fluke.

Their plan was to poison the emperor, this poison was to be added to a beef dish that Marcia would then serve to Commodus. Or alternatively a drink, according to Herodian. However, some frantic improvisation was required after Commodus, having eaten the poisoned beef, vomited it back up again. That had to be a hell of a heart pumping moment for the assassins, what to do if the emperor recovered and realised what they had done? The chance couldn't be taken, the emperor had to die. Although a quick solution was needed, the conspirators took the time to recruit somebody else to do the actual murdering, which is surprising given Laetus was the Praetorian Prefect and thus had free access to both men and weaponry. They settled upon a wrestler named Narcissus and whilst the emperor was bathing (presumably to clean himself up after the poisoning/vomiting incident) Narcissus entered and strangled him to death. And so was the end of the new Hercules.

Commodus is a slam dunk for worst emperor status; an overgrown child playing gladiators whilst his city faced such devastations as fire and plagues, an emperor who did not give a flying fig about the roles and responsibilities of the job and dumped everything he didn't want to do onto someone else. An emperor who systematically undermined, terrorised, murdered and humiliated a Senate who should have been his closest advisors. An emperor who created a reality that suited him, one where he was a chariot racer, a gladiator, a god!

You can't even go revisionist on his reputation[53] and claim our sources are making it all up. Cassius Dio and Herodian knew Commodus personally and both witnessed his eccentricities. Their accounts are backed up by the coin and inscription record that show that Commodus did employ a multitude of titles and he did start styling himself as an incarnation of Hercules.

That he lasted twelve years as emperor is testament to the inability of the senatorial class to organise a successful plot and the emperor's ability in forestalling them by wiping out their numbers on a regular basis. It is hardly surprising that Commodus' death was celebrated. But what that death unleashed was more mayhem and murder.

Five Stars

The year 69 CE is better known as the Year of the Four Emperors, the year after Commodus' death in 193 CE ups this ante as the Year of the Five Emperors. From which you might deduce we are entering into a period which can be described as 'interesting' or if you prefer, absolute bloody mayhem.

Commodus had left no heir. In similar circumstances in 69 CE and in 96 CE, after the death of Nero and the assassination of Domitian respectively, we find stepping on the scene an experienced, old pair of hands. In 69 CE this was Galba, in 96 CE Nerva and in 193 CE this old pair of hands was Pertinax.

Pertinax came with a heap of recommendations. 'This Pertinax was famous for his accomplishments, both civil and military; he had won many victories over the Germans and the Eastern barbarians and was the only survivor of the revered advisers appointed for Commodus by his father.'[54] He was also, interestingly, the son of a freedman which is quite a radical move, notably because this is casually commented on and Pertinax is generally happily accepted as emperor by all. The rules on who could be emperor had shifted, as becomes very apparent in the forthcoming centuries.

Pertinax got on with the job of cleaning up the mess both Commodus had left and his assassins, who had sneaked the emperor's body out of the palace disguised as laundry to avoid the Praetorian Guard discovering what they had done. Which is interesting given, as you'll remember, one of Commodus' assassins was the Praetorian Prefect. He clearly didn't rate his own powers of command.

Pertinax got on with the job that had been bestowed upon him with the sort of rigour and energy that had been entirely missing from Commodus' reign. But what else could one expect from one whose birth was greeted with an omen like this, 'The hour he was born a black horse climbed to the roof, and after remaining there for a short time, fell to the ground and died'.[55] One wonders how Pertinax's mother dealt with the double stress of giving birth and that damn horse getting on the roof again. It's really not what you need at that moment.

All in all, Pertinax was going a good job as emperor and 'everyone delighted in the rule of the Romans under Pertinax'.[56] What a shame that delight was only to last eighty-seven days. And whose fault was the end of the delighting? The Praetorian Guard, that's who. Yet again they seem to have forgotten the prime purpose of their role was to protect the emperor and they went and murdered him instead. Whoops. The reasons for this sudden and brutal execution (the guard burst into the palace and despite Pertinax making a very conciliatory speech at them that changed the minds of many of those guards present they murdered him anyway), is flimsy to the extreme. Herodian says: 'they plotted to remove Pertinax on the ground that he was a burden and a nuisance to them, and to choose an emperor who would restore to them their unbridled and uncontrolled power'.[57]

The *Historia Augusta* says they were displeased by his integrity and that the Praetorian Prefect Laetus, (who you'll remember was part of the plot to kill Commodus), 'regretted that he had made Pertinax emperor, because Pertinax used to rebuke him as a stupid babbler of various secrets'.[58] Cassius Dio agrees with Herodian on Pertinax being a pain. 'Since, now, neither the soldiers were allowed to plunder any longer nor the Imperial freedmen to indulge in lewdness, they both hated him bitterly.'[59]

In short, Commodus might have been a terrible emperor but that had personally suited them. They did not prefer competence; it was not to their taste. Having now offed the man in charge the Praetorians had found themselves in a dilemma; all their power stemmed from being the private bodyguard of an emperor. Only there was no emperor now, which meant they were all effectively unemployed. There was only one solution, they would have to find a new emperor.

Chapter 9

Didius Julianus (193 CE) – The Man who Brought an Empire

Didius Julianus became emperor in what is described in the book I am currently holding as, 'an event so extraordinary, tawdry and demeaning that even now it seems barely credible that the Roman Empire could have stooped so low'.[1] Which is an appetite wetter if ever I heard one.

The way Didius Julianus became emperor, of which more shortly, overshadows that he wasn't so bad a choice (on paper, definitely on paper). 'His mother was Aemilia Clara, his father Petronius Didius Severus, his brothers Didius Proculus and Nummius Albinus; another Salvius Julianus was his uncle',[2] says the *Historia Augusta*, whose word I'm going to take that this is an impressive lineage. The undisputedly good, and thus having no role in this book, Emperor Marcus Aurelius, saw something so impressive in the young Didius Julianus that he allowed him to be quaestor a year earlier than permitted. Clearly Julianus did not disappoint that emperor because he goes on to hold the full whack of public roles and gains the ultimate accolade 'He ruled Belgium long and well'.[3] Which I really hope he used whenever he was introduced to someone, 'Didius Julianus, I ruled Belgium long and well. And you are'?

All in all, Didius Julianus spent his foremost years doing what all men of the Roman elite did and he did it credibly. He could have lived out his years in a similar fashion, notching up positions, running provinces just as long and well as he had Belgium and died at a ripe old age satisfied that he had lived up to the example set by his ancestors. He could have. But he didn't. This is the tale of what he did instead.

The murder of Pertinax sent Rome into chaos. In the long history of emperor assassinations this takes the biscuit for being (a) the most pointless and (b) the least thought out. Pertinax had been proving himself as a good, capable emperor. He wasn't cruel like Caligula, nor paranoid like Domitian, nor did he believe he was the incarnation of Hercules and spend all day decapitating ostriches like Commodus. The worst thing he had done was say Laetus, the Praetorian Prefect was unable to keep a secret. Which for all we know was absolutely true. Laetus however had already removed one emperor, Commodus, and come up top trumps with a better one, Pertinax. Perhaps he hoped to repeat this until he found an emperor that suited him best.

Unfortunately finding a new emperor this time round was going to prove more difficult since, 'men of position went out to their estates which were farthest from the city, to avoid the danger of being present at the selection of the new emperor'.[4] Presumably in case they were the one who was handed the laurel wreath and told to get on with it; Pertinax's fate had made the top job distinctly unattractive.

This left the Praetorian Guard in quite a position, not least because aside from not spending any time thinking about who they would replace Pertinax with, nor any time on thinking about how the senators might react to their actions, the Praetorians hadn't given a modicum of their brain space to wondering how their emperor-murdering would go down with the people of Rome. It was going down like this, 'they ran about like madmen in their grief and rage. In the grip of unreasoning fury, the mob searched for the emperor's assassins'.[5] Oops.

So here we have it, the emperor is dead, the senators have fled to their country estates refusing to get involved, the people are in a fury and the Praetorian Guard who kicked all this off have headed back to their barracks on the Viminal Hill, 'shutting all the gates and blocking the entrances, they placed sentries in the towers and remained inside the walls to defend themselves if the mob should attack the camp'.[6] What a mess!

You will be unsurprised to learn that once news of events in Rome reached the provinces, that those provincial governors with legions under their command started to have thoughts about who should be emperor, because nobody else damn well was. But communication takes time in the ancient world and at this precise moment the murder of Pertinax and the resulting chaos hasn't reached them yet. Let us head back to Rome, where we left the Praetorian Guard hiding in their barracks.

They are still there hiding. However, they've come up with a fantastic idea on how to fill that emperor-shaped hole that will enable them to set foot outside their barracks and make them a bit of cash on the side. 'Bringing forward to the walls the men with the loudest voices, they made proclamation that the empire was for sale, promising to hand it over to the man who offered the highest price, and promising to conduct the purchaser safely to the Imperial palace under the protection of their arms.'[7]

The cynic in me sees this selling of the Imperial throne as the natural reverse of the usual situation upon the ascension of a new emperor when the Praetorians would receive a bounty to effectively buy their loyalty. This new method is surely more transparent revealing the naked truth as everyone knew it; the Praetorian Guard had the power to make emperors but also remove them, more so than the Senate who supposedly governed Rome.

The Praetorians new low was soon the topic of discussion everywhere, including at a dinner party one Didius Julianus was attending. We'll assume it was towards the end of this dinner after much food and delightful conversation had been had and everyone was a bit pissed, because it's absolutely the only explanation for this. 'His wife and daughter and a mob of parasites persuaded him to leave his dining couch and hurry to the wall of the camp to find out what was going on. All the way to the camp they urged him to seize the prostrate empire; he had plenty of money and could outbid anyone who opposed him.'[8]

Now many a poor group decision has been made at the end of an evening out, such as sambuca shots, 'borrowing' traffic cones or choosing to urinate under the full glare of CCTV whilst doing a thumbs up to the camera. But deciding you should be emperor and heading off to buy your way into the position is the sort of decision that is only made after a swimming pool of the red stuff. Only a drunk man surrounded by drunk men would dare to travel across Rome after dark to the home of the guards, who only days earlier had bloodily murdered the previous emperor, to take up an offer that could well just be dinner party gossip.

Julianus' behaviour when he reached the Praetorian camps backs up the theory that he was sozzled, for he stands outside the walls and bellows that he has loads of money, boxes crammed with silver and gold, all the money in the world! This was exactly what the Praetorians were eager to hear and still being too scared to open the gates they lowered a ladder over the wall which Julianus, full of drunk bravado, scaled into the Praetorian camp. Now safely inside, Julianus proves to be exactly the sort of emperor the Praetorians had hoped to reel in with their offer: 'Julianus promised to revive the memory of Commodus, to restore his honours, and to re-erect his statues which the Senate had pulled down; he further promised to restore to the Praetorians all the powers they had possessed under that emperor'.[9] And as the final proof, if more proof were needed (it's really not) that Julianus is totally off his face, he promises 'to give each soldier more gold than he asked for or expected to receive'.

The Praetorian Guard as a body have proven themselves throughout Roman history to be collectively grasping and greedy and with absolutely no understanding that money doesn't just appear because they feel they should have it. Nymphidius Sabinus, the Prefect that brought down Nero, promised his guards 30,000 sesterces each, a ridiculous sum that didn't exist but that did not stop the guards murdering Galba when he didn't deliver that non-existent coinage. That Julianus' bonus amount surprised the guard in its excess shows just how bonkers an offer it was. This new emperor was promising the world with all the confidence and bravado of a man who had drunk way too much. No doubt he revelled in the cheers and congratulations of his new chums. What a fabulous night this had been for him!

The Morning After The Night Before

The only problem with epic nights out, is there is a morning after. One without the comforting blanket of inebriation where anything and everything seems possible. One where the world must be faced sober, with a cracking headache and the growing realisation that you might have said and done a few things you probably shouldn't have.

Oh, to be a fly on the wall when Didius Julianus woke up the next morning and realised with a cold icy blast of horror what he had done the night before, because as Herodian bluntly puts it: 'the truth is that he did not have as much money in his personal possession as he had pretended to have'.[10] That's right, there were no strong boxes overflowing with gold and silver. Julianus had brought the position of emperor with money he did not have. And that generous bonus he had promised to every Praetorian Guard? No, he didn't have that either.

There he lay in his palace bed, emperor of Rome, surrounded by his heavily armed personal bodyguard who had murdered his predecessor and whom he had conned into believing he was going to enrich them, when he wasn't. It's a wonder they didn't burst in and murder him right then and there. Certainly, they had a greater cause for removing Julianus than they did Pertinax, but they don't. Perhaps they still naively believed the money promised to them might magically appear, perhaps they just wanted to see Julianus squirm. They were richly awarded in that at least.

Roman emperors don't tend to start off unpopular. Unpopularity, hatred even, is something that generally takes years to achieve. Congratulations then to Didius Julianus who was, we can say, successful at least in this one thing. This was the reaction of the people of Rome as Didius Julianus he made his way to the Senate House to formally be declared emperor. 'As he came down to the senate-house with the soldiers and senate, they heaped curses upon him, and when he performed the sacrifices, wished that he might not obtain favourable omens; they even hurled stones at him, though Julianus, with uplifted hand, continually sought to calm them.'[11]

To recap, the Praetorian Guard loathe Julianus for lying to them about his fortune. The Senate loathe Julianus because he was not their choice of emperor and the way he had been appointed greatly tarnished the reputation of the senatorial class as nobler and more moral than all the other social classes. The people of Rome loathe Julianus for not being Pertinax whom they see as the rightful emperor and for not being Commodus either and possibly for not being Marcus Aurelius – who knows. The Senate, the people and the guard were all united against Julianus. You'll remember these as the key groups that all emperors need to maintain the loyalty of to have any chance at remaining in position. It's not looking good, is it? And this is only day one of his reign!

Perhaps he could have pulled it back, made a success at being emperor and won everyone round. After all, as we noted Julianus was an experienced public official, he knew how things worked, he could have impressed all with his dedication to the job so that the disgraceful way he had acquired it would be forgotten. All was not lost! Surely?

However, Julianus faced a situation that was rapidly complicating. Remember those provincial governors with legions at their command? Well, the news about the Praetorian Guard and Julianus' shameful behaviour had now reached them and they were just as unimpressed as their fellow senators in Rome had been. So unimpressed that three of them, Pescennius Niger the governor of Syria, Septimius Severus the governor of Pannonia and Clodius Albinus the governor of Britain, all decided that they had better sort this mess out by making themselves emperor.

With Julianus facing not one, not two but three rival claimants to the job he'd so cheaply purchased (cheaply because he had no money to hand over) now was the time to see what he was made of, now was the time to redeem himself. Didius Julianus let's see what you're made of!

The Stuff that Emperors are Made Of

What Julianus was made of is probably best summed up in this Herodian quote, 'Julianus, dumb and witless, did not know how to handle the situation'.[12] He is urged to secure the Alps from the advance of Severus' army, but doesn't. He does put together an army to defend the city, it's made up of sailors 'who did not even know how to drill',[13] an army of elephants who, 'found their towers burdensome and would not even carry their drivers any longer, but threw them off, too', and the Praetorian Guard who alongside doing 'nothing worthy of their name and of their promise, for they had learned to live delicately', Julianus had also swindled out of money. Still, he could at least make a difference there.

Digging deep into the Imperial treasury, temple treasuries, his pockets and the pockets of his friends (whether these friends remained his friends is not commented upon) Julianus scraped together enough money to buy the

Praetorians loyalty against three rival claimants. A sensible strategy executed by a sensible emperor. The result of this sensible action? 'The Praetorians were in no way grateful to the emperor; they felt that he was not giving them a bonus but only paying them what he owed them.'[14] Oh.

Worse was to come, the men Julianus sent to intercept Severus on his march to Rome decided rather than fighting against Severus they would much prefer to fight with him and swapped sides, adding numbers to the army heading his direction.

With his soldiers swapping sides at the earliest opportunity, unable to depend on his own guard not to murder him, surrounded by a populace openly amused by his war preparations ('we would be overcome by laughter', reports man on the spot, Cassius Dio) and with elephants running amok on the streets of Rome, Didius Julianus emperor of Rome shut himself in the palace he had fortified.

But even this act caused merriment. 'But what caused us the greatest amusement was his fortifying of the palace with latticed gates and strong doors. For, inasmuch as it seemed probable that the soldiers would never have slain Pertinax so easily if the doors had been securely locked, Julianus believed that in case of defeat he would be able to shut himself up there and survive.'[15] Cassius Dio is proven correct, Severus' soldiers easily enter the palace, no doubt aided by the Praetorian Guard (who yes, as expected had abandoned the emperor at the first opportunity) and remove Julianus from the Imperial throne.

Julianus' final words we are told were, 'But what evil have I done? Whom have I killed'? According to the exact same source only a paragraph earlier, Laetus, Narcissus and Marcia, the assassins of Commodus and also 'many boys as a magic rite, believing that he could avert some future misfortunes if he learned of them beforehand'.[16] Proving to the very end that Didius Julianus was not a man whose word could be trusted.

Didius Julianus is a worst emperor. There is no argument on that score, there are no revisionist histories that attempt to paint his actions in a suddenly not reprehensible but entirely understandable light. Julianus was a terrible emperor. He became emperor in a truly shameful way and none of his actions after that could regain any respect from the Senate nor the army nor the people. Which is why Septimius Severus had such a cake walk into Rome to claim his throne to found Rome's newest ruling dynasty – The Severans.

Chapter 10

Geta (211 CE) – For-Geta-ble

'I am well aware, Constantine Augustus, that many besides Your Clemency may raise the question why I should also write the life of Geta Antoninus.'[1] So, the author of the *Historia Augusta* opens his chapter on Geta, the son of Septimius Severus. It's a fair question for there is very little that is interesting about the short-lived Emperor Geta, as the *Historia Augusta* chapter then goes onto prove.

Geta was fond of bright clothing 'so much so, in fact, that his father would laugh at him',[2] which is light on the mentally scarring compared to Caligula's childhood witnessing his family being picked off by Sejanus one by one. His dinner parties sound frankly ghastly. 'He was accustomed, moreover, to have skilful slaves serve meals, and especially dinners, according to a single letter of the alphabet, as, for instance, one in which there were goose, gammon, and gadwall, or, again, pullet, partridge, peacock, pork, poisson, and pig's-thigh.'[3] The *Historia Augusta* rather too kindly claims: 'for this reason he was considered a good comrade, even in his youth'. Which demonstrates that either expectations of Imperial dining had drastically plummeted since the era of Caligula's wife swapping affairs and Vitellius' epic gourmet evenings, or that the necessity of pretending everything the emperor did was marvellous was the one thing that hadn't changed over the centuries.

Elsewhere we find Geta enjoying his word games. 'It was a common practice of his to propound puzzles to the grammarians, asking them to characterize the cries of the different animals, as for example: the lamb bleats, the pig squeals, the dove coos, the hog grunts, the bear growls, the lion roars, the leopard snarls, the elephant trumpets, the frog croaks, the horse neighs, the ass brays, the bull bellows; and in proof he would cite the ancient writers.'[4] At which point we might imagine that Constantine Augusta summoned the author into his most private chamber and raised the question that yes, he would now really like to know now why he had also written the life of Geta Antonius, whilst giving him a hard loin cloth soiling glare.

You are probably asking the same question as Constantine Augusta, why does Geta, that good comrade who loved his word puzzles and dazzling tunics get a chapter in our collection of worst emperors? The simple answer is because he did not get on with his older brother. It's now time to unpack the deadliest brotherly rival since Remus laughed at Romulus' wall and was beaten to death for his cheek.

Two Little Boys had Two Little Toys and each wanted more.

Publius Septimius Geta was born on 7 March 189 CE, three years before his father became emperor. His brother Lucius Septimius Bassianus was born on the 4th April the previous year, making there a thirteen month gap between them. Age seven Bassianus was renamed Marcus Aurelius Antonius, an attempt by his newly made emperor father to link himself to the previous dynasty of those five good emperors. Our sources refer to him by this name, Antonius, but we better know him as Caracalla, a nickname given due to his fondness for wearing the style of hooded cloak known as a Caracalla. You will recall that the emperor Gaius gained the nickname 'Caligula' after a pair of boots he wore as a child. Based on this survey of two whole emperors, I conclude that nicknames derived from items of clothing have a terrible effect on sanity and the ability to rule as a good emperor.

According to all our sources the two brothers never got on. The *Historia Augusta* author, in his attempt to offer up some proof of the long-standing rivalry, comes up with the least convincing omen story ever put to papyri. 'Immediately after Geta was born someone announced that a purple egg had been laid by a hen in the palace. This egg was then brought in, and Bassianus his brother, seizing it, dashed it upon the ground, as a child would do, and broke it; whereupon Julia, it is said, exclaimed in jest, "Accursed fratricide, you have killed your brother".'[5]

It's far from subtle and if true, which it absolutely is not, was so obvious as to render the Imperial augurs obsolete. For as an omen it not so much foretells as slaps your cheek and yells in your face that *SPOILER ALERT* Caracalla would go onto murder his brother. It almost makes you yearn for the cryptic mystery of that horse that climbed onto the roof during Pertinax's birth and then dropped dead. What was that all about?

That Geta is murdered by his own brother, who not satisfied in snuffing him out in life, also snuffs out all references to him in all official documents, inscriptions, and statues by declaring *Damnatio Memoriae*,[6] overshadows accounts of Geta's life. He is doomed from the moment he was born, as seen in that terrible omen story, which lends him the tragic, ethereal quality of a man who is destined to disappear from history. However, there is enough in our sources to allow me to fully charge and convict Geta of being a worst emperor – tragic, inevitable end be damned!

There are some rather wonderful stories about the youthful, pre-emperor Geta. He is gloriously described as being 'incontinent in love' which is a magnificent way of saying he couldn't keep it in his loincloth. He showed 'boundless enthusiasm for shows, dancing, and chariot-driving'.[7] Which is portrayed by Herodian as some horrific character flaw, as opposed to being the natural activities of a young man in a society lacking big screen televisions, all you can eat buffets and premier league football. Significantly there is absolutely no mention of either Geta or Caracalla dressing up as yokels, hitting the taverns and beating the punters up. So, either that hobby beloved by Caligula, Lucius Verus and Commodus had gone out of fashion by the late second century or else the Severus boys were amateurs in the hell raising stakes. Although any excesses that they did show were the result of the fierce competition between the brothers in all matters, including how they chose to enjoy themselves.

In chariot racing if 'the one attached himself to a certain faction, the other would be sure to choose the opposite side'.[8] They did the same with cockfights and quail fight. Yes apparently quail fights were a thing. Let's face it if the Romans had had access to penguins, they'd have fitted them with razor blades and let them waddle towards each other betting thousands of sesterces on the result. The Severus boys also enjoyed hobbies which are referred to by Herodian variously as youthful pleasures, disgraceful practices, and new vices. Which is vague but intriguing. Thankfully Cassius Dio sheds light on these activities. 'They outraged women and abused boys, they embezzled money, and made gladiators and charioteers their boon companions, emulating each other in the similarity of their deeds, but full of strife in their rivalries.'[9]

What didn't help matters, and in fact made them a lot worse, was that each had their own group of 'friends', keen no doubt to make themselves popular with the next emperor by feeding the brotherly resentments and rivalry for their own benefit. Nobody ever got to be a favourite of an emperor by telling him to grow up and stop acting like a schoolboy. If they had the history of ancient Rome and, indeed the world would have been very different.

Septimius Severus despaired. Because you would, wouldn't you? For an emperor who spent much of his reign doing war stuff, Septimius Severus is oddly terrible at sorting out his wayward sons. I'd go as far as to say he is ineffectual, which is as withering a statement on someone's parenting skills as you will ever hear uttered. But really when he should be giving them the full hairdryer technique[10] he does this instead, 'Severus tried constantly to reconcile his sons and persuade them to live in peace and harmony. He kept reminding them of tales and plays of old, telling them time and again of the misfortunes suffered by royal brothers as a result of dissension.'[11] After which noble speech no doubt one of the little brats piped up, 'yeah but my bruv ain't building no city is he? So like what'? But in Latin.

'Severus tried to keep his sons under control and bring them into agreement. But the youths paid absolutely no attention to him.'[12] Like I said, ineffectual. The only notable stand he makes in controlling his sons was by punishing their friends. Although not in any way severely or that would have been worth a mention, perhaps he punished them with a dull, worthy lecture of their own.

Two Little Boys Become Two Little Emperors

Septimius Severus died in Eboracum, modern day York, on 4 February 211 CE. He had ruled Rome for eighteen years and done so rather well. When alive he had shown off this success to his sons: 'he showed them the treasuries and temples, overflowing with riches; he made it clear that they would never have to scheme abroad for money and power; resources at home were so plentiful that they could pay the soldiers with lavish generosity. The garrison at Rome had been quadrupled, and the army encamped before the city was so powerful that there remained no foreign army strong enough to rival it in number of troops, in physical prowess, or in the amount of money available for pay'.[13]

This was the empire that Severus bequeathed to his two sons to rule jointly, and it was quite a jewel. Caracalla was at his father's bedside as the emperor slowly slipped away, and as Severus took his final breath, that jewel was handed over. The first act of a new emperor sets the tone of their rule, and this is what Caracalla did. '[He] seized control and immediately began to murder everyone in the court.'[14] 'Everyone at court' is quite a wide criterion for Caracalla's first killing spree but still he manages to single quite a few out amongst the 'everyone', killing 'those men who had reared his brother and himself because they persisted in urging him to live at peace with Geta'.

That certainly set the tone for the new regime alright. The brotherly rivalry was not to be set aside simply because they were both emperors now and had a multitude of important empire running things to do. Instead, it was to intensify to such a burning heat that it was inevitable that only one of them would survive, and that wasn't necessarily Caracalla. For Geta, our puzzle-loving wearer of retina-scarring bright attire was not some innocent victim cruelly murdered by his own brother, he was just as likely to have been the one who did the murdering and all because they couldn't share.

Share and Share-alike

After Caracalla had murdered everyone at court, he attempted to convince the soldiers that they should make him sole emperor. They were having none of it though. 'For they remembered Severus and knew that the youths had been one and the same to him and had been reared as equals from childhood; consequently, they gave each brother the same support and loyalty'.[16] Caracalla had no choice but to rule jointly with Geta. A better man, a better emperor would have been conciliatory towards his fellow ruler, putting aside these differences for the good of Rome and those soldiers, who had made clear their loyalty. Neither Caracalla nor Geta were that better man.

During what had to be a very tense journey back to Rome from York the emperors, forced to share a carriage along with their mother, did not spend the time working out their differences and discussing how they could jointly make their empire better, instead they quarrelled constantly. Presumably their mother sat in-between them and periodically yelled out an exasperated, 'for pity's sake will you two cut it out'! But the brother's quarrelling was so much bigger than whose chariot team was victorious that day, or whose cock had pecked the others to death. It was even bigger than who did the most of that whatever it was that Herodian labels disgraceful practices. Caracalla's first act as emperor had, unsurprisingly (and understandably) made Geta nervous of him and the reverse was true too.

On this journey to Rome, 'they did not use the same lodgings or even dine together, since they were extremely suspicious of all they ate and drank; each feared that the other would secretly get prior access to the kitchens and bribe the servants to use poison'.[15] There's no mention of how Julia Domna handled this, did she dine one night with one son and one night with the other? Or just wash her hands of the exasperating pair and eat on her own?

When they reached Rome, this behaviour continued with the brothers deciding they couldn't peacefully co-exist in a palace the size of a small village. 'Each brother now took up residence in his half of the palace. Barricading the inner doors, they used in common only the public outer doors. Caracalla and Geta stationed their own private guards and were never seen together except briefly during their infrequent public appearances.'[17] I think it is fair for me to say that their feud was taking up so much of their time that completing the check list of things good emperors do did not even enter their heads, nor likely any of the training for the role they'd received from their father. This pointless rivalry consumed them both utterly, so much so that, 'anyone could see that something terrible was bound to result from the situation'.[18]

Still Caracalla and Geta manage to make one semi-mature decision together as emperors. Prepare to be as disappointed as Septimius Severus was with them every day of his life because it's nothing to do with conquering territories nor erecting impressive buildings or even a much-needed legal reform. No, the sole decision they managed to make as joint emperors was that they needed to get further away from each other than their division of a whopping big Imperial palace allowed. 'They concluded that it was best to divide the empire, to avoid remaining in Rome and continuing their intrigues. Summoning the advisers appointed by their father, with their mother present too, they decided to partition the empire: Caracalla to have all Europe, and Geta all the lands lying opposite Europe, the region known as Asia.'[19]

Having decided to split the empire between them, the two emperors actually cooperate in deciding how to make this work in practise, with Caracalla choosing Byzantium as his capital and Geta, Chalcedon (cities that are situated directly opposite each other, but with the Bosporus Sea as a handy barrier between them). European senators would stay in Rome but those from the Asiatic provinces would go with Geta (there's nothing on whether those senators were happy to do this – I'm presuming they were less than impressed to be told they had to uproot their whole lives because two brothers just couldn't get along). Caracalla's division would include the Moors and Numidians, whereas Geta would get the Libyans.

Which might have worked. Dividing the empire and ruling separate sides of it had certainly worked previously for Mark Antony and a pre-Augustus Augustus, right up until the point they went to war against each other. In future centuries joint rule of a split empire became the norm and was rather successful. So perhaps Caracalla and Geta could have made this work. You'll notice that I am using words like 'might' and 'perhaps' because this grand plan of dividing the empire never happens because that 'something terrible' happened.

The something terrible that happened

Ok, we all know what the something terrible was that happened because that purple egg-smashing omen gave it away. I've portrayed the brothers' disagreements as being somewhat childish and stupid, and yes, the whole thing is because neither side benefits from it all and anyone with any sense would just let it slide for the good of everyone involved and this empire they are supposed to be ruling together. But there is a darkness at the heart of this story, one that was demonstrated during that journey back from York where the brothers each feared the other would poison them.

Neither Caracalla and Geta are capable of letting their disagreements slide, and they build and build, no doubt egged on by their 'friends', until we reach a very black point that is far beyond a childish squabble and into full scale paranoia. 'They tried every sort of intrigue; each, for example, attempted to persuade the other's cooks and cupbearers to administer some deadly poison. It was not easy for either one to succeed in these attempts, however both were exceedingly careful and took many precautions.'[20]

This shines a different light on that dividing of the palace story, doesn't it? Less brothers unable to stand each other and more brothers barricading themselves away from the other for their own safety. Living under that constant paranoia is going to affect your mental health, is it any wonder then that this happened? 'Finally Caracalla decided to act and advance his cause by sword or slaughter or die in a manner befitting his birth.'[21]

Because if he didn't act then surely his brother would.

Caracalla would later claim to the Praetorians that Geta was forming a conspiracy against him; given their history of murdering emperors this was not unlikely. Perhaps Geta had got more organised in his campaigns against his brother, perhaps it was all in Caracalla's head. We will never know. But what is clear is that this conflict between the brothers had horrifically escalated. For Caracalla it was kill his brother or be killed by him: do or die.

The murder of Geta was not going to be easy because Geta was similarly affected by paranoia and had taken necessary precautions. 'Many soldiers and athletes, therefore, were guarding Geta, both abroad and at home, day and night alike.'[22] So how to do it? The plan Caracalla comes up with is particularly horrible because it involves the emperors' mother, Julia Domna. Caracalla had persuaded her that this time he was ready to reconcile with Geta and that she should invite them both to her chambers ready for the 'we're friends again, hug' moment.

When Geta arrived at the chamber of his mother for this big reconciliation he was set upon by centurions. 'Geta, at the sight of them had run to his mother, hung about her neck and clung to her bosom and breasts, lamenting and crying: "Mother that didst bear me, mother that didst bear me, help! I am being murdered".'[23] The centurions did not cease in the task they had been allotted and preceded to stab Geta to death as he clung to his mother. He was 22 years old.

Caracalla's reaction? 'Having succeeded in the murder, Caracalla ran from the room and rushed throughout the palace, shouting that he had escaped grave danger and had barely managed to save his life. He ordered the soldiers who guard the Imperial palace to protect him and escort him to the Praetorian camp, where he could be safely guarded.'[24]

Which I think shows the depths of the paranoia afflicting Caracalla, even after having murdered the chief source of that paranoia. It did not bode well for Rome to be under the now sole rulership of this man. But the subject of this chapter is not Caracalla, it's Geta.

Although after that whole murdering his brother in the actual arms of his mother event, you are probably wondering why Geta is a worst emperor and Caracalla is not. Well, I admit it was a close-run thing, but Geta is the winner in this particular bout, (which will be some consolation for him since his brother Caracalla was the ultimate victor in their lifelong tussles for superiority and attention), because he leaves so little imprint from his time as emperor. Yes, that is because he suffered *Damnatio Memoriae* and so any imprint he might have made was scrubbed out (see image 26 for an excellent example of this). But we do have written sources for his reign and what do they tell us about Geta's actions as emperor? They tell us that he used his time as one of the two most powerful men in the world thinking up ways to get at his brother and thinking up ways to protect himself from his brother.

In comparison when Caracalla finds himself sole emperor, he is fizzingly dynamic, not always in a good way for the populace, true,[25] but you can't deny he does stuff. He goes off to fight the Alamanni tribe in Germania, he declares war on the Parthians, he confers Roman citizenship to all in the empire and he builds some whopping big baths in Rome. He has a legacy, something that Geta does not. Which is why Geta is our worst emperor.

Chapter 11

Elagabalus (218 – 222 CE) – And Now for Someone Completely Different

Caracalla ruled for a further six years as emperor and was assassinated in 217 CE aged 29 whilst having a wee. He left no heir, which as we've seen repeatedly is always a dangerous moment for all concerned. The architect of his assassination, the Praetorian Prefect Macrinus (oh what a surprise a Praetorian involved in removing his boss!), nobly decided he may as well fill that gap as it was there (he'd put it there) and be emperor if he really had to (he forced everyone to swear allegiance to him).

But Macrinus had a rival for the Imperial purple and this one wasn't being championed by the senators, nor the army even, but rather the Imperial women. Julia Maesa, sister to Caracalla and Geta's mother, Julia Domna, put forward her grandson Varius Avitus Bassianus up against incumbent emperor Macrinus. Bassianus came with a ready-made claim of being the nephew of Septimius Severus, the cousin to Geta and the bastard son to Caracalla (or so claimed his grandmother, attempting to big up his right to be emperor).

Bassianus also came with a whole lot of other stuff that was going to make his time as emperor very interesting, but the soldiers fighting to make him their ruler had never met him. They were surprised as everyone else by the man who rocked up at the gates of Rome in the late summer of 218 CE after they had defeated Macrinus on his behalf.

This new emperor Varius Avitus Bassianus is more commonly known to us as Elagabalus. A name which given past Imperial nicknames, such as Caligula and Caracalla, you're probably assuming is a particularly natty style of tunic or a pair of woollen socks that Bassianus was fond of wearing. You'd be wrong. Elagabalus, or Heliogabalus as it is sometimes rendered, is the name of the Sun God, a deity young Bassianus had served as high priest to in his native homeland of Syria. Yep, that's right Varius Avitus Bassianus has come down through history with the name of a divine being – suck on that Bootykins!

If you're now thinking that the divine nickname given to Elagabalus means his rule must have been brimming with God-like acts and accomplishments, throw away that thought, because you'll only be bitterly disappointed by what follows. The *Historia Augusta* author is certainly disappointed, as shown by the opening line to his chapter on Elagabalus. 'The life of Elagabalus Antoninus, also called Varius, I should never have put in writing — hoping that it might not be known that he was emperor of the Romans were it not that before him this same Imperial office had had a Caligula, a Nero, and a Vitellius.'[1] Which is a hell of an opening paragraph.

The *Historia Augusta* goes onto say, 'the thoughtful reader may find himself some consolation for these monstrous tyrants by the reading of Augustus, Trajan, Vespasian, Hadrian, Pius, Titus, and Marcus'.[2] Screw that! Who wants to read about those good emperors doing good things? Hopefully not anyone reading a book entitled Ancient Rome's Worst Emperors. Bring on the depravity, the decadence, and the debauchery! Thankfully Elagabalus' reign is not short on any of these, think Caligula and then up the perversion factor by ten and you're only scratching the surface of the events of Elagabalus' rule. It was an interesting time, to put it mildly.

Our key sources for the reign of Elagabalus are, as mentioned, the *Historia Augusta*, a collection of emperor biographies written under the reigns of Diocletian and Constantine the Great (seventy years after Elagabalus' rule), our old friend Herodian who was alive during the events he described and Cassius Dio, who like Herodian was alive during the reign of Elagabalus and who, unlike Herodian, is a Roman senator.

Cassius Dio was our man on the ground during Commodus' reign, and very useful he was too on what it was like to be a senator serving an emperor who hated senators with a passion, unintentionally hilarious it turns out.[3] However, on assessing the rule of Elagabalus, Cassius Dio nails his colours to the wall with a very sturdy hammer by repeatedly referring to the emperor as The False Antonius.[4] Cassius Dio, as his repeated use of the False Antonius shows, believed Elagabalus was a usurper who had no right to be emperor. He is biased, let us say. He's also not our man on the ground this time either, as he himself admits, in a rather wonderful 'why I didn't do my homework' flavoured excuse. 'Thus far I have described events with as great accuracy as I could in every case, but for subsequent events I have not found it possible to give an accurate account, for the reason that I did not spend much time in Rome. For, after going from Asia into Bithynia, I fell sick, and from there I hastened to my province of Africa; then, on returning to Italy I was almost immediately sent as governor first to Dalmatia and then to Upper Pannonia, and though after that I returned to Rome and to Campania, I at once set out for home. For these reasons, then, I have not been able to compile the same kind of account of subsequent events as of the earlier ones.'[5]

So how did our master historian put together his account of the reign of Elagabalus? 'And let no one be incredulous of my statements; for what I have written about the other attempts of private citizens I ascertained from trustworthy men.' I am assuming these trustworthy men were pen pals given Cassius Dio's residence abroad. In the manner of pen pals the world over they likely tried to make their letters more exciting, if only to cheer up Cassius Dio from the relentless pressures of public duty, and to make themselves stand out from his other correspondents so he might remember them when they next needed a favour.

I am not saying we should dismiss Cassius Dio's account of Elagabalus altogether; he is a contemporary and so offers a valuable insight into what contemporaries felt about this emperor (very little in Cassius Dio's case), but this is one of the tales that these trustworthy men pass onto him. 'He carried his lewdness to such a point that he asked the physicians to contrive a woman's vagina in his body by means of an incision, promising them large sums for doing so.'[6] You might want to bear this in mind as we dig into the reign of Elagabalus, whilst also saying a private thank you to the pen pals for preserving such insane levels of gossip.

The *Historia Augusta* author, on the other hand, is made of less stern stuff, 'concerning his life many filthy anecdotes have been put into writing, but since they are not worthy of being recorded, I have thought I ought to relate only such deeds as illustrate his extravagance'.[7] Although the paragraphs that follow this rather pious statement on the emperors' extravagance are truly stupendous, triggering a frantic clanging of the 'so good it can't possibly be true' bell. Don't worry for we shall be examining these tales in detail and sorting the true from the could be true, the might be true, the well I suppose it's possible and the oh dear god that never happened!

The Teenager in Charge

Elagabalus was declared Emperor on 8 June 218 CE, at the tender age of 14. He wasn't the youngest ever to be declared emperor, that title falls on Diadumenian, the 9-year-old son of Macrinus, the man whose forces Elagabalus' troops had destroyed. Diadumenian, declared joint ruler with his father, only managed to hold power in his tiny hands for a single year. Elagabalus would achieve a reign four times this length. Which sounds impressive until you belatedly do the (simple) maths and realise that one times four is only four. Elagabalus as emperor burned brightly, but briefly.

Like Nero before him, who became emperor at 17 years old, Elagabalus owed his succession to the machinations of women. In the case of Nero this had been his mother, the wily Agrippina the Younger. Elagabalus owed his laurel wreath to two Julias, his mother Julia Soaemias and his grandmother, Julia Maesa. Both of these women are going to feature heavily in the rule of their puppet, sorry emperor.

There was great hope and excitement centred on this new emperor. 'After obtaining the Imperial power he despatched couriers to Rome, and there all classes were filled with enthusiasm, and a great desire for him was aroused in the whole people merely at the mention of the name.'[8] The Senate expressed the usual wishes for his long and happy reign. 'Such are the pious hopes of men, who are quick to believe when they wish the thing to come true which their hearts desire',[9] says, the *Historia Augusta* setting us up for the brutal disillusionment the Senate is later going to experience.

What of the new emperor on which all hopes were resting, what was he like? Over to Herodian. 'Bassianus, in the prime of youth, was the handsomest lad of his time. With physical beauty, bloom of youth, and splendour of attire combining to produce the same effect, the youth might well be compared to the handsome statues of Bacchus.'[10] That certainly makes a change from some of the previous holders of the post, Tiberius with his disfiguring skin disease, Galba and his crippling arthritis, Domitian and his 'hammer-toes'.[11] Image and appearance mattered in an emperor, which is why Suetonius in his biographies dedicates a whole passage discussing relative hairiness, protruding or non-protruding eyes and growing waistlines of the emperors he writes about. Statues, particularly of the Julio Claudian emperors remove such imperfections, displaying a manly vigour in even the most aged and decrepit of emperor.[12] Elagabalus' stunning attractiveness was an attribute to be harnessed therefore, if only to wow visiting dignities whose reports back home would surely open with a comment on the absolute gorgeousness of that king of the Romans.

However, the people of Rome would have to wait for their glimpse of the handsome young emperor because for now he was in the provinces doing that proper emperor thing of executing your enemies. The post-Macrinus era apparently required a great deal of mopping up, which is surprising given he barely ruled a year and so could have hardly built up a die-hard loyal faction who couldn't be persuaded to switch their allegiance to the new regime.

Still, we are told that Fabius Agrippinus was killed for his prior intimacy with Macrinus, Pica Caerianus for being slow to announce his allegiance to the new emperor and a certain Castius for the crime of being energetic and popular with the troops he commanded. Not to mention Sulla, who had intriguingly 'meddled in some matters that did not concern him'.[13] Which is gloriously unspecific and lends itself open to any interpretation you like.

Personally, I have Sulla down as organising a fabulous 'Hello New Emperor' party and annoying the palace entertainments department.

Or perhaps he wrote a letter to Elagabalus with lots of good advice on how to be emperor. Teenagers are seldom able to stomach being told what to do without a sulky exit complete with earth-trembling door slam. This is familiar emperor territory, cleaning out anyone whose loyalty was suspect and sending a message back to Rome that this was a strong emperor who wouldn't hesitate to remove you should you show anything less than full support and confidence in him.

Elagabalus' other activities in the east were a whole lot less familiar and unlikely to go down well in the still very conservative, Rome, 'when she saw what Heliogabalus was doing, Maesa was greatly disturbed',[14] as Herodian puts it. Which I'm going to leave hanging unexplained to create tension and anticipation for the rest of this chapter.

Elagabalus wasn't to reach Rome until 219 CE, a full year after he was first declared emperor. That was quite a period of time to build up a picture of what their new emperor would be like. Would he be military-minded like his alleged father Caracalla? Would he be strong willed and resolute like his (possible) Grandfather, Septimius Severus? Would he be a peace maker, desirous of harmony like his actual aunt Julia Domna? Nobody knew.

In the summer Rome was finally treated to the first sight of their handsome young emperor and this is what they saw, 'he wore the richest clothing, draping himself in purple robes embroidered in gold; to his necklaces and bracelets he added a crown, a tiara glittering with gold and jewels'.[15] Banging threads or what! Ones to compete with Commodus' purple gold-spangled gown and Caligula's foray into dressing up as the Goddess Venus, which I'm assuming involved similar use of luxurious fabric and precious jewels. This was Elagabalus, the young, handsome emperor resplendent in purple and gold ready to rule the empire. Let's see how he got on doing that.

Imperial Japes

Cassius Dio splits Elagabalus' actions as emperor into two distinct categories.

'He drifted into all the most shameful, lawless, and cruel practices, with the result that some of them, never before known in Rome, came to have the authority of tradition, while others, that had been attempted by various men at different times, flourished merely for the three years, nine months and four days during which he ruled.'[16] Essentially things that other worst emperors did and things that were so far out there that no emperor ever came close to replicating them. Which, thank you Cassius Dio, is actually a very helpful categorisation and one I shall shamelessly steal.

In that first category, the things 'that had been attempted by various men at different times' we find some familiar motifs. There is the taste for over the top, but apparently still edible, delicacies 'he frequently ate camels-heels and also cocks-combs taken from the living birds, and the tongues of peacocks and nightingales'.[17] Which he consumed on couches made of solid silver and gave out as party gifts for departing guests 'eunuchs, or four-horse chariots, or horses with saddles, or mules, or litters, or carriages, or a thousand aurei or a hundred pounds of silver'.[8]

Where we cross over into Cassius Dio's second category of things 'never before known in Rome' is with the pranks Elagabalus allegedly pulled on his guests. This one I'm sure had them all in stitches or else miserably shaking with fear and clinging onto their party gift eunuch all the way home. 'Among his pets he had lions and leopards, which had been rendered harmless and trained by tamers, and these he would suddenly order during the dessert and the after-dessert to get up on the couches, thereby causing an amusing panic, for none knew that the beasts were harmless.'[19] Only slightly less amusing than Commodus jape of feeding his guests poo.

It was a joke he clearly did not tire of playing for when any of his friends got that bit too drunk. 'He would often shut them up, and suddenly during the night let in his lions and leopards and bears — all of them harmless — so that his friends on awakening at dawn, or worse, during the night, would find lions and leopards and bears in the room with themselves.'[20]

Picture if you will the worst hangover you have ever experienced. The type of hangover where even your eyeballs pulsate with pain and your head is afflicted with a constant fuzzy buzzing. The type of hangover where you lay utterly still, not daring to move any part of your body for fear that your lurching stomach will heave last night's excesses all over the floor. The type of hangover that leaves you feeling that you surely must have been poisoned, for it surely cannot be possible to feel this ill on booze alone. Are you picturing it? Good. Now throw in a bear in your bedroom on top of all that and the sound of the emperor sniggering outside your door. Horrific doesn't cover it. As the *Historia Augusta* bluntly puts it, 'some even died from this cause'. I do not doubt that.

Another way Elagabalus manages to kill off his party guests can be best described as 'death by flowers' and is the subject of a painting by Victorian chappie, Sir Lawrence Alma-Tadema (see image 30). 'In a banqueting-room with a reversible ceiling he once overwhelmed his parasites with violets and other flowers, so that some were actually smothered to death, being unable to crawl out to the top.'[21] In Alma-Tadema's painting, Elagabalus and chums recline on couches dispassionately watching as the killer blossoms cascade onto the helpless guests. How long this took you do have to wonder. Elagabalus doesn't strike me as the sort of man who could sit for hours watching flowers fall from the ceiling slowly filling the room. He couldn't even sit through your average dinner party without throwing in a bear to make it more interesting. As a method of death, I'm not convinced it would work, would the flowers combined weight really reach a level that could smother a man?[22]

On the more believable scale of anecdotes, was Elagabalus' joke of letting the air out of his party guests' cushions so that they found themselves suddenly sliding off the couch and under the table, no doubt accompanied by Imperial laughter. Really, it's a wonder the roads out of Rome weren't jammed solid with people fleeing the prospect of having to attend another Imperial banquet.

But what comes across loud and clear from these tales of Elagabalus' 'jokes', whether they are strictly true or not, is the juvenile nature of them. Take this one as an example, 'he used, too, to play jokes on his slaves, even ordering them to bring him a thousand pounds of spiders-webs'.[23] You can imagine the scene, a long-wet afternoon lying in front of the bored adolescent when his eyes fall mischievously on the slaves positioned around his chamber. Time to have a bit of fun. It's all very childish.

Caligula's 'jokes' you'll recall were deliberately and calculatingly sadistic. Elagabalus' are childish because he is a child. That is worth bearing in mind as we trawl our way through the outlandish tales of Elagabalus' reign, for some of these can be seen as the result of giving a jar of glitter to a toddler and telling him not to open it. The moment you're out of the room he is going to unscrew that lid for sure, glitter is going to go everywhere and he's going to be standing there laughing as you do your back in sweeping up all the mess.

The most excessive of sexual excesses

Back to those things 'that had been attempted by various men at different times', and another motif of the worst emperor we are now familiar with, same-sex shenanigans. Or rather same-sex shenanigans in a manner that upset the ancient Rome notions of what was proper. What was proper in ancient Rome is often the reverse of what is considered proper in our own society, sexual relations with pre-adolescent boys being the example that stands out the most. The anecdotes presented on Elagabalus' relations with men are very much geared to strike every single note on the moral degeneracy xylophone. It's an entire scale all the way from C to G, with the sharp notes thrown in for good measure.

You'll recall that acceptable sexual relations for an elite Roman male involve him being the penetrator, never the penetrated. You'll be unsurprised to learn that Elagabalus is portrayed as the penetrated. But to distinguish him from other emperors who've had this accusation thrown at them (which up to this point is absolutely all of them with the notable exceptions of Vespasian and Claudius. And presumably Elagabalus' immediate predecessor Diadumenian, on account of him being 9) we get this extra sprinkle of depravity dust.

'He himself would take the role of Venus, and suddenly drop his clothing to the ground and fall naked on his knees, one hand on his breast, the other before his private parts, his buttocks projecting meanwhile and thrust back in front of his partner in depravity.'[24]

According to the *Historia Augusta*, Elagabalus would put in the effort during these relations to model his expression on that of the actual Venus, as depicted in art. Although you'll also recall according to the *Historia Augusta*: 'concerning his life many filthy anecdotes have been put into writing, but since they are not worthy of being recorded, I have thought I ought to relate only such deeds as illustrate his extravagance'.[23] We may all laugh cynically and slightly manically now after having read the preceding seventeen chapters of extremely filthy anecdotes. The *Historia Augusta* is not, as you'll gather, a reliable source. But all credit to them for managing to craft an anecdote incorporating passive homosexuality, cross dressing and offending the gods. A triple whammy of degeneracy! But there's more. 'To the other posts of distinction he advanced men whose sole recommendation was the enormous size of their privates.'[26]

Elagabalus is a sacrilegious, transvestic passive homosexual who favours large penises and overlooks the entire senatorial and equestrian class to fill the public positions that they believe are rightfully theirs. The latter you have to suspect is the truth that is lurking behind these extraordinary slurs (which only get more extreme, you'll be pleased to know). For Elagabalus did not think much of those august senators. 'He often showed contempt for the senate, calling them slaves in togas.'[27] Which when you think about it is a very apt description, although hardly one that will gain you many friends in that quarter.

Cassius Dio's tales, or rather the tales he's been told by his attention seeking pen pals go even further. Not only is Elagabalus a highly effeminate passive homosexual, but he also sets himself up as a rent boy! 'He set aside a room in the palace and there committed his indecencies, always standing nude at the door of the room, as the harlots do, and shaking the curtain which hung from gold rings, while in a soft and melting voice he solicited the passers-by. There were, of course, men who had been specially instructed to play their part.'[28]

Even more offensive to Roman minds than taking part in sodomy was Elagabalus' marriage to a Vestal Virgin. Breaking the divinely ordained sanctity of a Vestal was a very big deal. Historically Rome had suffered terrible misfortune when Vestals had broken their vows, as we've mentioned in a previous chapter.[30] Elagabalus' knowing breaking of a Vestal's chastity was therefore not only an affront to decency but threatened the survival of the city and the empire itself.

But he didn't only sully a priestess of Vesta, he also committed a great sacrilege against the goddess herself by entering a part of the temple that only her priests were permitted to enter. Even worse, Elagabalus removed the holy shrines from Vesta's temple. We are told he wanted to take this sacrilege further by extinguishing the holy fire Vestals were charged with never letting go out on pain of death. The gods protected Rome, but they could also punish Rome if displeased, Elagabalus' fragrant disregarding of religious protocol was felt as a very real threat by the citizens of Rome.

It's difficult to contemplate how much lower Elagabalus the emperor could sink, but never fear because our sources have handily scraped their barrels for us of the most unimaginable things that a ruler could get up. As a useful experiment, as you read the following summary, picture your own prime minister or president behaving in this way. The horror/amusement you will experience is akin to what the ancient Romans felt.

Elagabalus married many women including a Vestal Virgin; aside from his wives (of which there were four) he never had sex with the same woman twice.[31] He took a charioteer named Hierocles as his long term lover, in a single day he visited every single prostitute who worked the public spaces and gave each a gold aureus, he wore a hairnet and other women's attire and 'planned, indeed, to cut off his genitals altogether, but that desire was prompted solely by his effeminacy; the circumcision which he actually carried out was a part of the priestly requirements of Elagabalus'.[32]

Phew, that's quite a catalogue of depravity and one designed to hit just about everything that could offend an ancient Roman. Circumcision was not practised by Romans, they considered it barbaric and akin to castration. The law stated that anyone found to have circumcised themselves or their slaves were liable to exile and having their property confiscated by the state. Any doctor found to have performed the operation faced execution. That the emperor himself was circumcised was very shocking indeed.

Alongside the emperor having practised a custom that was non-Roman, we find some further descriptions of the clothes Elagabalus was fond of wearing that again highlight this non-Romaness. 'He went about in barbarian dress, wearing long-sleeved purple tunics embroidered with gold which hung to his feet; robes similarly decorated with gold and purple covered his legs from hip to toe, and he wore a diadem of varicoloured precious gems.'[33] Elagabalus, we are told, loathed Greek and Roman clothes, he preferred to dress Eastern style despite his grandmother begging him to dress in a tunic and toga. Let us give this non-Romaness a more familiar word, one that isn't going to upset my spell checker something rotten; foreign. Elagabalus dressed like a foreigner, he took up foreign customs and he worshipped a foreign god. This was a problem for the Romans.

The Exotic Emperor

Rome was a city made up of hundreds of thousands of people, the majority of whom had probably started life elsewhere in the world. Thousands more likely arrived every year ready to take advantage of what Rome offered or were brought there forcibly in chains as slaves. It was a true multi-cultural society, a mass of people of different skin colours, religions, and beliefs. However, every single damn one of those people, whether they had come from Spain or Syria, Romania or North Africa, would have worn a tunic or stola, dripped garum sauce[34] all over their dinners and complained loudly about those trouser-wearing barbarians who were hogging access to the drinking fountain. Much as Martial does in this poem:

> *German, this is our aqueduct*
> *And not the Rhine. Barbarian clot,*
> *How dare you elbow and obstruct*
> *A thirsty boy from drinking? What!*
> *Jostle a Roman from his place!*
> *This is the conqueror's fountain, not*
> *A trough for your defeated race.*[35]

Martial himself is from Spain, another one of those defeated races.

To be a Roman, with all the superiority and sophistication that came with it, you needed to act like a Roman. As mentioned previously, as early as the reign of Rome's fourth emperor, Claudius, we find foreigners in the shape of Gauls admitted to the Senate. Trajan and Hadrian, emperors number thirteen and fourteen, were both Spanish. Septimius Severus hailed from Libya. Being Roman no longer meant hailing from that city in central Italy, it was a much wider term than that, it was a culture that anyone could adopt as their own. Except that Elagabalus did not, as was clearly demonstrated to all by his 'barbarian' dress.

There were other barbarian behaviours of Elagabalus that got those Roman tongues tutting on full volume. There was his fondness for eunuchs, long considered a sign of eastern decadence, who Elagabalus had given jobs in 'the administration of the finances and in procuratorships'.[36] His successor as emperor, Alexander Severus, makes a big show of removing these eunuchs from their posts and reassigning them to what he considers more suitable work for their kind, working in the women's baths. Alexander is said to have limited the number of eunuchs in Imperial service, suggesting that Elagabalus' court had been full to bursting with the testes-free chaps. Another clear sign of Elagabalus' foreignness in Roman eyes

But the most noticeable sign of Elagabalus' otherness was his adherence to the God that would ultimately name him for posterity. Foreign gods went down as well as other foreign things in Rome, they were the highly suspect product of cultures not nearly as good as Rome. Evidence of the emperor's favourite god's weird foreign-ness was everywhere. 'The circumcision which he actually carried out was a part of the priestly requirements of Elagabalus, and he accordingly mutilated many of his companions in like manner.'[37]

The way the emperor worshipped his god was also weird. 'Accompanied by flutes and drums, he went about performing, as it appeared, orgiastic service to his god.'[38] Cassius Dio mentions these performances too, although apparently these performances leaked out into his everyday life. 'He used to dance, not only in the orchestra, but also, in a way, even while walking, performing sacrifices, receiving salutations, or delivering a speech.'[39] Although now I'm wondering if Elagabalus was just dying for a wee.

Foreign gods were not entirely new to Rome, some had even been allowed to hang out with the Roman gods and their worship incorporated into the state religion. The goddess Cybele, sometimes known as the Great Mother, was a Turkish goddess who was brought over to Rome. A Temple dedicated to her was built on the Palatine Hill, next door to the Temple of Apollo, a god the Romans had nicked from the slightly nearer Greece. The cult that surrounded the worship of Cybele was about as foreign as you can get; it involved eunuchs, who Romans never really got the hang of, acting as the priests of Cybele. These Galli, as they were called, would dance about the streets of Rome to the accompaniment of tambourines and clashing cymbals, beating themselves with pinecones until they bled as they pulled an effigy of the goddess to the Circus Maximus during the spring festival of Megalesia.

The Galli became eunuchs by a personal act of self-castration in honour of Attis, the consort of Cybele, who hacked his genitals off with a piece of flint after being driven mad by a nymph. Which you wouldn't think would be a suitable subject for poetry, but Ovid gives it good shot.

Elagabalus (218–222 CE) – And Now for Someone Completely Different

> 'Ah! Let the parts that harmed me, perish!
> Let them perish!' cutting away the burden of his groin,
> And suddenly bereft of every mark of manhood.
> His madness set a precedent, and his unmanly servants
> Toss their hair and cut off their members as if worthless.[40]

A foreign goddess served by very foreign priests who had committed a very foreign act upon themselves the cult of Cybele might have been, but there was one key difference between Cybele's worship and that of Elagabalus' new god, Cybele had the sanction of the Roman state.

Cybele had found her way to the city after a crushing humiliation for Rome. It was the time of the second Punic war and Carthage had the upper hand after wiping out 70,000 Roman soldiers at the battle of Cannae. In Rome itself, ill portents were showing themselves everywhere and worse still there was a famine. All this misfortune was a clear sign that the gods were deserting Rome, or at the very least sufficiently annoyed with the city as to not lift a finger to assist. The question on everyone's lips was how to make the gods happy. Luckily there was somebody they could ask or rather something, the Sibylline books.

The Sibylline books were a collection of sayings in Greek that were consulted in times of great peril in the hope they contained a better suggestion on what they should do that nobody else had come up with.[41] Like a magic 8 ball really. Just like a magic 8 ball the Sibylline books tended to come up with suggestions that on the surface make no sense. There are numerous interventions to prevent famine and to recover from a humiliating military defeat that you can't help but think might be of more practical use than sending a delegation, to what is now modern-day Turkey, to collect an enormous effigy of a goddess and heave it all the way back to Rome. But you can't argue with the results of that seemingly mad expedition, Rome went on to win the second Punic war and its sequel the unimaginatively named third Punic war, the famine ended and there weren't any more meteor showers to be had.

Cybele's introduction to Rome was debated in the Senate, official documents consulted, and a state sponsored delegation sent to bring her to Rome. Elagabalus on the other hand rocked up to Rome and installed his own god. Consultation was not had, and you can tell that really narked folk by the stories our friendly historians come out with. Cassius Dio alleges, 'The offence consisted, not in his introducing a foreign god into Rome or in his exalting him in very strange ways, but in his placing him even before Jupiter himself'[42] Before bringing up the circumcision thing again.

The *Historia Augusta* claims that Elagabalus built a temple to his god on the Palatine Hill in which, 'he desired to transfer the emblem of the Great Mother, the fire of Vesta, the Palladium, the shields of the Salii, and all that the Romans held sacred, purposing that no god might be worshipped at Rome save only Elagabalus'.[43] Note that 'he desired to' rather than actually did.

Herodian adds to these tales with this beauty. 'Not content with making a mockery of human marriage, he even sought a wife for the god whose priest he was.'[44] The first wife found for this statue was not pleasing enough and so Elagabalus had the Carthaginians send over an effigy of their goddess Urania. When the bride-to-be arrived, lavish feasts and festivals were held to celebrate the nuptials. Herodian portrays this as if this were a very peculiar thing, but in the context of Roman religion whose calendar of festivals included the aforementioned self-castrating eunuchs, a ritual involving naked young men running about the city whipping young ladies to grant them improved fertility, burning torches tied to the tails of foxes who were then released into the Circus Maximus and the wholesale slaughtering of dogs to please the gods,[45] it really wasn't. Elagabalus' statue god getting it on with an effigy of Urania is positively winsome in comparison.

As you might have gathered, our sources for Elagabalus' reign are all very concerned with the emperor's extravagances and 'eccentricities' as Herodian terms the most fantastical of Elagabalus' alleged behaviour. This certainly makes for a very entertaining read, but the barrage of anecdotes also makes it very difficult to ascertain exactly what Elagabalus does as emperor. You are left yearning for Suetonius' master hand and skill at weaving together the extreme sexploits of emperors with the minor improvements they made to standing laws. Caligula, for instance, committing incest with all three of his sisters whilst also beginning work on a new aqueduct and revising the list of equestrians. There is sparse mention in our sources of Elagabalus doing anything so useful.

If we believe our sources (and we shall get into it shortly as to whether we should) there was a reason why Elagabalus had quite so much time for debauchery, someone else was undertaking all the duties of an emperor. In fact, two people were: Julia Maesa and Julia Soaemias, Elagabalus' grandmother and mother. 'He was wholly under the control of his mother so much so, in fact, that he did no public business without her consent.'[46]

But Elagabalus took it further than merely listening to his mother and doing what she said. 'When he held his first audience with the senate, he gave orders that his mother should be asked to come into the senate-chamber. On her arrival she was invited to a place on the consuls' bench and there she took part in the drafting — that is to say, she witnessed the drawing up of the senate's decree. And Elagabalus was the only one of all the emperors under whom a woman attended the senate like a man, just as though she belonged to the senatorial order.'[47]

You can just feel the disgust dripping off the page. Women in the Senate House! This was a serious afront to the natural order of things, one beyond even Elagabalus' desire to own a vagina. Although clearly his mother attending the Senate wasn't a regular thing since Elagabalus sets up a women's Senate for her to rule over. From what the *Historia Augusta* has to say about it, this women's Senate was never going to rival the men's for political influence. 'Absurd decrees were enacted concerning rules to be applied to matrons, namely, what kind of clothing each might wear in public, who was to yield precedence and to whom, who was to advance to kiss another, who might ride in a chariot, on a horse, on a pack-animal, or on an ass.'[48] Which is a bit rich given that the (proper) Senate in the past had taken the time to debate and pass a law limiting how much women could spend on clothes and banning them from wearing multi coloured dresses.[49]

Elagabalus' reliance on the advice of and elevation of his womenfolk beyond what was deemed suitable for women in ancient Rome was yet another thing for the Senate and Rome at large to grumble about alongside the deeply unfunny pranks, the promotions based on penis size and that brothel he'd set up in the palace.

The Truth behind the scandal?

So far, we have viewed Elagabalus' rule through the eyes of our tutting historians, and it's been terrific fun, but now it is time to turn our attentions to other sources available to us, such as archaeological finds and coins from the era. Do they corroborate the picture we've formed of Elagabalus as a transvestite, penis-obsessed, flower killer? Let's hope so!

The coins issued by Elagabalus during his short reign do actually corroborate two of the stories that our hostile band of disapproving historians mention. The Vestal Virgin, Aquilia Severa, that Elagabalus was said to have married does appear on coins and medallions as empress, including one coin in which she is depicted alongside her husband, their hands clasped together. Another coin with Severa's image on bears the word Vesta, the name of the goddess she had been ripped away from serving.[50]

That Elagabalus was a priest of the Syrian god of the same name is proven by surviving inscriptions that refer to the emperor as holding the traditional religious title of Pontifex Maximus alongside being described as 'the most elevated priest of the sun god Elagabul'. His priesthood also makes it onto his coins too. Clearly Elagabul was of primary importance to the emperor, but did he really insist upon this deity being worshipped and no other, to the extent that even Jews and Christians were to be forced to transfer their loyalty to Elagabalus' god?

Emperors were known to have favourite gods, Domitian was highly devoted to Minerva for instance, but what is striking about Elagabalus' god is that after the year 220 CE he is the only god depicted on coins. No Jupiter, no Juno, no Minerva, no anybody but Elagabul. The emperor himself appears on a coin making a sacrifice to Elagabul whilst wearing a pair of Parthian trousers. Trousers were one of the key ways Romans distinguished themselves from barbarians. Romans wore tunics, only barbarians wore trousers. Which would appear to back up all those statements from the likes of Cassius Dio about Elagabalus' barbarian dress.

However, surviving records show that people are being appointed to the usual priesthoods. A temple was built to Elagabul true, but the temples of the other gods were not destroyed as you might expect during the forced imposition of a single god. The Christian writer Eusebius, whose history of the church is one long depressing list of how awful Christians were treated by Roman emperors, passes over Elagabalus' reign without comment. In comparison he has plenty to say about Caligula's attempt to insert his own image into the Jewish temple. From which we may conclude Elagabalus may have placed his god centre stage, he may have promoted him endlessly, but the old gods were still there and being worshipped as normal.

One of the stories our historian sources are fond of is Elagabalus' promotion of his favourites, 'the emperor was driven to such extremes of lunacy that he took men from the stage and the public theatre and put them in charge of the most important Imperial business'.[51] Excluding the emperor himself, here is a list of all the consuls appointed during Elagabalus' reign; Q Tinius Sacerdos, P Valerius Comazon, C Vettius Gratus Sabianius and M Flavius Vitellius Seleucus.

Comazon had been commander of one of the legions that had helped Elagabalus to the throne, Sacerdos was a former governor of Bithynia and pro consul of Asia, Sabianius' previous roles included responsibility for securing Rome's food supply. We know nothing about Seleucus, perhaps he was the theatre actor Herodian complains about being promoted, because for sure the other consuls Elagabalus appointed were upstanding citizens of Rome. I suppose there is always the possibility that alongside being successful generals and provincial governors that Comazon and co also possessed large penises; sadly we have no way of corroborating this. Pity.

Elsewhere those favourites of Elagabalus, such as his charioteer-lover Hierocles, feature nowhere in the historical records of posts, honours and dedications that have survived. There is nothing surviving to support Herodian and our other sources claims that Elagabalus was placing the likes of actors in positions of extreme Imperial power.[52] It might have felt to the senatorial class that the emperor valued men from what they considered the lowest dregs of society over them by the amount of time he spent consorting with them, but this was certainly not translated into granting them any official positions that allotted them power and influence.

Of the other accusations tossed at Elagabalus, sadly there is no tangible way to confirm that he wore a hair net and really wanted a vagina. Although we can say that the extravagant building programme described in the *Historia Augusta*, 'he constructed baths in many places, bathed in them once, and immediately demolished them, merely in order that he might not derive any advantage from them. And he is said to have done the same with houses, Imperial headquarters, and summer-dwellings',[53] is likely exaggerated given what the archaeological record tells us. And also given what the author of *The Historia Augusta* tells us himself. 'However, these and some other things which surpass credence, I believe to have been fabricated by those who wished to vilify Elagabalus in order to curry favour with Alexander.'[54] Thanks for clearing that up.

Too Eccentric by far

You may be wondering how all this was going down with Romans, by all this I mean the trouser wearing, vestal marrying, strange god worshipping, big penis hunting antics of the emperor. The answer is not terribly well, as Elagabalus' grandmother Julia Maesa was fully aware of. Having sampled the sweet taste of power Julia Maesa was not prepared to let it go without a fight. Failing miserably to get her grandson to tone it down even slightly, she hit upon an idea that would solve everything. 'She tried to persuade the youth, who was in every respect an empty-headed young idiot, to adopt as his son and appoint as Caesar his first cousin and her grandson, the child of her other daughter, Mamaea.'[55]

The cousin was named Severus Alexander and at only 12 years old, was malleable to Maesa's machinations. That Elagabalus didn't clock that his grandmother, in conjunction with his aunt, Alexander's mother Julia Mamaea, were lining up a plan B in the (highly likely) event of his overthrow is probably down to, as Herodian neatly summarises above, him being an empty-headed young idiot. How else to explain how easily he falls for his grandma's reasoning as to why he should appoint his cousin to a position of extreme power. 'She told the emperor what it pleased him to hear, that it was clearly necessary for him to have time to attend to the worship and service of his god and to devote himself to the rites and revelries and divine functions, but that there should be another responsible for human affairs, to afford him leisure and freedom from the cares of empire. It was not necessary for him, she said, to look for a stranger or someone not a relative; he should entrust these duties to his own cousin.'[56]

Elagabalus actually believes this, and Alexander is appointed Caesar to his Augustus. A decision he soon regrets as Alexander's mother, Julia Mamaea refuses to let him play with his new Caesar chum. 'After adopting Alexander as Caesar, Heliogabalus undertook to teach him his own practices; he instructed him in dancing and prancing, and, enrolling him in the priesthood, wanted the lad to imitate his appearance and actions. But his mother Mamaea kept Alexander from taking part in activities so disgraceful and unworthy of an emperor.'[57]

It's at moments like these that you might want to flick back to the chapters on Galba, Vitellius, Domitian and Nerva to remind yourself that there had been a time not so long back when an emperor stepped into the job with decades of public and military service under his belt. Right now, we have a 16-year-old boy in the top job whose heir is only just scratching at puberty. Boy have things changed!

He may have been only 12 years old, but it didn't take long for Alexander Severus' appeal as an alternative to Elagabalus to occur to those around the throne. 'The Praetorians were angered and disgusted. They were annoyed when they saw the emperor, his face painted more elaborately than that of any modest woman, dancing in luxurious robes and effeminately adorned with gold necklaces. As a result, they were more favourably disposed toward Alexander, for they expected great things of a lad so properly and modestly reared.'[58]

As a further assurance of the scheme, Julia Mamaea sprinkled the Praetorian Guard with coinage, with the result that they were even more favourably inclined towards her son over the emperor. The history of the Praetorian guard has demonstrated again and again that not only are they to a man venal and self-serving but also physically unable to intrigue for longer than a day (the one exception being Sejanus who alone of all of them could play the long game). You sense that their boredom threshold is quite low which is why you find them getting a brilliant idea and enacting it instantaneously without giving it any proper thought. Think back to Pertinax's murder, the result of a Praetorian whim. So, no, as expected they weren't terribly good at hiding their switching of loyalties. 'They welcomed Alexander with enthusiastic cheers but ignored the emperor.'[59]

Elagabalus (218–222 CE) – And Now for Someone Completely Different

This did not please Elagabalus who made the fatal error of being cross at the Praetorians for this. So they murdered him and his mother, Julia Soaemias, bringing to an end one of the most colourful and strangest rules of any Roman emperor.

To conclude

What are we to make of Elagabalus as emperor? Somebody help me out here because I haven't got a clue!

Elagabalus didn't so much as tear up the book on traditional values as set it on fire and determine to use a stick of celery instead. Clearly, he's the victim of extremely hostile sources who have exaggerated his behaviour beyond anything even vaguely believable, but as we have seen some of these behaviours can be corroborated in part by other evidence. Elagabalus may not have worn a 'tunic made wholly of cloth of gold'[60] and insisted on having jewels embedded into his shoes, but he is depicted wearing very un-Roman attire. He may not have made his god the one true god and insisted everyone worshipped him, but he did promote that god to the exclusion of all others. He may not have promoted actors and eunuchs to official positions, but there were clearly enough of them hanging about the emperor to breed discontent and resentment, along with being something for the next emperor to sort out.

Elagabalus may not have been as full on extravagant as to construct 'a mountain of snow in the pleasure-garden attached to his house, having snow carried there for the purpose'[61] but he was certainly extravagant in his gifts to the people, he spent what is estimated to be 113 million sesterces in handouts to the populace.[62]

How Elagabalus comes across in our sources is not with the sadistic cruelty of a Caligula or a Vitellius, (bar those executions before he reaches Rome there are no sudden removals of senators, or nasty and novel methods of death meted out to perceived enemies), but rather more like a child given the keys to a big box of dressing up clothes. He's playing.

'He got himself up as a confectioner, a perfumer, a cook, a shopkeeper, or a procurer, and he even practised all these occupations in his own house continually.'[63] You'll also remember the *Historia Augusta* passage where Elagabalus 'plays' at being a prostitute too. Remember the pranks too and how childish they are. A teenager giggling at making fun of his elders and betters with a joke cushion, although he missed a prime opportunity to invent the whoopie cushion.

I think we can conclude that Elagabalus was too young to be emperor, coupled with being not terribly bright and possessed of that very teenage trait of not listening to what your mum, and in this case also your grandmother, tell you to do. Never mind, perhaps Alexander Severus will be able to sit quietly and not dance about whilst he's told what to do as emperor.

After the glamour, the grit

Alexander Severus does alright as emperor compared to his cousin. He styles himself almost as the anti-Elagabalus, 'he wore a plain white robe without any gold, just as he is always depicted, and ordinary cloaks and togas'.[64] He removed all of Elagabalus' hangers on from the palace staff, he treated the Praetorians as extra special allowing their Prefects to enter the Senate and memorised every detail he could about the soldiers who served him. 'Even in his bedchamber he had records containing the numbers of the troops and the length of each man's service, and when he was alone he constantly went over their budgets, their numbers, their several ranks, and their pay.'[65] Now you can't imagine Elagabalus doing that, can you? He got up to much more interesting things in his bedchamber.

Elsewhere *The Historia Augusta* tells us Alexander Severus was brilliant at geometry, astrology and divination. He wrote poetry, he painted, he sang and played the lyre, the clarinet and the organ. Is it wrong that I quite hate Alexander Severus and long for the return of his cousin?

Alexander Severus is exceedingly dull to read about in comparison to Elagabalus, his reign is one long list of dutiful doings. I got momentarily excited by this line. 'He did have one kind of amusement in the palace which gave him the greatest pleasure and afforded him relief from the cares of state'[66]; only to be bitterly disappointed by the following paragraph on how Alexander set up an aviary in the palace grounds. Yes, just when you think he can't get any duller they throw in that he's a bird fancier.

Alexander Severus managed to rule in this not terribly exciting fashion for thirteen years and nine days before being brutally murdered by his own troops because they 'despised Alexander as a mother's boy'.[67] We should perhaps enjoy the quiet, dutiful dullness of Alexander Severus' reign because it's going to get mighty interesting for the next hundred years, exhaustingly so. That Alexander Severus ruled for thirteen years is something that will seem like a fantastical achievement shortly, for we are going to enter a period known as the third-century crisis.

Part III

The Third Century – Where Any Man Can be Emperor (briefly), 222 CE–284 CE

The Crisis

Between the death of Alexander Severus in 235 CE and the ascension of the emperor who would eventually sort it all out in 284 CE, there were twenty-one emperors. To put this in context, there were the same number of emperors in this thirty-nine-year period as in the entire first and second centuries combined. Calculators at the ready! Twenty-one emperors in thirty-nine years makes the average length of reign a paltry 2.333333 years. There's really not a lot you can get done in 2.33333 years.

In this era there aren't any dynasties because no emperor stays in the job long enough to found one. In some cases, the emperor barely has the time to have his full titles read out to him before WHAM he's been deposed and there's a new emperor. Historical accounts of this era are thin on the ground, both Cassius Dio and Herodian very inconveniently die before the chaos really gets cracking.[1] We still have the *Historia Augusta*, which comes into its own in this era for unreliability and rather gloriously contradicting itself, often in the same chapter. Similarly, the manic nature of the times means the archaeological evidence is thin on the ground too.

Despite these limitations I have managed to gather a collection of worst emperors from the third century, who are all there (mostly) for one reason and one reason only; a total inability to hold onto power. 2.33333 years is our average length of reign but as we shall see that was an ambitious target for a great many third-century emperors. Bring on the roll call of nonentities who for the briefest of moments were the most powerful man on the planet!

The Brief and not Brilliant Rulers of the Third Century

The third century crisis begins properly with the assassination of Alexander Severus in 235 CE for being both a mummy's boy and exceedingly dull. The soldiers who murdered the emperor did so because, 'they considered the current reign burdensome because of its long duration'.[2] There was no profit to be made by these soldiers in peaceful times and no fun to be had either. If this sentiment sounds vaguely familiar to you it's because we've hit it before. Remember back in 69 CE those Rhine legions who could be talked into civil war because, 'the men now wanted campaigns and set battles, as the prizes here were more attractive than their normal pay'.[3]

There's one big difference between what happened in 69 CE and what happens now in 235 CE; who the legions choose to lead them into insurrection. In 69 CE the very able military commanders, Valens and Caecina, needed a figure to get behind, they settled on Vitellius because he had the right credentials; namely he was malleable, and his father had been consul three times. In 69 CE Verginius Rufus was discredited as a potential emperor because he is from an equestrian family and as Tacitus rather bluntly puts it, 'his father was a nobody'.[4]

In 235 CE this is who the legions supported as emperor. 'They say that as a boy he was a shepherd, but that in his youthful prime he was drafted into the cavalry because of his size and strength. After a short time, favoured by Fortune, he advanced through all the military ranks, rising eventually to the command of armies and the governing of provinces.'[5] His name was Maximinius Thrax and his family is described as 'half barbarian' by Herodian. The gods know what Tacitus would have made of a half barbarian with no consuls in his family, who hadn't followed the proper order of public roles becoming emperor! He wouldn't have liked it, that's for sure. This biography though, of military positions held but not administrative ones, of a family background lacking in distinction is going to become a lot more familiar in this century.

What recommended Thrax to the legionaries was not how many consuls he could count in his family, because there were none, nor his impressive background in holding important positions, because outside of the military he hadn't done. But rather something else; Thrax was impressive. There is no other word for a man who allegedly stood over six feet eight inches tall and who, 'could drag waggons with his hands and move a laden cart by himself'.[6] He was also known for his party trick of punching horses so that they fell to the ground, which had to make him unpopular with the cavalry section of his legion.

Thrax was the physical embodiment of a demigod, he was Hercules reborn in a much more likely guise than Commodus. That Thrax became emperor is a direct consequence of the reigns of both Elagabalus and Alexander Severus. The soldiers wanted an emperor they could personally respect, one who didn't wear makeup and didn't do everything his Mummy told him to, one who could punch out a horse; in Thrax they found it.

He ruled for three years, sort of. The Senate never accepted him as emperor, which is not terribly surprising and threw themselves behind alternative candidates (as we shall shortly see). Thrax, therefore spent most of his rule as emperor fighting other would-be emperors. We've had the year of the four emperors 69 CE, we've had the year of the five emperors 193 CE, we now have in 238 CE the year of the six emperors and the first of our third-century worst emperors.

Chapter 12

Gordian I (238 CE) – He Came, He Did Not Conquer and Then He Went

The horse punching, half barbarian Thrax for some reason did not appeal as an emperor to the Senate, I suspect they might have been a bit frightened of him. I don't blame them. Thrax, raised up by the legions, was quick to reward his soldiers at the expense of everyone else. Those with the biggest pockets found them emptied the quickest. 'It was thus possible every day to see men who yesterday had been rich, today reduced to paupers, so great was the avarice of the tyrant, who pretended to be ensuring a continuous supply of money for the soldiers.'[1]

Meanwhile in Africa the appointed procurator[2] was trying to get himself noticed by this new emperor by emulating Thrax's severe and money grabbing tactics. It was not a popular move, this we can say for sure because he was stabbed to death by, what Herodian describes as aristocratic youths. Demonstrating just how unpopular a policy it was because Roman youths of the upper classes are not generally this energetically political. Not when they could be disguising themselves as peasants, hitting the taverns and getting duffed up.

Although very typical of their age these youths hadn't thought through the consequences of their actions. 'The success of their plan immediately put the youths in a desperate situation; they realized that a single avenue of safety lay open to them: to add to their bold act deeds even bolder.'[3] This even bolder move was to get the governor on side for a full-scale rebellion and he could be emperor instead of Thrax and everyone would forget about them brutally murdering a Roman official.

It probably would have been a kindness to talk the governor in question, a man named Gordian, first about how he felt about being emperor or maybe send him a letter with their arguments laid out as to why they felt he'd be a cracking ruler. Instead, they turned up at Gordian's home. 'Accompanied by the entire band with drawn swords, the youths overpowered the guards on duty at the gates and burst into the house, where they found Gordian resting on a couch. Standing around him, they draped him in a purple cloak and greeted him with the Imperial honors.'[4] Frankly they were exceedingly lucky Gordian didn't keel over from a stroke right then. The astounded governor suggested to these home invaders that he perhaps wasn't the best choice of emperor given his age (did I mention that Gordian was in his 80s?). The youths held their swords to his throat and told him he could either be emperor or he could be dead. Upon which Gordian decided he could perhaps be emperor after all.

Gordian and the sudden entourage he had acquired, which included 'the tallest of the city's youths'[5] presumably to show off that Thrax wasn't the only one with a bit of leg length, headed to Carthage where the new emperor set to work. First up was a letter to the Senate informing them of his eventful day and then, 'he promised the Romans moderation in all things: he would banish informers, provide new trials for the unjustly condemned, and return exiles to their own lands. To the Praetorians he promised more money than anyone had given them before, and he announced gifts for the people'.[6] This is the stuff of Augustus' 'How to be an Emperor' checklist. Credit to Gordian for getting his Imperial head together so quickly.

Also: 'arrangements were made for the early execution of the commandant of the Praetorian Guard in Rome, a man named Vitalianus'.[7] Another sensible policy decision guaranteed to appeal to the Senate! However, what went down less well was when Gordian, flexing his Imperial signing hand, decided to replace the Numidian Governor, Capellanus with someone he hadn't once been involved in a lawsuit with. Because if you can't get revenge for a petty grievance when you're an emperor, when can you?

Capellanus did not step down as governor and exit his province in an orderly fashion as instructed. After all he had been appointed to his position by Thrax, who was the emperor as far as Capellanus was concerned. In no mood to follow any orders from this man calling himself emperor 'the governor marched toward Carthage at the head of a huge army of young, vigorous men equipped with every type of weapon and trained for battle by military experience gained in fighting the barbarians'.[8]

Still, all is not lost, Gordian had those tall youths at his disposal to counter Capellanus' forces and those Carthaginians were certainly up for a scrap, 'aroused by the news and thinking that their hope of victory lay in the size of a mob rather than in the discipline of an army, went forth in a body to oppose Capellianus'.[9] And so, all were ready for a full-on fight to decide who out of Gordian and Thrax was the true emperor, and whether Capellanus still had a job.

This would have been a good moment for Gordian to make a rousing speech to his amateur but enthusiastic soldiers, to stir them up before battle, except Gordian was elsewhere. 'When he considered the size of Maximinus'

Gordian I (238 CE) – He Came, He Did Not Conquer and Then He Went

army and reflected that there were no forces in Africa strong enough to match it, he hanged himself.'[10] Oh. He had reigned for but a month.

So as not to damper the spirit of the Carthaginian mob, whose over confidence had them fully believing they could smash up a highly-skilled, highly-trained and highly-armed army, nobody told them that the emperor they were fighting for had given up before anyone could get into battle formation. It likely wouldn't have made any difference to the result if they had known Gordian was currently hanging from the rafters, it was total annihilation. 'They easily routed the huge Carthaginian mob; without waiting for the Numidians' charge, the Carthaginians threw down their arms and fled. Crowding and trampling one another underfoot, more Carthaginians were killed in the crush than fell by enemy action.'[11]

Gordian makes our list of worst emperors for making a catastrophic decision and then not sticking around to face the hell he'd caused by that decision. At a bare minimum you would've have thought he could have tried to get his mob to stand down, knowing as he did how futile and hopeless their situation was. Instead, he let them run into a sure massacre whilst ensuring his own death was more composed and less bloody. Herodian hedging his bets repeats an 'others say that' tale that has Gordian hanging himself after the battle, which paints him in a marginally better light I suppose, but not enough to save him from worst emperor status.

Gordian's death and the death of his son, the appointed co-emperor known as Gordian II, in that battle with Capellanus' Numidians sent the Senate into a panic. They had thrown their weight behind the Gordians as an alternative to the half barbarian Thrax, now their great hopes were gone and they knew that Thrax, all six feet eight of him, was likely to be quite cross at them and what's more he was on his way to Rome with his army. What to do? Get some more emperors sharpish that can see off Thrax!

They chose a double act of emperors named Balbinus and Pupienus who did manage to clock up a longer reign than Gordian. It took them a whole ninety-nine days to piss off the Praetorian Guard enough to lead to their horrible murders. They were succeeded by the grandson of Gordian, Gordian III who at thirteen was a safe bet not to annoy the Praetorians for a number of years. Instead after six years of rule he went into battle with the Persians, who he presumably annoyed quite a lot because he never returned. Either that or one of his own side fancied a go at being emperor. At 19, Gordian III wasn't so dependent on those advisors who steered him in his early years, which could well have been behind his mysterious disappearance.

If you're wondering what happened to that scary giant Thrax, he was murdered by his own troops in 238 CE alongside his son and many others.

'Their bodies were handed over to those who wished to trample and mutilate them, after which the corpses were exposed to the birds and dogs.'[12] Which was one of the big problems of letting the legions choose emperors, they are not terribly patient and have a tendency to murder them and move onto declaring the next guy emperor at the first sign that they might not get as rich as they hoped they would.

The death tally continues onwards in a shuffling deck of cards of emperors who are raised up by the troops and then brutally cut down by the same troops when they stop being pleasing. It's a wonder that anyone wants to be emperor in this era, although I suppose the short life expectancy means that the paperwork is minimal. In such conditions it's not so hard to find a worst emperor, it's deciding which of the many, many rulers that utterly fail to hold onto power and achieve absolutely nothing of note should make our list.

I may as well have put a list of third century emperors on the table, closed my eyes and randomly picked one. Just to be clear I didn't do that, although I may as well have, and it would have saved on an awful lot of research. Although for our next worst emperor there isn't any research I could've done, his name is Silbannacus and he is the phantom emperor.

Chapter 13

Silbannacus (253 CE) – The Phantom Emperor

Sometime in the mid third century there was a man named Silbannacus, who became emperor. Except nobody apparently noticed this, or if they did, they didn't have a pen to hand to jot it down, because Silbannacus is entirely missing from the written record. The only reason we know he was emperor is because of two coins that were discovered in the twentieth century (see image 34).[1] Until then he had been entirely forgotten about, which is quite something when you think about it. How undistinguished do you have to be to not even get a single line noting the fact that you were the boss? Even his death, presumably shortly after he became emperor, had to be not worth recording; his supporters shrugging it off as just one of those things before going off to find another emperor to rally around.

If a tree falls in a wood with no one to hear it, did it ever fall? Silbannacus poses the question if a man is emperor but nobody remembers it, was he ever emperor?

Chapter 14

Quintillus (270 CE) – Easy Come, Easy Go

Marcus Aurelius Quintillus became emperor in 270 CE and died that same year. His reign was so brief and so insignificant that nobody can quite decide how long it went on for. Some sources say only seventeen days, which makes it more like work experience than an actual job. Others are more favourable to Quintillus' ability to hold onto power and give him a generous seventy-seven days. Most modern historians sum up his reign as 'a few months', thus hedging their bets.

Unlike most of the emperors in this era Quintillus isn't some army commander randomly raised up by his troops, he is the brother of the previous emperor Claudius Gothicus. Claudius Gothicus, true, had come to power in exactly that manner, but had managed to rule relatively successfully for two whole years. What's more Gothicus hadn't been overthrown and decapitated by his own troops, nor had he been hacked to death by the Praetorian Guard. Rather he had died of wholly natural causes, succumbing to an outbreak of plague, making him somewhat unique for this era.

This peaceful, though likely still horrible death for him, raises Gothicus up to be noteworthy. The *Historia Augusta* even finds some very nice things to say about him, 'the valour of Trajan, the righteousness of Antonius, the self-restraint of Augustus, and the good qualities of all the great emperors, all these were his to such a degree'.[1] But enough of Gothicus and his goodness at being emperor, let's bring on his brother!

When his brother died, Quintillus happened to be hanging out in Northern Italy with a load of soldiers. On receiving the news of Claudius Gothicus' death those soldiers promptly proclaimed Quintillus emperor. Although *The Historia Augusta* says that this had nothing whatsoever to do with Quintillus being the brother of the deceased emperor, claiming the role, 'was offered him by the judgement of all, not as an inherited possession, but because his virtues deserved it; for all would have made him emperor, even if he had not been the brother of the Claudius their prince'.[2] Which I guess in an era where pretty much anyone can have a go at being emperor is believable.

Coins was issued in Rome but also minted in Italy, Croatia and Turkey showing a geographical spread of support for Quintillus that was not just limited to the troops he happened to be commanding in Italy.[3] Quintillus, with two sons offered the tantalising prospect of a stable and stabilising dynasty for once. Which possibly motivated the Senate into proclaiming him emperor as well. One of Quintillus' first, and indeed few acts as emperor, was to deify his brother. He was now related to the gods, a tactic used very successfully you'll remember by Augustus and one over utilised by Domitian who made his entire family into gods and set up a nice temple to the Flavians where he, sorry, they could be worshipped.

So here we are with Quintillus, a man whom *The Historia Augusta* at least, would have us believe was brim full of *virtus*, was the brother of an emperor who was (again according to *The Historia Augusta*) 'marvellous and admirable',[4] who had the support of both the Senate and troops, and who had ample experience in warfare (a necessity in this era). What a set up!

However, immediately it became clear that there was a rival claimant, Lucius Domitius Aurelian. Aurelian was a pal of Claudius Gothicus, not least for plotting to remove Gothicus' predecessor as emperor, Galleinus. A grateful Gothicus had made him master of the horse (the coolest sounding of all Roman positions), sent him off to sort out barbarian issues in the provinces and, Aurelian claimed, asked him to be the next emperor.

What was Quintillus' response to this threat to his throne? Apparently, he tried for a few days to contest Aurelian's claim to be emperor and then he died. How he died matters a great deal in how we view Quintillus' short reign. The *Historia Augusta* says he was killed by his own troops 'as Galba had been and Pertinax also, because he had shown himself stern and unbending toward the soldiers and promised to be a prince in very truth'.[5] However, this noble end to the too noble for this earth, Quintillus is disputed by another source, 'when it was known that Aurelian was emperor, he was abandoned by all his army; and when he had made a speech attacking Aurelian and the soldiers refused to listen, he severed his veins and died on the twentieth day of his rule.'[6] That source being *The Historia Augusta* in the following chapter to the one in which they say Quintillus was murdered.

Most accounts have Quintillus committing suicide and I'm going with that one because I don't trust *The Historia Augusta* in the slightest on either Quintillus or his brother. They are suspiciously glowing in their praise of the pair, witness this toe-curling sentiment on Gothicus: 'for what was there in him that was not admirable? that was not pre-eminent? that was not superior to the triumphant generals of remote antiquity'?[7] *Raises hand* Please sir, I can think of lots of things.

That Quintillus gives up quite so easily is telling. Aurelian is in the Danube region; it's going to take some weeks for him to be a literal physical threat to

Quintillus. Quintillus is in Northern Italy, he has the chance to get to Rome and cement his rule whilst Aurelian's soldiers are packing their rucksacks and strapping their best marching sandals on.

As we've seen, Quintillus has absolutely everything going for him, so why give up only days into his reign? I think the answer is likely simply that he wasn't made of emperor material. He certainly wasn't any good at inspiring speeches since his troops desert him very quickly after Aurelian launches his claim. He seemingly makes no attempt to muster together a force to fight for his throne, it's almost as if he doesn't really want it, not enough to make a stand against the likes of Aurelian. For caving in so rapidly and for using none of the advantages he had at his disposal and for not wanting to be emperor, Quintillus gets worst emperor status.

Restorer of the World

In comparison to his predecessor, Quintillus, Aurelian does marvellously well as emperor, he reconquers Gaul and Palmyra who had taken the opportunity of Rome's chaotic state to break away from the empire, he defeats the Goths, the Vandals and the Alamanni. He reunifies what was a very broken empire and for his efforts he's given the title 'Restorer of the World'.

Obviously, he still gets assassinated, because every emperor does in this era, but it's not for anything he does wrong, rather it was for something that his messenger, Eros, had done wrong. What that something was we have no idea, but it was bad enough that Eros felt it necessary to have Aurelian killed before he could find out about whatever that something was. I'm assuming there was a high embarrassment factor here for Eros or else he was particularly sensitive about being yelled at by the boss.

With 'The Restorer of the World' gone there was once more a gaggle of men with armies waiting to make themselves emperor. But this time not for long, because along came another man, another 'Restorer of the World' by the name of Diocletian and he would prove more successful at not getting murdered than any Roman emperor ever.

Part IV

Sorting It All Out – The Tetrarchy and Beyond, 284 CE–455 CE

The third century crisis had been battering for Rome. The constant instability of civil war had led to all manner of problems for the empire; financial woes caused by the disruption of crucial trade routes that led to a devaluation of the currency, a power vacuum caused by the constant changing of leaders that had allowed the province of Gaul and city of Palmyra to break free from the empire and declare themselves independent,[1] and famines/plagues aplenty. It had also created new enemies nipping on Rome's borders: those troublesome Persians, those murderous Goths, the really quite angry Vandals. That you've likely heard of all three of these, as opposed to some of Rome's enemies in previous centuries such as the Chatti and the Helvetii, demonstrate how much of a bigger threat these enemies were compared to the past.[2]

The Augustan way of governing had proved no match for the events of the third century. We've seen how the men who became emperor in this era were radically different to what had come before, they were careerist soldiers from humble backgrounds without the experience of having served in public positions. The man who steps into Rome's history now is another of these men, his name was Diocletian, and he was from a humble background but had risen through the military ranks. In 286 CE he was proclaimed emperor by his troops when the previous emperor mysteriously died.[3]

You're probably all expecting him to now get murdered by his troops or hacked to pieces by the Praetorian Guard or commit suicide when a rival turns up with a bigger army. That's not what happens. Instead, Diocletian is the guy who sweeps up the mess of the third century and in the process changes what it is be emperor.

From Principate to Dominate

What Augustus created is referred to as the Principate; a model where the Princeps, or first citizen, worked with the 600 men that made up the Senate to rule the empire. It was a model that had not worked for decades now. Change was needed.

The third century had brought a wave of problems to the empire which maybe would have been solvable by the old system had there not been the constant stream of usurpers. The result was that any emperor in this era spent most of his time playing whack a mole, smacking down hard on the heads of the would-be emperors, with one eye constantly twitching as yet another one popped up in his peripheral vision. It didn't leave a lot of time for anything else, like sorting out all those other problems the empire was facing. Those other problems not getting sorted lead to discontent, which lead to more moles popping up promising better things until there was nothing left of the lawn. It's all endless mole holes as far as you can be seen, policed by a wide-eyed man clutching a club who looks like he hasn't slept in a decade. He likely hasn't.

Diocletian recognised the reality of this situation; it was too much for one emperor to manage. He instituted a new system called the tetrarchy that divided power between two senior emperors, who had the title of Augustus and two junior emperors called Caesars. Dishing out the responsibilities between four men rather than one meant that whilst one Caesar was busy repelling barbarian incursions into Roman territory, the other Caesar could be fighting off a would-be emperor and an Augustus could be sorting out the grain supply. Leaving one Augustus to handle the 'any other business' on the agenda.

The 'any other business' was to separate out military from civil posts, preventing any future provincial governor having the brainwave of using the legions in his province to make him emperor. An original idea way back in the first century CE, but one that had become boringly predictable in the third century. Splitting these functions meant that the man in command of the troops was not the same man who was paying the wages of those soldiers and the man who was paying the soldiers wasn't in command of them.

Now freed of the temptation to make himself emperor, the civil provincial governor had the time to do some actual governing of his province and all that paperwork that had built up over the preceding fifty years. His military counterpart, likewise, freed of this temptation, could concentrate his efforts on fighting the enemies of the empire, rather than battling Rome itself.

But Diocletian's admin frenzy went further than this, he redrew the map of the empire, splitting provinces into smaller chunks to make them easier to administrate for his new civilian posts. There was also a widespread effort to codify the many laws that had built up over the centuries into volumes of text that were to be made available across the empire. It's difficult for us to understand how hugely important a project this was. In an empire as huge as Rome's. the law was whatever documents could be found to support it, here now were all the laws available for all to access. It had to be reassuring after so many decades of seeming lawlessness.

Alongside reforming the empire's bureaucracy, Diocletian tackled the taxation system, setting in place a fixed cycle for the census that had previously been somewhat erratically and randomly held. This ensured a stable and predictable income for the tetrarchy's use. Diocletian is very much the man you'd want organising your office Christmas do. Not only would he source a great venue, but he'd also have factored the waiter's tip into the kitty and arranged rides home with the local cab company. Likely he'd also be the main source of Alka Seltzer the morning after too.

Under Diocletian and his supporting act of emperors, the city of Rome was no longer the centre of power. This was something that had been bubbling away for some time, you'll remember that the emperor Domitian in the first century greatly favoured his Alban palace, spending an increasing amount of time there. In the third century there were emperors who never made an appearance in Rome, because generally they were horribly murdered before they could make the journey. Diocletian was emperor for twenty-one years, yet he only made it to Rome twice in those years; he preferred to hang out in Nicomedia, in modern day Turkey.

Nicomedia as a residence for an emperor made much more sense than Rome. The trade routes from the east to the west ran through this area, and it was also neatly positioned should Diocletian happen to need to top up his troops from the large number of legionaries stationed nearby. Not that Diocletian spent all his time in Nicomedia, like his three co-emperors he travelled from one city to another, sorting out bubbling issues and then moving on to the next city – not unlike that dog in The Littlest Hobo. Maybe tomorrow Diocletian might just settle down or maybe tomorrow he'll just keep moving on to sort out the next problem on his massive to do list.

The result of this moving on was that the Senate was of far less importance, they simply didn't have the inner access to the emperor's ear that they used to. Unlike Domitian, whose Alban palace was only a short distance from Rome and thus easy for the Senate to travel with him, the third century emperors were frequently hundreds of miles away sorting stuff out. What use would they have been anyway to an emperor whose main tasks involved such a lot of fighting? The ladder of public offices involved sparse military service, certainly of insufficient length or value to offer up any useful insights on how the emperor might fight off the Persians, the Goths and three other men saying they were emperor.

The Senate was no longer the breeding ground for emperors, it hadn't been for decades, the emperors that rose now came directly from the army with the skillset that provided them with. Diocletian's appointment of other emperors to serve alongside him hammered home the insignificance of the Senate, it was also a message to the army to stop creating new emperors of their own. Emperors made emperors. Nobody else. Got that? I'll underline it for you if you like.

Diocletian was so successful in cleaning up the mess that was the third century that in 303 CE he does something no other emperor had ever done before: he retires. So satisfied with his life's work and the strength of the system he introduced, Diocletian heads back to his private estates in Nicomedia to grow cabbages. Which sounds like a euphemism for something else, but no, he genuinely grows cabbages. Or at least he did until the tetrarchy system he created spectacularly imploded and he was begged to leave his cabbages behind and sort it all out.

Diocletian wasn't keen returning, 'If you could see at Salonae the cabbages raised by our hands, you surely would never judge that a temptation'.[4] From which we may deduce that Diocletian's cabbages were worthy of a Guinness World Record. The tetrarchy which seems such a logical, practical solution to the problems of the third century had crashed and burned, principally due to the nature of man, one born of the nursery and carried ever forward with him: but I don't want to share!

When Diocletian stepped down to go off into the sunset and grow cabbages, his successors eyed each other up nervously and jealously. As did the two men who thought they were going to be named as Caesars in Diocletian's retirement speech, Constantine and Maxentius, but who, despite being the sons of tetrarchy emperors, were overlooked. When Constantine's father, Constantius Chlorus died in 306 CE, his son decided he'd give himself the job instead. Which naturally gave the similarly overlooked Maxentius ideas too. You can see where this is headed.

The seemingly perfect system of the tetrarchy disintegrates as emperor brothers turn into emperor rivals. Just as the era of the emperor and the Senate sharing power, or at least pretending to, was at an end, so was the seemingly perfect system of a tetrarchy of appointed, skilled emperors. Left standing in the flattened dustbowl of Diocletian's dream was Constantine the Great. He kept power well and truly in the family, founding his own dynasty who ruled up to 363 CE. They were followed by other family dynasties; the Valenteniac and the Theodosian.

Power now lay indisputably in the hands of the emperor and was handed over by him to his own blood. Which means our criteria for what makes a best or worst emperor must also change, grandiose, egotistical behaviour is now what is expected of an emperor rather than being something to castigate him for. Also employing a load of eunuchs to do the filing is no longer considered decadently eastern and un-Roman but rather more ordinary – although those emperors who let their eunuchs become too powerful are in for a battering in our sources. Oh, and venerating the gods and showing them proper care and attention is no longer one of the duties of an emperor because from the rule of Constantine the Great (306–337 CE) onwards Rome is now a Christian empire.[5]

The emperors of the 4th century CE may be of a different religious bent to those we have looked at previously, but they were no less cruel, greedy, lustful or ineffectual. Which is handy for us, let us go find some more worst emperors!

Chapter 15

Valentinian II (375–392 CE) – The Boy Emperor

Remember Augustus training up his young male relatives in a variety of public and military positions, so they had the exact skill set to be emperor? Remember the Five Good Emperors when the best men in all the empire were chosen and adopted by their predecessor? Remember the tetrarchy whereby the emperors chose their Caesars based on talent and ability? Remember even the third-century crisis where men became emperor because they were skilled in military matters and charismatic enough to persuade an army to follow them? Those days are well and truly gone. Valentinian II became emperor aged four.

I think it's fair to say that he hadn't held any public nor military positions, nor was he the most talented man to be found in all the empire. Although I may be doing young Valentinian a disfavour, perhaps he was a child prodigy along the lines of Mozart but composing sensible laws rather than arias in the nursery. Prodigious political talent certainly ran in the family, Valentinian II's older half-brother Gratian had become emperor aged eight, so a bit of a late developer.

What qualified both boys to be emperor, sadly, was not some innate precocious talent in statecraft, rather they were both the sons of an emperor, Valentinian I. Which is disappointing in the extreme because I have such an entertaining picture in my head of baby Valentinian II breaking off from sucking on his rusk to re-write the empire's entire foreign policy and compose a couple of peace treaties before nap time.

Valentinian I had done his best to expose Gratian to as much of the emperor life as possible. The boy was sent by Daddy Emperor to fight the Quadi, one of the fearsome German tribes. Later we find him as a teenager campaigning with his father against another one of Rome's many enemies in this era and yet another fearsome German tribe, the Alamanni. Gratian performed well enough in the ensuing battle to receive from his father the titles of Germanicus Maximus and Alamanicus Maximus, which added a kick-ass end to any time he was introduced at a formal event.

This is quite a fighty period, Valentinian I had been busy battling the Alamanni, the Quadi and the Sarmatians. Whilst his younger brother and co-emperor in the East, Valens had been seeing off the Persians, the Saracens, the Goths and Isaurians. Remember those days when Caligula's staff had to pretend that some of his own German bodyguard were enemy tribesman in order for him to have someone to fight? Yeah, those days are long gone. There was no need for an emperor to seek out an enemy to fight, they were leaping out of cupboards at him wherever he went. Valentinian I was able to expose young Gratian to the kind of hard front-line experiences that were lacking in some of the earlier emperors we've covered.

In November 375 CE the Quadi had had enough of fighting and decided they'd much rather be at peace with the Romans. They were granted an audience with Valentinian I, where rather than throw themselves on the floor before the emperor and humbly beg him for peace, which I suspect was the sort of thing Valentinian I was expecting, they instead added, 'as a sufficient justification for what had happened that the rage of the country folk had been aroused by the wrongful and untimely attempt to build a fort'.[1] Essentially saying to the emperor that it was all his fault that they'd run at him and his troops with sharp weapons repeatedly during the previous months.

It is fair to say that Valentinian was not pleased by this speech. He was, in fact, quite cross about it. But as the historian, Ammianus Marcellinus tells us, Valentinian I was in general a cross man, '[who was] never content with a slight punishment and often ordered a proliferation of bloody trials'.[2] So really the Quadi should have known better. Valentinian I true to his personality became very cross. Ammianus Marcellinus describes it as a. 'paroxysm of anger', that the emperor was, 'boiling with fury' and 'in noisy and abusive language he accused the whole nation of ingratitude and the forgetfulness of past favours'.[3]

I think we can all picture the scene; the Quadi delegation standing with flushing cheeks as the emperor yelled in their faces exactly how he felt about their peace terms before going on to explain how he felt about their appearance, their manner and the past careers of their mothers (probably). The spittle was likely flying from his mouth with all the force of a decent power shower. Before anyone could get towelled off though, the emperor, 'was struck as if by lightening'. He hadn't been struck by lightning. Unlike Emperor Carus who was struck by lightning in 283 CE and killed.[4] From what Ammianus Marcellinus says next it sounds like Valentinian I had suffered a stroke, one that turned out to be fatal.

Valentinian's son, co-emperor and intended heir, Gratian was at that moment preparing for another one of his father's study trips on how to kill your enemies in the city of Trier. Which was sufficiently far away for the officials currently standing over the corpse of Valentinian I to have a collective panic. 'Anxious fears were felt about the attitude of the Gallic troops who were not always loyal to the lawful prince and regarded themselves as arbiters in the choice of emperor.'[5] Fearing a coup, 'all felt that they were in the same boat and likely to share in any danger that arose'.[6] After what we're told is a careful deliberation they decided on the best course of action; to proclaim 4-year-old Valentinian II emperor.

You do have to wonder how careful these deliberations were given that the solution they came up with to face down the threat of a highly trained and heavily armed army making their own choice of emperor, was to pre-empt them by giving the job to a pre-schooler. It is true that 4-year-old boys can be very determined and fierce, particularly when you don't cut the crusts off their sandwiches, but they are also somewhat erratic in their decision making and tend to fall over a lot while running. Those careful deliberations likely involved a map and a ruler. as the officials worked out that although Gratian was currently 600 miles away, Valentinian II was only 100 miles away and that was quicker to get from. Valentinian II arrived six days later to accept his throne, and jam sandwiches with the crust cut off.

What did Gratian make of this? Ammianus Marcellinus tells us that although it was thought he would take it amiss, he apparently didn't mind because Gratian was a nice guy who, 'treated his kinsman with great affection and supervised his upbringing'.[7] Or rather Gratian realised at only 16 years old he was in no position (yet) to take on those officials who could now rule through his younger half-brother. Which puts the supervision and affection shown towards Valentinian in a different light; Gratian needed to stay close to his brother to ensure his own survival.

The boy on the throne

So far, this chapter has been heavy on Gratian details, and I could continue on this theme for young Gratian is an exceedingly busy fellow; he goes off to fight the Alamanni and the Goths, he intercedes in disputes within the Christian church, a big fan of rhetoric and grammar, Gratian sends forth teachers into the empire to force the rest of the population to become big fans of it too. But this chapter isn't about Gratian, it's about Valentinian II. More's the pity because it's really hard work finding anything to say about him.

Valentinian II is barely featured in the historical record, probably because our historians of this era are more concerned by invading Goths and schisms in the church rather than the smaller more personal conquests of childhood. Nobody bothers to record anything that Valentinian II is up to. Which is a shame because I would have welcomed a break from elder church leaders debating stuff and yet more battles with whatever tribe is now harassing the empire narrative for an update on Valentinian II's triumphant completion of his Maths homework.

Whilst Valentinian II was busy with his homework, 'Probus, a man of consular dignity, had the chief administration of affairs',[8] and his mother, Justina ran things. For Justina this involved developing an intense hatred for Ambrose the Bishop of Nicene, who she disliked so much she had him banished. Although it's tempting to think that Ambrose had one of those irritating goatee beards or a really boring voice, what was behind his exile was the far more mundane topic of religious interpretation. Justina proscribed to a different interpretation of Christianity and wished to promote this interpretation across the empire, a move Ambrose did not approve of, hence his exile from court. But yet again we are talking about the actions of people other than Valentinian II, who is not creating schisms within the Christian church and getting heavy with bishops. But fear not because something exciting, or terrifying depending on your viewpoint, is going to happen to Valentinian II; he faces a rival claimant for his throne.

It's not an entirely unexpected set of events, what with Valentinian II being a child and his co-emperors busy fighting the multiple threats facing the empire, he was always a bit of a sitting duck for any ambitious man to take a shot at. The ambitious man who did was the wonderfully named Magnus Maximus, which translates roughly as the Greatest Great. A man with such a moniker could hardly fail and the Greatest Great decided to do something befitting to his name by first orchestrating the murder of Emperor Gratian and then putting together an army and marching it into Italy to take on the other emperor, Valentinian II.

Maximus claimed he was doing so to prevent Justina's religious innovations from destroying the church. Which nobody believed at the time either. Although, the Greatest Great's move had the desired effect. 'From Fear of him Justina ceased persecuting Ambrose'.[9]

Despite the whole murdering an emperor and marching an army towards the remaining western emperor, the Greatest Great was keen not to appear like one of those third-century emperors who used their army to force people to make them emperor, despite doing exactly that. 'He was watching and intriguing for the Imperial rule in such a way that it might appear as if he had acquired the Roman government by law, and not by force. Valentinian was compelled by the exigencies of the times to recognize the symbols of his rule.'[10]

Valentinian didn't stick around for the getting to know your new co-emperor meeting, but soon after, in fear of suffering, fled with his mother

Justina, and Probus, the Praetorian Prefect in Italy, to Thessalonica'.[10] Why Thessalonica? Having googled images of the Greek city I can see plenty of reasons, it all looks very pleasant, but for Valentinian II, Thessalonica had an added attraction, it was where Theodosius, the successor to the Eastern half of the empire was.[11] Theodosius later earns himself the moniker The Great, which tells you that he was exactly the sort of person you should flee to when threatened by a desperately trying to appear non-threating political rival.

Theodosius, proving that he was exactly the right man to flee to in a crisis, received Valentinian II and his Mum, and promptly went off to sort out their Maximus problem for them. Theodosius' determination and clear intent (and the words 'the great' hovering above his head at all times) panicked the soldiers of Maximus and they killed their leader. Of all the battles Theodosius faced in his fighting life, this one had to be the easiest. Which had to make Valentinian feel even smaller than he was (he was fifteen at this time).

Still, he had learnt at the feet of a master a good lesson of how to be a good emperor – be so frightening and intimidating that an enormous army would rather kill their leader and back down than face you. A big party/triumph was called for and Theodosius very kindly let Valentinian join in, even though he'd done sod all and arguably it was his fault for not being scary.

With Maximus dead, Theodosius restored Valentinian II to his throne and then suggested he go do some emperor work of his own in his provinces, though not entirely on his own. 'His mother accompanied him, to supply, as much as was possible in a woman, the prudence which his youth required'.[12] Of course she did. But the time was coming when Valentinian II would have to step out from behind his mother's skirts and become fully emperor. That time came in 388 CE when Justina died. Which was helpful for the busy Theodosius, 'he restored order in the churches of Italy, for the Empress Justina was dead'.[13]

The man on the throne

This was it, the crunch time for Valentinian II to finally show what kind of emperor he was. The court settled in Vienna, Valentinian II was now his own boss, no more being told what to do by anyone. Except here now enters our story, a man named Arbogast. A Frank by birth, he had risen high in Theodosius' court, now he was in Vienna and hoping to make a similar mark. He had plenty to recommend himself for a position at court and to the soldiers who surrounded Valentinian almost too much, because quietly Arbogast, 'assumed the command without the emperor's permission. Being thought proper for the station by all the soldiers under him, both for his valour and experience in military affairs, and for his disregard of riches, he attained great influence'.[14] Looking, in other words, like a much better candidate for emperor than a spotty teenage boy.

But just like Maximus before him, Arbogast was not about to take on Theodosius. Besides he didn't need to, he had all the power he needed to rule. 'He thus became so elevated, that he would speak without reserve to the emperor and would blame any measure which he thought improper.'[15] Arbogast had instigated a first for Rome, a bloodless coup.

What did Valentinian II do about this official vastly overstepping the mark? 'He opposed him on several occasions, and would have done him injury had he known how to effect it.'[16] Didn't know how to effect injury on Arbogast! Is Valentinian II really so ignorant of the powers of emperor that he doesn't know of that standard Imperial task of offing people who threaten/annoy you?

Clearly not, since this is how he deals with Arbogast. 'When Arbogast was approaching him as he sat on the Imperial throne, [he] looked sternly upon him, and presented him with a writing, by which he dismissed him from his command.'[16] He doesn't even dare tell him! He has to write it down! It would be laughable if it wasn't so pathetic. Arbogast's reaction to this pathetic display of Imperial power was exactly what you'd expect, he told the emperor: 'You neither gave me the command, nor can deprive me of it', and having said this, tore the writing to pieces, threw it down, and retired.[17]

Having failed at dismissing Arbogast by note, Valentinian II turns to plan B, (which no, it isn't sending the Imperial bodyguard to Arbogast's house and slitting his throat), rather he writes a series of letters to Theodosius asking him to come and sort out Arbogast for him like he sorted out Maximus. Which somehow is even more pathetic than the note incident.

Theodosius was far too busy being great in the East to write back, but a short while later he received a quite different letter from Vienna. 'While Theodosius was thus occupied in the wise and peaceful government of his subjects in the East, and in the service of God, intelligence was brought that Valentinian had been strangled.'[19] Valentinian was but 21 years old.

I know what you're thinking, you're thinking that fellow Arbogast might have been involved. Or maybe not. 'Others assert, however, that Valentinian committed the fatal deed with his own hands, he did not deem it worthwhile to live; for although an emperor, he was not allowed to do what he wished.'[20] Which sounds like a tall story devised to disguise the heinous murder of an emperor, however knowing what we know about Valentinian II it does sort of fit. A weak leader faced with a stronger rival, one he couldn't run away from this time, one that Theodosius couldn't or wouldn't help him with, without his mother around to advise him and with Arbogast much more popular with the army than him, I can see how Valentinian, isolated in Vienna might see no other way out. Alternatively, I can quite see Arbogast strangling him with his own bare hands in front of Valentinian's own soldiers who decline to intervene.

The Church historian Sozomen has this to say about Valentinian II, 'it is said that the boy was noble in person, and excellent in royal manners; and that, had he lived to the age of manhood, he would have shown himself worthy of holding the reins of empire, and would have surpassed his father in magnanimity and justice.'[21] To which I say, nah.

Valentinian II was 21 years old at his death, a young man not a child. You'll remember that Octavius fellow who raised an army and fought the killers of Julius Caesar at 19 and the Imperial histories brim with similar tales of impressive deeds at ridiculously young ages. Whatever age Valentinian II had lived to, whether it was 21 or 81 you can't help but feel it would have been underwhelming. He well deserves his place in our list of worst emperors for being so weak a ruler who relied on others to rescue him rather than fight his enemies himself.

Chapter 16

Petronius Maximus (455 CE) – Evil Genius

Petronius Maximus was emperor for two months in the year 455 CE, which is as disappointing for me as it likely was for him, because his path to becoming emperor is a really very good story. I'd go as far as to say it's by far the best becoming emperor tale we've had so far, but I'll let you be the judge of that. Enter the master of all plotters!

'Were the fate of all princes before and after him left out of the account, this Maximus of yours would alone provide the maximum of warning',[1] so says Sidonius Apollinaris writing to his friend, Senanus. From this letter we can put together Petronius Maximus' pre-emperor career. 'He had scaled with intrepidity the prefectorian, the patrician, the consular citadels; with an unsated appetite for office, he took for a second term posts which he had already held.'[2]

Sidonius goes on to describe him as a great figure, 'with his conspicuous way of life, his banquets, his lavish expense, his retinues, his literary pursuits, his official rank, his estates, his extensive patronage.'[3] I'm assuming the conspicuousness of his life involved a tendency to wander about the streets with his retinue talking loudly about the fabulous soiree he held last night which all the best people attended and where he performed his latest poem to the delight of all.

All in all, Petronius Maximus was living the very good life, he'd held a number of jobs which he'd evidently been very good at, he had pots of money, he had pots of admirers and lovely estates he could escape the pressures of his public life to and indulge himself in his hobby, writing.[4]

However, it appears that this ancient version of the Dolce Vita was not enough for Petronius Maximus, he wanted more. Perhaps it was down to that effortless success in every other sphere of his life that convinced Petronius Maximus that he should be emperor or perhaps as Sidonius believes, he simply got too big for his boots; 'his head swam beneath the diadem at sight of that enormous power'.[5]

Revenge is a dish best served by somebody else on your behalf

John of Antioch has an entirely different tale of why Petronius Maximus set himself on the path of becoming emperor, one that is less a morality tale of how conceit and hubris can lead to your own destruction and more the plot of any decent western, *The Outlaw Josey Wales* for preference. Yes, our theme is revenge, vengeance and something around getting justice in an unorthodox way.

In John's tale, Emperor Valentinian III had fallen in love with Petronius Maximus' wife and in a somewhat bewildering set up that involves Valentinian showing Maximus' wife her husband's ring (which he had won in a dice game earlier), the emperor had his way with Maximus' missus. Possibly the involvement of the ring leads her to believe her husband is dead or that her husband has ordered her to sleep with the emperor. I have no idea, insert your own preferred version of the tale here.

The important part of the story is not the ring, although I'd still jolly well like an explanation about that, but rather Petronius Maximus' reaction; he was not best pleased. 'After the lovemaking the wife went to meet her husband as he came, wailing and reproaching him as her betrayer. When he learned the whole story, he nursed his anger at the emperor.'[6]

Let us picture Petronius Maximus at that moment, sitting in the dark his features lit only by the faint glow of a nearby oil lamp, hands cupped around his wine goblet, his eyes narrowing as he plots his revenge against the emperor who has dishonoured his wife. It's a far better story than Sidonius' 'he got a bit greedy and big headed', is it not?

Petronius Maximus, a man who had excelled at everything he had ever turned his hand to, proved similarly successful at enacting his revenge on Valentinian III. If you're expecting the kind of stabby, bloody, extremely messy removal of an emperor we've encountered earlier with the likes of Caligula, Domitian, Geta and Elagabalus for once upgrade your expectations, because it's far better than that.

Petronius Maximus was a clever man, and he went about his revenge in a very clever way with the patience and foresight of the super villain who successfully secures planning permission off the council for his underground lair without a single objection from the neighbours. He recognised that to get close to the emperor, close enough to enact his revenge, he needed to get rid of the emperors closest and most able man, Flavius Aetius.

Aetius was another impressive man who was supremely good at what he did; in his case what he did was successfully repel no less an enemy than Attila the Hun, as well as numerous other barbarian types who were threatening the empire. This is well and truly an era where you need good generals[7] and Aetius was the best there was. He was so good that Imperial favour was lavished all over him and his son was betrothed to the emperor's daughter. Aetius was also the sort of clever man who could sniff out a threat to the emperor and destroy it like an energetic cockapoo with his favourite ball. He had to go, but obviously in a way that did not thwart Petronius Maximus' ultimate goal of avenging his wife.

The assassination of Flavius Aetius, the most successful Roman general of his era, is unique. It's unique because it's not carried out by Petronius Maximus nor any henchman paid by Petronius Maximus; Flavius Aetius was killed by Emperor Valentinian III himself.

It occurred on the 21 September 454 CE during what Aetius had assumed was a standard planning meeting and it was, until the any other business section when the emperor suddenly jumped up and declared that he, 'could no longer bear being the victim of so many drunken depravities'.[8] Given that immediately prior to this Aetius had been explaining the projected tax revenues, I think we can all agree Aetius was fully entitled to be as stunned as a fish who only moments before was swimming happily along with his fishy friends and now suddenly finds itself on a river bank with three men armed with mallets standing over him. However, Aetius had faced off Attila the Hun, so he's made of sterner stuff than you or I, instead his reaction was to marvel 'at this unexpected outburst'.

Unfortunately, Aetius didn't have much time to marvel because, 'Valentinian drew his sword from his scabbard, and together with Heraclius, who was carrying a cleaver under his cloak...for he was head chamberlain, fell upon him. They both rained down blows on his head and killed him, a man who had performed so many brave actions against enemies both internal and external'.[9]

Jeepers, is all I can say, and much like Flavius Aetius briefly thought before being stabbed to death by his boss, what the hell is going on? What drunken depravities? And no doubt something around the tax revenues not being that bad.

What the hell was going on? Because emperors stabbing to death their employee during a meeting is very out of the ordinary. Not least because getting rid of underperforming, or in the case of Flavius Aetius, over performing staff is something emperors usually outsource to the palace guard. If only to save ruining his Imperial Majesty's regal outfit with those hard-to-get-out blood stains.

Behind this extraordinary event there was our pal Petronius Maximus. He was in league with Heraclius, the eunuch who'd handily been standing by with that cleaver under his cloak to help the emperor in his murdering. According to the historian John of Antioch, '[they] were both hostile to Aetius on the same pretext; both men attempting to substitute their own power for Aetius'.[10] There's no mention here of Petronius Maximus' dishonoured wife as the motivation, but then Heraclius the eunuch likely couldn't care less about Maximus' missus so needed a better reason for entering into this conspiracy – a bigger office with a nicer desk is reason enough for him.

With the great Flavius Aetius now dead, Petronius Maximus went to the emperor and offered his services to fill that vacuum. Valentinian III said no. Petronius Maximus was stunned, not as stunned as Aetius no doubt had been when he saw the emperor running at him with a sword, but still it was a surprise and not a nice one. Particularly given Maximus had spent a lot of time talking the emperor into murder when he could have been enjoying nice banquets and writing poetry.

Behind this refusal was Maximus' fellow conspirator Heraclius, who had suggested to the emperor that after removing one powerful threat to his rule it was silly to hand over so much power, so soon, to another. Valentinian, wound up by weeks of being told how dangerous Aetius was to him, easily agreed with the eunuch.

Revenge Part II

Petronius Maximus did not take this blow well. It made him rather cross. So cross that he immediately entered into another conspiracy; this time the plan was to murder the emperor. His co-conspirators were two men named Optelas and Thraustelas who as pals to Aetius, were easily persuaded that the emperor's brutal killing of their friend determined retribution. 'They would reap the greatest rewards, he said, if with justice they exacted revenge when the opportunity arouse.'[11] Note again, as with Aetius' death, that Petronius Maximus is playing no part in the gruesome bit of the plot, he's staying well away from any blood splatter to his, no doubt expensive, sandals.

A few days later the emperor set off on an outing to the Field of Ares accompanied by Optelas and Thraustelas. When he dismounted from his horse and was walking off to practice archery, Optelas and his followers made for him and, drawing the swords at their sides, attacked him. Optelas struck Valentinian across the side of his head and, when he turned to see who struck him, felled him with a second blow to the face.'[12]

Ouch. After Valentinian was well and truly dead, 'a swarm of bees appeared and drew up the blood flowing from his body into the earth. They sucked up all of it'.[13] Which I'm mentioning for no other reason than it's a bit weird and an omen for what follows. Possibly.

So that's the empire's greatest general and the emperor out of the way and standing ready in the wings is the man who has engineered the entire situation, Petronius Maximus. God he's good, isn't he? He's removed the two most powerful people in the empire without getting his hands bloody at all. This is genius level of plotting beyond anything we've seen so far – generally because what we've seen so far are some very poorly thought-out assassinations. He's more than avenged his wife, if that ever was his motive and frankly, I'm doubting it given it's only John of Antioch from our sources who mentions it and because of one of the first actions of this new emperor – which we shall come to shortly.

Petronius Maximus wasn't a total shoe in, there were other men put forward to step into Valentinian's shoes but his, 'bribes nevertheless surpassed all and so he won the palace'.[14] All hail Emperor Petronius Maximus. He had out schemed and out brought everyone to obtain the one title missing from his CV, that of emperor.

Being Emperor

So there was Petronius Maximus, he had achieved the ultimate; he was emperor. But being emperor was a bigger step up than the endlessly successful Maximus had imagined. 'He soon discovered that the business of empire and a senatorial ease are inconsistent with each other.' As Sidonius puts it, concluding 'his rule of it was from the first tempestuous, with popular tumults, tumults of soldiery, tumults of allies'.[15]

It was pretty much on day one of Petronius Maximus' reign as emperor that he made the decision that would bring his rule crashing down and comprehensively demolishes that ring story. He announced his intention to marry Valentinian III's widow, Eudoxia. You can sort of see why he thought this was a good idea, it would link him to the previous dynasty strengthening his right to be emperor. What he hadn't factored into this clever piece of politicking was how Eudoxia might feel about this. Very unhappy is the answer,

Something else that Petronius hadn't thought about during his path to the top job was how the deaths of Aetius and Valentintian III might be seen in the rest of the empire. Why would he when he was so consumed with his own success and so sure of his own abilities?

Whilst Petronius Maximus had been living his best life, Aetius and Valentinian III had been negotiating a peace deal with Gaiseric, the ruler of the fearsome Vandals. A peace deal that had been cemented with an engagement between Valentinian III's daughter Eudocia to Gaiseric's son, Huneric. The murder of Valentinian III was therefore, for Gaiseric, very much considered a family matter (or at the very least a useful pretext for having a go at those Romans again).

A further incentive for rampaging was handed to Gaiseric by Euxodia who it was said begged him to invade Rome and rescue her from being forced to marry Petronius Maximus. Gaiseric set his Vandals on the road to Rome.

Starting a war with an enemy of Rome that had been subdued after decades of hostilities and careful negotiations was not a great start to the reign of Petronius Maximus. But he's an experienced politician and as we've previously established, a very clever man, no doubt he has a heap of ideas and schemes and plans to deal with this unexpected turn of events.

'When Maximus learned that Gaiseric's army was positioned at Azestos (this was a place near Rome) he became very fearful. He mounted his horse and fled. The Imperial bodyguard and the freedmen who he used to trust the most deserted him; when they saw him riding away, they mocked and berated his cowardice. Just as he was about to leave the city, someone threw at stone at the side of his head and killed him.'[16]

I don't know about you but I'm proper disappointed in Petronius Maximus, as disappointed as those Imperial bodyguards and freedmen were. Facing his first real test as emperor he completely loses his nerve and does a runner. It makes us look back at those assassinations he was behind with new eyes; perhaps it wasn't him being clever getting other people doing his dirty work, perhaps Petronius Maximus' was a cringing coward reliant on others to do what he himself did not dare to do.

Coward or not, Petronius Maximus quickly learnt that being emperor was not how he imagined it would be. Sidonius has a neat analogy for what Petronius Maximus discovered, 'behold a bare sword, swinging from the ceiling right over his purple-mantled shoulders, as if every instant it must fall and pierce his throat'.[17]

I'm reminded of the Emperor Domitian. 'He used to say that the lot of princes was most unhappy, since when they discovered a conspiracy, no one believed them unless they had been killed.'[18] Petronius Maximus had uncovered the secret, that to be emperor did not necessarily make you happy, it was far more likely to make you unhappy. Not least because of the target it painted on your forehead for your poor decisions, or as Sidonius put it better, that bare sword swinging from the ceiling above your head at all times.

Petronius Maximus is a worst emperor for sure, worse even than Didius Julianus. For at least Didius Julianus had plans to beat back Septimius Severus' invading army; they were terrible plans, true but it was more than Petronius Maximus had. In the cruellest way possible Petronius Maximus discovered he was not made of emperor material, no matter what his background, no matter what his experience, no matter his wealth and his bounteous friends, none of it prepared him for the reality of the job. You'll recall Gordian? I had a similar moment of stark realisation that he wasn't up to the job when faced with an invading army, although he took a slightly more honourable route (in Roman eyes) by committing suicide. Petronius Maximus' response to this realisation was to run away. Is it any wonder the mob gave his corpse a good kicking? A more shameful end is difficult to imagine.

Petronius Maximus' legacy was an event that left an indelible stain on Rome and is the subject of numerous paintings; the sacking of Rome by the Vandals in 455 CE. It's hard to think of a greater consequence for Rome of having a worst emperor in charge.

Conclusion

I hope you have enjoyed our tour of 500 years of Roman history and some truly terrible rulers. But is there anything we can learn from having spent 200 odd pages in the company of Rome's worst emperors? Something that maybe our leaders today, presidents and prime ministers could perhaps learn from our journey? Probably not. But I called this chapter 'conclusion', so I'd better come to one.

It's probably wise to make sure your ruler is not in possession of a fatal character flaw that will be acerbated by the pressures of holding high office, think Caligula's sadism and Domitian's paranoia, neither of which might have been revealed had they not found themselves as emperor. Handing the most important job in the empire over to someone simply because of who their father was turns out to also be a chronically bad decision which brought Rome the likes of the not terribly bright Commodus, the petty Geta and the terminally weak Valentinian II.

Forcing men into the role of ruler such as with Vitellius and Gordian I, and likely Quintillus and Nerva too, is unlikely to result in a lengthy rule. Probably best not to appoint an emperor sight unseen, such as happened with Elagabalus and selling off the job to the highest bidder is unlikely to find someone worthy of the post, certainly not Didius Julianus. On the other hand, even the best qualified candidate, the one with the most experience and ability, such as Galba and Petronius Maximus, can turn out to be a crushing disappointment when actually handed the job.

So, I guess what I'm trying to say is that there is no hard rule for predicting who will be a worst emperor. Now good emperors on the other hand, but that's a whole other book....

Authors Note

For those of you who skipped from the contents page straight to this note with angry finger-turning pages wanting to know why I haven't included Tiberius/Nero/A.N. Other emperor you feel is a dead cert for a worst emperor, the reason is that this turned out to be a far bigger topic than I initially anticipated. Edits had to be made and several worst emperors I had been intending to include had to be cut out entirely.

This, however, probably worked in the books favour because those emperors who survived that edit I feel demonstrate a wide breadth of what makes a worst emperor. From dangerous personality flaws like Caligula's sadism and Domitian's paranoia, to emperors who were overtaken by events and swept along with them, such as Vitellius and Nerva, and onwards to the likes of Gordian I and Petronius Maximus, who both realised at the worst possible moment that they had been drastically over promoted.

I'd like to give a big thank you and tons of appreciation to Dr Emma Southon for sending me some truly fabulous material for my Caligula chapter and for watching the 1979 Caligula movie, so I didn't have to (once was more than enough for me). A big thanks also to Scott Rowland for the use of his holiday snaps of Rome in this book. And a thank you to all of you on social media who kept my spirits soaring and my typing fingers crackling over the keyboard at extremely odd hours in the morning.

L.J. Trafford

Notes

Introduction
1. The thumbs down to denote death is an invention of the movies. As is the idea that every gladiator bout ended in an emperor or otherwise appointed death.
2. Calculating the number of Roman emperors is not as straight forward as you might think. There are heated arguments to be had around when a usurper ceases to be a troublesome problem and qualifies as an emperor. For clarity I have totted up the western Roman emperors listed in Michael Grant's book *The Roman Emperors*.

Chapter 1: The Basics, What is an Emperor?
1. Res Gestae, 34.
2. It was partly the pressure from having such a successful ancestor that pushed the younger Brutus into taking part in the assassination of Julius Caesar. According to the historian Plutarch, graffiti started appearing regularly on the statue of Brutus the Liberator bemoaning the lack of Brutus when a Brutus was so needed now. I suspect a certain Cassius was sneaking about at night with a paint can, to apply that extra nonce of persuasion on Brutus the younger. Fair due to him, that did actually work and Brutus joined the rank of conspirators.
3. Livy, *the History of Rome*, 1.59.
4. One such issue was that of land reform. Small farmers had been increasingly pushed off their land so that the senatorial class could build up mega farmers of their own. Unsurprisingly the senators as the beneficiaries of this policy didn't see any hurry in resolving it. It remained whatever the Roman equivalent of a political hot potato is, maybe a turnip. This political hot turnip was used by multiple politicians to whip up a good mob when they required one.
5. Julius Caesar was Governor of Gaul for eight years, a time he spent doing plenty of conquering and then writing his own account of this conquering in case anybody in Rome had missed the amazing conquering he was doing. Pompey earned his 'The Great' tag for the four years of conquering he did in the wealthy East that helped enrich Rome.
6. The Late Republican period is one of increasing political violence. In the 50s BCE Pompey the Great used his mob to pour manure over the head of his political rival, Bibulus. Later Tribune of the Plebs. Clodius Pulcher used his mob to follow Pompey around, shouting insults at him and intimidating Pompey back into his house. In 53 BCE the city erupted in full out warfare between rival mob owners, and the would-be elected praetor and consul for the year, Clodius and Milo. The elections had to be abandoned due to the level of violence on the streets. In 52 BCE a scuffle between Clodius and Milo's gangs on the Appian way road into Rome led to Clodius' death and a very public trial for Milo.

7. The drama behind crossing the Rubicon is due to it being the symbolic boundary of the city, rather than the actual crossing of the river, which is a disappointing and non-dramatic trickle of water.
8. Octavius, a great nephew of Julius Caesar was adopted as his son in Caesar's will. Octavius liked to pretend that this legal adoption meant he inherited Caesar's powers as well as his name. It didn't. But deifying his murdered father does give Octavius the opportunity to style himself as the son of a god. Which is something Mark Antony couldn't do in their battle of one-upmanship.
9. Res Gestae 34.
10. Clodius used his time as tribune of the plebs to wage a personal vendetta against the famous Roman statesman Cicero. After having Cicero exiled and demolishing his house just for the fun of it, Clodius found himself at a loose end and without a decent enemy to torment. He turned his attention to Pompey the Great, who he had followed around by a mob every time he left the house. This mob would shout various insults at Pompey that 'the Great' found upsetting. Well, you would, wouldn't you?
11. Livy, *History of Rome*, 32.5.
12. Livy, *History of Rome*, 32.6.
13. Livy, *History of Rome*, 2.33.
14. Res Gestae, 5.
15. Tacitus, *Annals of Imperial Rome*, I.2.
16. Res Gestae, 8.
17. In an attempt to compete with his fellow triumvirs, Pompey and Caesar, and match their glorious conquests in the East and Gaul, Marcus Licinius Crassus had marched three legions into the territory of the Parthian empire in 53 BCE. All three legions were annihilated by the skilled Parthian archers. Tiberius' diplomatic mission was to recover the standards for each legion from the Parthians, a highly significant and symbolic task.
18. Tacitus, *Annals of Imperial Rome*, I.2.
19. The Optimates, or good men, were the traditionalists who were of the opinion that Rome was doing so damn well, why change the recipe? The Populares sought to mix things up by reforming legislation.
20. Olivia Coleman's Oscar acceptance speech is a good example of this self-effacing attitude in the face of an enormous triumph. She praises others who did not win as her idols, states 'this will never happen again' and is very thankful to many people for her success. Nowhere does she acknowledge that she won because she was a better actress than everyone else who was nominated.
21. Res Gestae, 1.
22. Res Gestae, 12.
23. Res Gestae, 9.
24. Suetonius, *Life of Augustus*, 8.3.
25. Res Gestae, 15.
26. Res Gestae, 15.
27. Res Gestae, 18.
28. Suetonius, *Life of Claudius*, 18.2.
29. Res Gestae, 22.
30. Res Gestae, 3.
31. Res Gestae, 15.
32. Res Gestae, 30.

182 Ancient Rome's Worst Emperors

33. Res Gestae, 27.
34. Res Gestae, 26.
35. Res Gestae, 26.
36. Res Gestae, 25.
37. Res Gestae, 31.
38. Galen, *The affections and errors of the soul*, 10.55–56.
39. Galen famously demonstrated for an audience that the brain controlled functions of the body. He did this by dissecting a live pig and noting which nerve he cut that ceased it's no doubt deafening, squealing. He then went on to test his theory on a menagerie of other animals. Proving that you should never hire Galen as your pet sitter.
40. Res Gestae, 6.
41. Suetonius, *Life of Augustus*, 86.2.
42. Res Gestae, 3.
43. Res Gestae, 2.
44. Suetonius, *Life of Augustus*, 73.
45. Res Gestae, 20.
46. Res Gestae, 25.
47. Res Gestae, 8.
48. Statius, court poet to the Emperor Domitian, particularly excels at this, 'Is it you I gaze at, as I sit here, sovereign of all the lands, Great father of a world conquered, dear to the gods, hope of all mankind'? Silvae book IV.2. It is indeed, because Statius has been invited to an Imperial banquet during which he nearly explodes with joy all over his patron.
49. Entry to the equestrian order required a fortune of 300,000 sesterces. To be a senator you needed a minimum of 1 million. These are very large sums.
50. Jones, Brian W, *The Emperor Domitian*, p181.
51. Emperors who were deified post death include Julius Caesar, Augustus, Claudius, Vespasian, Titus and Nerva. Amongst many others, it has to be said.

Chapter 2: Caligula – How Absolute is Absolute Power?
1. Informers bringing a successful charge were awarded a quarter of the estate of the condemned. Given the wealth of the senatorial class this could be a sizable sum.
2. Suetonius, *Life of Tiberius*, 58.
3. There are all manner of stories regarding what Tiberius got up to on the island of Capri, of which Suetonius says, 'he acquired a reputation for still grosser depravities that one can hardly bear to tell or be told, let alone believe'. Suetonius helpfully lists all of these depravities, which are pretty much the worst you will read about any emperor, even Caligula. It is however highly unlikely any of them are true, if only because Tiberius was in his seventies when he retired to Capri and it is difficult to believe he would possess the necessary stamina to commit even a third of what he is accused of.
4. Suetonius, *Life of Tiberius*, 75.
5. Sejanus is the first of what will quickly become a theme; dodgy, double crossing Praetorian Prefects. Sejanus convinced Tiberius that Agrippina and two of her sons were plotting against him; all three were exiled and died. The Prefect had his eye on Agrippina's only surviving son, Gaius, as his next target when Tiberius was finally made aware of his Prefect's duplicitous nature, which included an affair with Tiberius' daughter in law, Livilla and the murder of Livilla's husband, the emperor's son Drusus. Sejanus was executed. Livilla was said to have been bricked up in a room in the palace by her own mother, Antonia, and left to starve to death.

6. Germanicus, whilst in the East, had fallen out with the governor of Syria, Gnaeus Calpurnius Piso, When Germanicus fell ill and died at the extremely tender age of 33, Piso was suspected of poisoning him and put on trial in Rome. As Piso was a close confident of Tiberius the big question on everyone's lips was whether Piso had murdered Germanicus under Tiberius' orders. It was a big question that was never answered for Piso committed suicide during the trial. Which was seen as suspiciously handy for Tiberius. Modern scholars think it most likely that Germanicus had simply died of a fever, which is a distinctly less dramatic story and a bit of a bummer for Piso, who it turns out hadn't done anything wrong.
7. Suetonius, *Life of Caligula*, 3.1.
8. Suetonius, *Life of Caligula*, 13.
9. Suetonius, *Life of Caligula*, 13.
10. Suetonius, *Life of Caligula*, 16.
11. Suetonius, *Life of Caligula*, 15.
12. Suetonius, *Life of Caligula*, 15.
13. Suetonius, *Life of Caligula*, 16.
14. Suetonius, *Life of Caligula*, 17.
15. Suetonius, *Life of Caligula*, 17.
16. Suetonius, *Life of Caligula*, 17.
17. Cassius Dio, *The History of Ancient Rome*, LIX.1.
18. Suetonius, *Life of Caligula*, 21.
19. Suetonius, *Life of Caligula*, 22.
20. Suetonius, *Life of Caligula*, 22.
21. As noted previously, plain Gaius Octavius passed on a suggestion that he take the name Romulus because Romulus had been a king. That stirring speech of Brutus the Liberator was still very dear to the Romans, and they held a firm conviction that they would never be ruled by kings again.
22. Suetonius, *Life of Caligula*, 52.
23. Suetonius, *Life of Caligula*, 36.
24. Caligula's great grandfather, Augustus, had brought in a series of morality laws that penalised exactly the sort of behaviour Caligula is displaying here. Namely adultery with married freeborn women.
25. Suetonius, *Life of Caligula*, 54.
26. Suetonius, *Life of Caligula*, 27.
27. So keenly felt was the loss of these legions that Augustus 'for several months in succession he cut neither his beard nor his hair, and sometimes he would dash his head against a door, crying: "Quintilius Varus, give me back my legions!"' Suetonius, *Life of Augustus*, 23.
28. Suetonius, *Life of Caligula*, 30.
29. Suetonius, *Life of Caligula*, 22.
30. Suetonius, *Life of Caligula*, 56.
31. Julius Caesar is the classic example of this. Early in his career he was accused of submitting sexually to King Nicomedes of Bithynia, a charge his political rivals manage to keep in the public discourse for decades after the alleged offence. Which shows a dedication to gossip that is truly heroic.
32. Seneca, *Controversies*, 4.
33. Suetonius, *Life of Nero*, 26.
34. Juvenal, *Satires*, VI.

35. Ironically this statue was made from melted down bronze coins of Caligula, after the Senate decreed anything with his image on should be destroyed. We might commend Messalina for her recycling efforts here.
36. Cassius Dio, *The History of ancient Rome*, LX 22.3.
37. Suetonius, *Life of Caligula*, 55.
38. Suetonius *Life of Caligula*, 36.
39. Suetonius, *Life of Caligula*, 25.
40. Suetonius, *Life of Caligula*, 40.
41. Suetonius, *Life of Caligula*, 38.
42. Suetonius, *Life of Caligula*, 38.
43. Suetonius, *Life of Caligula*, 45.
44. Suetonius, *Life of Caligula*, 56.
45. Plutarch, *Life of Brutus*, 8.
46. Suetonius, *Life of Caligula*, 58.
47. Suetonius, *Life of Caligula*, 58.
48. About the Production; 1980 Press Notes on Caligula Film, Page 2.
49. About the Production; 1980 Press Notes on Caligula Film, Page 2.
50. From Robert Ebert reviews website.
51. The Washington Post, Caligula and the courting of an expert witness, S. Schoenbaum, 10/08/1980.
52. The Harvard Crimson, Professors testify in Caligula case, Burton F. Jablin, 05/08/1980.
53. The Guardian, Caligula's sex and excess is bizarre and depressing, Peter Bradshaw, 28/08/2008.
54. The Making of Caligula, Alan Royce https://filmstarfacts.com/
55. Josephus, *History of the Jewish War*, Xix.1.
56. Tacitus, *Annals*, XII.3.
57. Tacitus, *Annals*, XI.26.
58. Quoted in Taylor, L. R. (1929). Tiberius' Refusals of Divine Honors. Transactions and Proceedings of the American Philological Association, 60, 87–101.
59. Cassius Dio, *History of Ancient Rome*, LI.20.
60. I like to believe there was some sort of threesome between the Empress, Suetonius and Clarus. Or alternatively Suetonius read his chapter on those interesting Tiberius Capri years out loud to the Empress, which her husband thought unsuitable reading material. On the more boring side Suetonius may simply have breached court protocols by addressing the empress more casually than was dictated.
61. Cassius Dio, *History of ancient Rome*, LIX.8.
62. Philo, *On the Embassy to Gaius*, 2.14.
63. Graves, Robert, *I Claudius*, p.332.
64. Suetonius, *Life of Caligula*, 24.
65. Cassius Dio, *History of ancient Rome*, LIX.11.
66. Martial, *Epigrams*, 9.XCI.
67. Cassius Dio, *History of ancient Rome*, LXI. 13.
68. Cassius Dio, *History of ancient Rome*, LXI.16.
69. Cassius Dio, *History of ancient Rome*, LXI.16.
70. Cassius Dio, *History of ancient Rome*, LXI.11.
71. Ferell, Arthur, *Caligula, Emperor of Rome*, p.128.
72. Winterling, Aloys, *Caligula*, p.118.
73. Suetonius, *Life of Caligula*, 60.

Chapter 3: Galba – The Man who Should be King
1. Suetonius, *Life of Galba*, 3.
2. Suetonius, *Life of Galba*, 4.4.
3. According to Pliny the Elder, a certain Gaius Caecilius Isidorus was in possession of 4116 slaves on his deathbed. *Natural History Xxxiii*.
4. Suetonius, *Life of Galba*, 7.
5. Suetonius, *Life of Galba*, 8.
6. Suetonius, *Life of Galba*, 7.
7. Tacitus, *The Histories*, 1.49.
8. Plutarch, *Life of Galba*, 15.
9. Plutarch, *Life of Galba*, 15.
10. Mark Antony's attempt to invade the Parthian empire was as similarly disastrous as Crassus' had been 17 years before. Under constant harassment of those Parthian archers that had wiped out Crassus' legions, Antony was forced into a humiliating retreat. During this campaign Antony decimated part of his own force on a charge of cowardice and fleeing from the enemy, which in the light of the retreat that Antony himself later orders, seems jolly unfair.
11. Suetonius, *Life of Galba*, 14.
12. Suetonius, *Life of Galba*, 21.
13. Plutarch, *Life of Galba*, 2.
14. Plutarch, *Life of Galba*, 9.
15. Tacitus, Annals, XV.71.
16. Plutarch, *Life of Galba*, 14.
17. Suetonius, *Life of Galba*, 16.
18. Tacitus, *Histories*, 1.2.

Chapter 4: Vitellius – No Appetite for Power
1. Suetonius, *Life of Vitellius*, 13.
2. Suetonius, *Life of Vitellius*, 14.
3. Suetonius, *Life of Vitellius*, 4.
4. Suetonius, *Life of Vitellius*, 4.
5. Suetonius, *Life of Vitellius*, 5.
6. Arminius was the Romanised German who had led Varus and his legions into that ambush. The Germans are still pretty proud of his actions, enough to have a twenty-four-metre statue constructed of him which is situated near the town of Detmold.
7. Tacitus, *Histories*, 1.51.
8. Tacitus, *Histories*, 1.55.
9. Tacitus, *Histories*, 1.52.
10. Tacitus, *Histories*, 1.62.
11. Tacitus, *Histories*, 1.74.
12. Lacking quick access to the legions stationed in the provinces, Otho had put together a ramshackle army consisting of raw recruits, the Praetorian guard and, proving how desperate he truly was for men, gladiators. Ramshackle they may have been but swayed by Otho's charisma they fought extremely hard against the vastly superior numbers of the professional soldiers of the Rhine legions and had some successes.
13. Tacitus, *Histories*, 1.71.
14. Tacitus, *Histories*, 1.71.
15. Tacitus, *Histories*, 1.87.

16. Suetonius, *Life of Vitellius*, 13.
17. Suetonius, *Life of Vitellius*, 13.
18. Livy, *History of Rome*, 1.
19. Plutarch, *Life of Aemilius Paulus*, 1.
20. Plutarch, *Life of Cato the Elder*, 16.5.
21. Tacitus, *Histories*, 1.64.
22. Tacitus, *Histories*, 2.29.
23. Tacitus, *Histories*, 2.29.
24. Tacitus, *Histories*, 2.88.
25. Tacitus, *Histories*, 2.93.
26. Tacitus, *Histories*, 2.93.
27. Tacitus, *Histories*, 1.48.
28. Suetonius, *Life of Otho*, 2.
29. Tacitus, *Histories*, 2.96.
30. Tacitus, *Histories*, 3.36.
31. Tacitus, *Histories*, 3.54.
32. Suetonius, *Life of Vitellius*, 15.
33. Tacitus, *Histories*, 3.66.
34. Tacitus, Histories, 3.68.
35. Tacitus, *Histories*, 3.68.
36. Tacitus, *Histories*, 3.70.
37. Suetonius, *Life of Vitellius*, 17.
38. Tacitus, *Histories*, 3.85.
39. Tacitus, *Histories*, 3.85.

Chapter 5: Domitian – A Swirling Paranoia
1. Suetonius, *Life of Vespasian*, 12.
2. Pliny the Younger, *Panegyricus*, 52.
3. Pliny the Younger, *Letters*, 9.13.
4. The scandal in this tale (such as there was) for the Romans was not necessarily the incest element (although that is still scandalous), but rather Domitian's hypocrisy in partaking in adultery whilst passing new morality laws aimed at clamping down on the very thing he was allegedly doing with Julia.
5. Suetonius, *Life of Domitian*, 2.
6. Suetonius, *Life of Vespasian*, 2.
7. This is not so novel or ingenious as it might appear. The very same tactic had been used by the governor of Africa, Clodius Macer, the previous year. It hadn't proved very effective for Macer either, given he was executed in October 68 CE.
8. Tacitus, *Histories*, 3.85.
9. Tacitus, *Histories*, 3.86.
10. Tacitus, *Histories*, 3.74.
11. Tacitus, *Histories*, 3.74.
12. Tacitus, *Histories*, 4.2.
13. Tacitus, *Histories*, 4.44.
14. Suetonius, *Life of Domitian*, 1.
15. Tacitus, Histories, 4.51.
16. Suetonius, *Life of Domitian*, 1.

17. Augustus by now had become synonymous with being emperor, Caesar as a title was handed out to the junior partner in empire ruling.
18. Suetonius, *Life of Domitian*, 2.
19. Suetonius, *Life of Domitian*, 2.
20. Cassius Dio, *History of ancient Rome*, LXVII.2.
21. Suetonius, *Life of Domitian*, 2.
22. Suetonius, *Life of Domitian*, 2.
23. Suetonius, *Life of Titus*, 1.
24. Suetonius, *Life of Domitian*, 7, 8, 9.
25. Suetonius, *Life of Domitian*, 5.
26. Suetonius, *Life of Domitian*, 6.
27. Suetonius. *Life of Domitian*, 4.
28. Suetonius *Life of Domitian*, 9.
29. Statius, *Silvae*, Book IV.3.
30. Martial, *Epigrams*, 7.LXI.
31. Suetonius, *Life of Claudius*, 21.
32. Suetonius, *Life of Domitian*, 4.
33. Suetonius, *Life of Domitian*, 10.
34. Suetonius, *Life of Domitian*, 13.
35. Cassius Dio, *History of ancient Rome*, LXVIII5.
36. Suetonius, *Life of Domitian*, 13.
37. Cassius Dio, *History of ancient Rome*, LXVII4.
38. Suetonius, *Life of Domitian*, 19.
39. Pliny the Younger, *Panegyric*, 52.6.
40. Cassius Dio, *History of ancient Rome*, LXVII.11.3.
41. Suetonius, *Life of Domitian*, 10.2.
42. Suetonius, *Life of Domitian*, 10.2.
43. Suetonius, *Life of Claudius*, 29.
44. Tacitus, *Agricola*, 2.
45. Tacitus, *Agricola*, 45.
46. Pliny the Younger, *Letters*, 1.5.
47. Pliny the Younger, *Letters*, 4.11.
48. Cassius Dio, *History of ancient Rome*, LXVII.9.
49. Imperial freedmen get a terrible write up in our sources likely due to class snobbery and the distaste at them having once been slaves. Also, perhaps jealousy for their proximity to the emperor and the trust he placed in them.
50. Martial, *Epigrams*, 12.XI.
51. Martial, *Epigrams*, XVIII.
52. Martial, *Epigrams*, 5.V.
53. Cassius Dio, *History of ancient Rome*, LXVII.15.
54. Suetonius, *Life of Domitian*, 17.
55. Suetonius, *Life of Domitian*, 21.
56. Suetonius, *Life of Domitian*, 10.
57. Suetonius, *Life of Domitian*, 12.
58. Eusebius, *The History of the Church*, 20.2.
59. Pliny, *Letters*, 4.XLIII.
60. Suetonius, *Life of Domitian*, 10.2.
61. Suetonius *Life of Domitian*, 10.2.

62. Suetonius, *Life of Domitian*, 14.
63. Suetonius, *Life of Domitian*, 21.
64. Suetonius *Life of Domitian*, 3.
65. Suetonius, *Life of Domitian*, 14.4.
66. Suetonius *Life of Domitian*, 14.
67. Suetonius, *Life of Nero*, 49.
68. Suetonius, *Life of Domitian*, 17.
69. Cassius Dio, *History of ancient Rome*, LXVII.15.

Chapter 6: Nerva – The Hinge
1. Gibbon, Edward, *Decline and Fall of the Roman Empire*, p.83.
2. Caligula, Claudius, Galba, Vitellius and Domitian are murdered. Nero and Otho commit suicide. Augustus was rumoured to have been poisoned by his wife Livia (highly unlikely). Tiberius was rumoured to have been smothered by the Praetorian Prefect Macro under the orders of Caligula (slightly more likely) and Titus was rumoured to have been killed not by a fever but by his brother Domitian (unlikely).
3. Cassius Dio, *History of ancient Rome*, LXVII.15.
4. Suetonius, *Life of Galba*, 6.
5. Suetonius, *Life of Galba*, 6.
6. Cassius Dio, *History of* ancient *Rome*, LXVIII.1.
7. Tacitus, *Annals*, XV.48.1.
8. Tacitus, *Annals*, XV.58.
9. Tacitus, *Annals*, XV.72.
10. Traditionally, as we have seen, there were two posts of consul each year. However, to share around the glory and aiming to ingratiating himself with the Senators probably, Augustus had introduced a system whereby the consuls elected at the beginning of the year would step down after six months. There would be a further election process for these *suffect* consuls. As noted Vespasian named himself and one of his sons as ordinary consul except on four occasions.
11. Cassius Dio, *History of ancient Rome*, LXVIII.3.
12. Cassius Dio, *History of ancient Rome*, LXVIII.1.
13. Cassius Dio, *History of ancient Rome*, LXVIII.2.
14. Cassius Dio, *History of ancient Rome*, LXVIII.2.
15. Cassius Dio, *History of ancient Rome*, LXVIII.2.
16. Cassius Dio, *History of ancient Rome*, LXVIII.3.3.
17. Cassius Dio, *History of ancient Rome*, LXVIII.3.3.
18. Cassius Dio, *History of ancient Rome*, LXVIII.3.3.
19. Pliny the Younger, *Panegyric*.
20. Gibbon, Edward, *Decline and Fall of the Roman Empire*, p.80.

Chapter 7: Lucius Verus – Overshadowed
1. Historia Augusta, *Life of Lucius Verus*, 4.4.
2. Historia Augusta. *Life of Lucius Verus*, 3.4.
3. Historia Augusta, *Life of Lucius Verus*, 5.11.
4. Historia Augusta, *Life of Lucius Verus*, 5.11.
5. Historia Augusta *Life of Lucius Verus*, 10.
6. Historia Augusta, *Life of Lucius Verus*, 10.
7. Historia Augusta, *Life of Lucius Verus*, 10.

8. Historia Augusta, *Life of Lucius Verus*, 10.
9. Historia Augusta, *Life of Marcus Aurelius*, 1.
10. Historia Augusta, *Life of Marcus Aurelius*, 2.6.
11. Historia Augusta, *Life of Marcus Aurelius*, 8.
12. Historia Augusta, *Life of Lucius Verus*, 1.

Chapter 8: Commodus – Monstrous Ego
1. Cassius Dio, *History of ancient Rome*, LXIII.36.
2. Cassius Dio, *History of ancient Rome*, LXXIII.16.
3. Historia Augusta, *Life of Commodus*, Part 2.19.
4. Historia Augusta, *Life of Commodus*, 19.
5. Cassius Dio, *History of ancient Rome*, LXXIII.15.
6. Cassius Dio, *History of ancient Rome*, LXXIII.4.
7. Cassius Dio, *History of ancient Rome*, LXXIII.3.
8. Cassius Dio, *History of ancient Rome*, LXXIII.2.
9. Herodian, *Roman History*, 1.6.1.
10. Cassius Dio, *History of ancient Rome*, LXXIII.2.
11. Herodian, *Roman History*, 1.7.1.
12. Horace, *Ars*, 161–5.
13. Cassius Dio, *History of ancient Rome*, LXXIII.1.
14. Herodian, *Roman History*, 1.8.1.
15. Herodian, *Roman History*, 1.8.2.
16. Herodian, *Roman History*, 1.9.1.
17. Herodian, *Roman History*, 1.9.6.
18. Cassius Dio, *History of ancient Rome*, LXXIII.9.2.
19. Cassius Dio, *History of ancient Rome*, LXXIII. 10.2.
20. Historia Augusta, *Life of Commodus*, 6.
21. Historia Augusta, *Life of Commodus*, 6.
22. Historia Augusta, *Life of Commodus*, 7.
23. Herodian, *Roman History*, 1.12.4.
24. Herodian, *Roman History*, 1.12.5.
25. Herodian, *Roman History*, 1.13.3.
26. Herodian, *Roman History*, 1.6.1.
27. Historia Augusta, *Life of Commodus*, 5.
28. Cassius Dio, *History of ancient Rome*, LXXIII.14.
29. Historia Augusta, *Life of Commodus*, 5.
30. Historia Augusta, *Life of Commodus*, 5.
31. Historia Augusta, *Life of Commodus*, 10.
32. Historia Augusta, *Life of Commodus*, 11.
33. Historia Augusta, *Life of Commodus*, 9.
34. Historia Augusta, *Life of Commodus*, 11.
35. Historia Augusta, *Life of Commodus*, 10.10.
36. Herodian, *Roman History*, 1.15.5.
37. Herodian, *Roman History*, 1.15.6.
38. Herodian, *Roman History*, 1.15.7.
39. Herodian, *Roman History*, 1.15.7.
40. Herodian, *Roman History*, 1.8.6.
41. Herodian, *Roman History*, 1.8.7.

42. Cassius Dio, *History of ancient Rome*, LXXIII.5.3.
43. Herodian, *Roman History*, 1.14.9.
44. Cassius Dio, *History of ancient Rome*, LXXIII.20.
45. Cassius Dio, *History of ancient Rome*, LXXIII.20.
46. Cassius Dio, *History of ancient Rome*, LXXIII.20.
47. Cassius Dio, *History of ancient Rome*, LXXIII.20.
48. Cassius Dio, *History of ancient Rome*, LXXIII.21.
49. Cassius Dio, *History of ancient Rome*, LXXIII.21.
50. Herodian, *Roman History*, 1.14.7.
51. Cassius Dio, *History of ancient Rome*, LXXIII.17.
52. Historia Augusta, *Life of Commodus*, 8.
53. Although John S McHugh in his book *The Emperor Commodus: God and Gladiator* has a crack at rehabilitating Commodus' dire reputation as the natural result of overlooking the senatorial class for positions and executing them a lot. However, even he doesn't dispute Commodus' grandiose behaviours such as renaming all the months after himself.
54. Herodian, *Life of Commodus*, 2.1.4.
55. Historia Augusta, *Life of Pertinax*, 1.
56. Herodian, *Roman History*, 2.4.3.
57. Herodian, *Roman History*, 2.5.1.
58. Historia Augusta, *Life of Commodus*, 10.9.
59. Cassius Dio, *History of ancient Rome*, LXXIV.5.

Chapter 9: Didius Julianus – The Man who Brought an Empire
1. *Praetorian: The Rise and Fall of Rome's Imperial Bodyguard*, Guy De La Bedoyere, p. 2.
2. Historia Augusta, *Life of Didius Julianus*, 1.
3. Historia Augusta, *Life of Didius Julianus*, 1.7.
4. Herodian, *Roman History*, 2.6.3.
5. Herodian, *Roman History*, 2.6.1.
6. Herodian, *Roman History*, 2.5.9.
7. Herodian, *Roman History*, 2.6.4.
8. Herodian, *Roman History*, 2.6.7.
9. Herodian, *Roman History*, 2.6.10.
10. Herodian, *Roman History*, 2.7.2.
11. Historia Augusta, *Life of Didius Julianus*, 4.
12. Herodian, *Roman History*, 2.12.3.
13. Cassius Dio, *History of ancient Rome*, LXXIV.16.
14. Herodian, *Roman History*, 2.11.8.
15. Cassius Dio, *History of ancient Rome*, LXXIV 16.4.
16. Cassius Dio, *History of ancient Rome*, LXXIV.16.2.

Chapter 10: Geta – For-geta-ble
1. Historia Augusta, *Life of Geta*, 1.
2. Historia Augusta, *Life of Geta*, 5.
3. Historia Augusta, *Life of Geta*, 5.
4. Historia Augusta, *Life of Geta*, 5.4.
5. Historia Augusta, *Life of Geta*, 3.
6. The Severan Tondo is a beautiful and rare work of Roman painting, currently housed in Berlin. It depicts Emperor Septimus Severus, Empress Julia Domna and their two

young sons. Only the boy on the left, Geta, has had his face entirely scrubbed out as part of the *Damnatio Memoriae* inflicted on him by his brother. See Image 26.
7. Herodian, *Roman History*, 3.10.3.
8. Cassius Dio, *History of ancient Rome*, LXXVII.7.
9. Cassius Dio, *History of ancient Rome*, LXXVII.7.
10. Sir Alex Ferguson, ex-manager of Manchester United football club, brought the hairdryer technique to prominence. It's a method for improving the performance of players on the pitch by yelling their shortcomings and what you think about them right in their face, along with a hefty injection of really quite inventive swearing and insults. You can't deny it worked for Sir Alex, Manchester United did very well under his managership.
11. Herodian, *Roman History*, 3.13.3.
12. Herodian, *Roman History*, 3.13.5.
13. Herodian, *Roman History*, 3.13.4.
14. Herodian, *Roman History*, 3.15.4.
15. Herodian, *Roman History*, 4.1.1.
16. Herodian, *Roman History*, 3.15.5.
17. Herodian, *Roman History*, 4.1.5.
18. Cassius Dio, *History of ancient Rome*, LXXVIII.1.
19. Herodian, *Roman History*, 4.3.5.
20. Herodian, *Roman History*, 4.4.2.
21. Herodian, *Roman History*, 4.4.2.
22. Cassius Dio, *History of ancient Rome*, LXVIII.2.
23. Cassius Dio, *History of ancient Rome*, LXVIII.2.3.
24. Herodian, *Roman History*, 4.4.3–4.
25. Most notably a massacre of civilians he ordered in Alexandria after he heard they were making jokes about him, one of which centred around his fratricide.

Chapter 11: Elagabalus – And Now for Someone Completely Different
1. Historia Augusta, *Life of Elagabalus*, 1.
2. Historia Augusta, *Life of Elagabalus*, 1.
3. See the chapter on Commodus for an account of Cassius Dio stuffing his own toga into his mouth to try and stop himself from laughing at the Emperor.
4. He also refers to him as Avitus, Sardanapalus and Tiberinus in his account. Elagabalus gains the name Tiberinus after his death because that was where his corpse was thrown: in Rome's River Tiber. Which well and truly demonstrates how much Cassius Dio did not like Elagabalus.
5. Cassius Dio, *History of ancient Rome*, LXXX. 1.2.
6. Cassius Dio, *History of ancient Rome*, LXXX.16.7.
7. Historia Augusta, *Life of Elagabalus*, 18.
8. Historia Augusta, *Life of Elagabalus*, 3.
9. Historia Augusta, *Life of Elagabalus*, 3.3.
10. Herodian, *Roman History*, 5.3.7.
11. Suetonius, *Life of Domitian*, 17.
12. The statues of Galba, for instance, are utterly unlike the physical descriptions preserved of him. See image 8 for an example.
13. Cassius Dio, *History of ancient Rome*, LXXX.4.5.
14. Herodian, *Roman History*, 5.5.5.

15. Herodian, *Roman History*, 5.5.3.
16. Cassius Dio, *History of ancient Rome*, LXXX.3.
17. Historia Augusta, *Life of Elagabalus*, 20.4.
18. Historia Augusta, *Life of Elagabalus*, 21.6.
19. Historia Augusta, *Life of Elagabalus*, 21.
20. Historia Augusta, *Life of Elagabalus*, 25.
21. Historia Augusta, *Life of Elagabalus*, 21.5.
22. A fascinating discussion on the social media site Reddit tackles the very important question of exactly how many flowers would be necessary to smother a dinner party. Assuming the number of guests to be 20 and the room 18 x 10 x 3 metres in size the answer, the poster concludes, after some Maths that is way beyond my GCSE grade C, is that 51,333,333 flowers would be required to fill the room. Which is about 70 hectares worth of blooms or half-ish of Regents Park in London. Which makes the story thoroughly unbelievable before we even get to working out the logistics of transporting 70 hectares worth of flowers to Rome and into the palace.
23. Historia Augusta, *Life of Elagabalus*, 26.6.
24. Historia Augusta, *Life of Elagabalus*, 5.
25. Historia Augusta, *Life of Elagabalus*, 18.
26. Historia Augusta, *Life of Elagabalus*, 12.
27. Historia Augusta, *Life of Elagabalus*, 20.
28. Cassius Dio, *History of ancient Rome*, LXXX .13.
29. See the chapter on Domitian.
30. Historia Augusta, *Life of Elagabalus*, 6.6.
31. One of Suetonius' many cracking stories is about the emperor Nero never wearing the same outfit twice. I suspect the *Historia Augusta* author has read the same anecdote and adapted/reimagined it for his own means.
32. Cassius Dio, *History of ancient Rome*, LXXX.11.
33. Herodian, *Roman History*, 5.3.
34. Garum is the ketchup of the ancient world, they poured it on everything and there was a lucrative trade for producers of this condiment. Which is all the more surprising given garum was essentially fermented rotten fish.
35. Martial, *Epigrams*, 9.XCVI.
36. Historia Augusta, *Life of Alexander Severus*, 23.4.
37. Cassius Dio, *History of ancient Rome*, LXXX.11.
38. Herodian, *Roman History*, 5.5.4.
39. Cassius Dio, *History of ancient Rome*, LXXX.13.3.
40. Ovid, *Fasti*, 4.4.
41. Previous occasions in which the Sibylline books were consulted include a plague in 348 BCE, a shower of stones in 345 BCE and when Appius Claudius' army kept getting hit by lightning in 295 BCE.
42. Cassius Dio, *History of ancient Rome*, LXXX.11.
43. Historia Augusta, *Life of Elagabalus*, 3.4.
44. Herodian, *Roman History*, 5.6.3.
45. This was the festival of Lupercalia held in February each year. The Ceriala festivities, also in mid-April, included a ceremony where foxes with blazing torches tied to their tails were released into the Circus Maximus. Robigalia on 25th April involved the ritual sacrifice of dogs.
46. Historia Augusta, *Life of Elagabalus*, 2.

47. Historia Augusta, *Life of Elagabalus*, 4.
48. Historia Augusta, *Life of Elagabalus*, 4.3.
49. The Lex Oppia of 215 BCE restricted what was seen as the ostentatious display of wealth by women.
50. Icks, Martin *Crimes of Elagabalus*, p.32.
51. Herodian, *Roman History*, 5.7.6.
52. Icks, Martin *Crimes of Elagabalus*, p.23.
53. Historia Augusta, *Life of Elagabalus*, 30.7.
54. Historia Augusta, *Life of Elagabalus*, 30.8.
55. Herodian, *Roman History*, 5.7.1.
56. Herodian, *Roman History*, 5.7.2.
57. Herodian, *Roman History*, 5.7.4–5.
58. Herodian, *Roman History*, 5.8.1–5.8.2.
59. Herodian, *Roman History*, 5.8.7.
60. Historia Augusta, *Life of Elagabalus*, 23.
61. Historia Augusta, *Life of Elagabalus*, 23.8.
62. Icks, Martin, *Crimes of Elagabalus*, p.24.
63. Historia Augusta, *Life of Elagabalus*, 30.
64. Historia Augusta, *Life of Elagabalus*, 4.
65. Historia Augusta, *Life of Elagabalus*, 21.6.
66. Historia Augusta, *Life of Elagabalus*, 41.
67. Herodian, *Roman History*, 6.8.3.

Part 3: The Third Century – Where Any Man Can Be Emperor (briefly)
1. Cassius Dio died in 235 CE. Herodian in 240 CE.
2. Herodian, *Roman History*, 6.8.5.
3. Tacitus, *Histories*, 1.51.
4. Tacitus, *Histories*, 1.52.
5. Herodian, *Roman History*, 6.8.1.
6. Historia Augusta, *Life of Thrax*, 6.8.

Chapter 12: Gordian I – He Came, He Did Not Conquer and Then He Went
1. Herodian, *Roman History*, 7.3.3.
2. A procurator was the official in charge of the finances of a province.
3. Herodian, *Roman History*, 7.5.1.
4. Herodian, *Roman History*, 7.5.3.
5. Herodian, *Roman History*, 7.6.2.
6. Herodian, *Roman History*, 7.6.4.
7. Herodian, *Roman History*, 7.6.4.
8. Herodian, *Roman History*, 7.9.3.
9. Herodian, *Roman History*, 7.9.4.
10. Herodian, *Roman History*, 7.9.4.
11. Herodian, *Roman History*, 7.9.7.
12. Herodian, *Roman History*, 8.5.9.

Chapter 13: Silbannacus – The Phantom Emperor
1. The British Museum acquired one of these coins in 1937. See image 34.

Chapter 14: Quintillus – Easy Come, Easy Go
1. Historia Augusta, *Life of Claudius Gothicus*, 2.2.
2. Historia Augusta, *Life of Claudius Gothicus*, 12.
3. Grant, Michael, *The Roman Emperors*, p.181.
4. Historia Augusta, *Life of Claudius Gothicus*, 2.5.
5. Historia Augusta, *Life of Claudius Gothicus*, 12.5.
6. Historia Augusta, *Life of Aurelian*, 37.
7. Historia Augusta, *Life of Claudius Gothicus* 2.2.

Part 4: Sorting It All Out – The Tetrarchy and Beyond
1. The Gallic Empire lasted from 260 – 274 CE. It was Aurelian who sucked it back into the empire, one of the reasons he was called the Restorer of the World. Palmyra, led by Queen Zenobia was an independent state from 270–273 CE, again Aurelian was the one to recapture the Syrian city. What a guy! Shame on Eros!
2. The Persians had scored a massive victory over the hated Romans when they captured the Emperor Valerian in 250 CE; he had a miserable time at the court of King Sharpur being used as a foot stool and forced to perform other humiliating acts.
3. Emperor Carus who managed to hold onto power for possibly a full year before dying from a lightning strike. Allegedly.
4. Aurelius Victor, *Epitome de Caesaribus*, 39.6.
5. Although the last of Constantine the Great's dynasty, Julian who ruled from 361–3 CE was a pagan and tried with absolutely no success to overturn Christianity as the religion of the empire.

Chapter 15: Valentinian II – The Boy Emperor
1. Ammianus Marcellinus, *The Later Roman Empire*, 30.6.1.
2. Ammianus Marcellinus, *The Later Roman Empire*, 30.8.1.
3. Ammianus Marcellinus, *The Later Roman Empire*, 30.6.1.
4. Details on how Carus died are sketchy. Our old friend *The Historia Augusta* has this to say about it, 'he met his death, according to some, by disease, according to others, through a stroke of lightning'. Which is quite a divulgence of opinion. On Carus' staff happened to be a young man named Diocletian, who shortly thereafter becomes emperor. Talk about being in the right place at the right time! Yes, it's borderline suspicious and for all my bigging up of Diocletian's administrative bent he was quite as ruthless as any other Roman emperor.
5. Ammianus Marcellinus, *The Later Roman Empire*, 30.10.
6. Ammianus Marcellinus, *The Later Roman Empire*, 30.10.
7. Ammianus Marcellinus, *The Later Roman Empire*, 30.10.4.
8. Sozomen, *Ecclestical history*, VII.13.
9. Socrates, *Church History*, V.
10. Sozomen, *Ecclestical history*, VII.14.
11. If you're wondering what happened to Valens, the permanently cross Valentinian I's younger brother, he was killed at the Battle of Adrianople fighting the Goths.
12. Zosimus, *New History*, 4.47.2.
13. Sozomen, *Ecclestical history*, VII.14.
14. Zosimus, *New History*, 4.53.1.
15. Zosimus, *New History*, 4.53.1.
16. Zosimus, *New History*, 4.53.1.

17. Zosimus, *New History*, 4.53.2.
18. Zosimus, *New History*, 4.53.2.
19. Sozomen, *Ecclestical history*, VII.22.
20. Sozomen, *Ecclestical history*, VII.22.
21. Sozomen, *Ecclestical history*, VII.22.

Chapter 16: Petronius Maximus – Evil Genius
1. Sidonius Apollinaris, *Letters*, 2.X111.
2. Sidonius Apollinaris, *Letters*, 2.X111.
3. Sidonius Apollinaris, *Letters*, 2.X111.
4. Given that Sidonius mentions it in his list of 'good things Petronius Maximus had going for him' I think it's safe to say he at least wasn't terrible at and maybe even half good a poet/playwright/essayist.
5. Sidonius Apollinaris, *Letters*, 2.X111.
6. John of Antioch (*fr*.200.1: Gordon trans., p.51).
7. Those enemies of Rome weren't getting any fewer with the Huns being added to the list of marauding Goths, Vandals etc
8. John of Antioch, 69.
9. John of Antioch, 69.
10. John of Antioch, 69.
11. John of Antioch, 71.
12. John of Antioch, 71.
13. John of Antioch, 71.
14. John of Antioch, 71.
15. Sidonius Apollonaris, *Letters*, 2.X111/
16. John of Antioch, 71.
17. Sidonius Apollonaris, *Letters*, 2.X111.
18. Suetonius, *Life of Domitian*, 21.

Bibliography

Barrett, Anthony A., *Caligula's Quadrans Issue*. Latomus, vol. 57, no. 4, Societe d'Etudes Latines de Bruxelles, 1998, pp. 846–52.
Bedoyere, Guy De La, *Praetorian, The Rise and Fall of Rome's Imperial Bodyguard*. Yale University Press; 2018.
Bird, H. W., *Diocletian and the Deaths of Carus, Numerian and Carinus*. Latomus, 35(1), 123–132. 1976.
Bond, Shelagh M., *The Coinage of the Early Roman Empire*. Greece & Rome, vol. 4, no. 2, 1957, pp. 149–159.
Beard, Mary, *SPQR; A History of Ancient Rome*. Profile Books, 2016.
Cassius Dio, *Roman History* (translated by Earnest Cary). Loeb Classical Library, Harvard University Press, 1914 thru 1927.
Collins, Andrew W., *The Palace Revolution: the assassination of Domitian and the accession of Nerva*. Phoenix, vol. 63, no. 1/2, 2009, pp. 73–106. JSTOR.
Eusebius, *The History of The Church*. Penguins Classics, 1989.
Eutropius, *Abridgement of Roman History*, (translated by Rev. John Selby Watson). Henry G. Bohn, York Street, Convent Garden, 1853.
Ferrill, Arther, *Emperor of Rome*. Thames and Hudson, 1991.
Freisenbrugh, Annelise, *The First Ladies of Rome*. Jonathan Cape, 2010.
Galen, *Selected Works* (translated by P.N. Singer). Oxford University Press, 1997.
The Fragmentary History of Priscus, Attila, the Huns and the Roman Empire AD 430–476 (translated by John Given). Evolution Publishing, 2013.
Gibbon, Edward, *The History of the Decline and Fall of the Roman Empire*. Penguin Books.
Grainger, John.D, *Nerva and the Roman Succession Crisis of AD 96–99*. Routledge, 2003.
Grant, Michael, *The Roman Emperors*. Phoenix Giant, 1996.
Graves, Robert, *I, Claudius*. Penguin Classics.
Herodian of Antioch's History of the Roman Empire (translated by Edward C Echols). Berkeley and Los Angeles, 1961.
Historia Augusta, Lives of the Later Caesars (translated by David Magie). Loeb Classical Library, 1921.
Holland, Richard, *Augustus; Godfather of Europe*. Sutton Publishing Ltd, 2004.
Icks, Martin, *The Crimes of Elagabalus*. I.B. Taurus & Co Ltd, 2011.
Jones, Brian W. Jones, *The Emperor Domitian*. Routledge, 1993.
Josephus, Flavius *The Jewish War, (translated by William Whitson, A.M, Ed.)*
Juvenal, *The Sixteen Satires* (translated by Peter Green). Penguin Books, 2004.
Levick, Barbara, *Tiberius the Politician*. Thames and Hudson, 1986.
Livy, *The Early History of Rome* (translated by Aubrey De Selincourt). Penguin Classics, 1971.
Livy, *Rome and the Mediterranean* (translated by Henry Bettenson). Penguin Books, 1976..

Kemezis, Adam, *The Fall of Elagabalus as Literary Narrative and Political Reality: A Reconsideration*. Historia: Zeitschrift Für Alte Geschichte 65, no. 3 (2016): 348–90.
Kulikowski, Michael, *Imperial Triumph*. Profile Books, 2018.
Kulikowski, Michael, *Imperial Tragedy*. Profile Books, 2019.
Maranon, Gregorio, *Tiberius – A study in resentment*. Hollis and Carter, 1956.
Marcellinus, Ammianus, *The Later Roman Empire* (translated by Walter Hamilton). Penguin Classics, 1986.
Martial, *The Epigrams* (translated by James Michie). Penguin Books, 1978.
McHugh, John.S, *The Emperor Commodus; God and Gladiator*. Pen and Sword Military, 2015.
Ovid, *Fasti* (translated by A.J. Boyle and R.D. Woodard). Penguin Books, 2004.
Penthouse Magazine, *Caligula Special*. May 1980.
The Works of Philo of Alexandria (translated by Charles Duke Yonge). London, H. G. Bohn, 1854–1890.
Pliny the Elder, *Natural History: A Selection* (translated by John Healey). Penguin Books, 1991.
Pliny, *The Letters of the Younger Pliny* (translated by Betty Radice). Penguin Books, 1969.
Plutarch, *Roman Lives* (translated by Robin Waterfield). Oxford World's Classics, 1999.
Potter, David, *The Emperors of Rome*. Quercus, 2007.
Seneca, *Letters from a Stoic* (translated by Robin Campbell). Penguin Books, 2004.
Sidonius Apollinaris, *Letters* (translated by O.M. Dalton). Oxford at the Clarendon Press, 1915.
Southon, Emma, *Agrippina: Empress, Exile, Hustler, Whore*. Unbound, 2018.
Southern, Patricia, *Ancient Rome; The Empire 30 BC–AD 476)*. Amberley Publishing, 2011.
Southern, Patricia, *Domitian: Tragic Tyrant*. Routledge, 1997.
Sozomen, *Ecclesiastical History* (translated by Chester D. Hartranft). Nicene and Post-Nicene Fathers, Second Series, Vol. 2. Edited by Philip Schaff and Henry Wace. Buffalo, NY: Christian Literature Publishing Co., 1890.
Statius, *Complete Works*. Delphi Classics, 2014.
Suetonius, *The Twelve Caesars (*translated by Robert Graves). Penguin Books, 1989.
Svyanne, Ilkka, *Caracalla, a military biography*. Pen and Sword Military, 2017.
Syme, Ronald, *The Roman Revolution*. Oxford University Press, 1960.
Tacitus, *The Annals of Imperial Rome* (translated by Michael Grant). Penguin Books, 1989.
Tacitus, *The Histories* (translated by Kenneth Wellesley). Penguin Books, 1995.
Taylor, L. R., *Tiberius' Refusals of Divine Honours*. Transactions and Proceedings of the American Philological Association, 60, 87–101, 1929.
The Res Gestae, Deeds of the Divine Augustus (translated by P. A. Brunt & J. M. Moore). Oxford, 1969.
Trafford, L.J., *Sex and Sexuality in Ancient Rome*. Pen and Sword History, 2021.
Wallace-Hadrill, Andrew, *The Emperor and His Virtues*. Historia: Zeitschrift Für Alte Geschichte, vol. 30, no. 3, 1981, pp. 298–323.
Wallace-Hadrill, Andrew, *Suetonius*. Bristol Classical Press, 1995.
Wellesley, Kenneth, *The Year of the Four Emperors*. Routledge, 2005.
Winterling, Aloys, *Caligula*. University of California Press, 2001.
Zosimus, *New History*. W. Green and T. Chaplin, 1814.

Index

Actors and the theatre, 8, 27-28, 53, 72, 143, 145
Aetius, Flavius, 172-74, 175
Agrippina the Elder, 21, 22, 40, 182 n 5
Agrippina the Younger, 22, 34-5, 40, 44, 64, 131
Alexander Severus, 138, 143-4, 146, 147, 148
Antonia, mother of Claudius, grandmother of Caligula, 22, 182 n.5
Arbogast, 168-70
Army, 2-3, 5-6, 8, 11, 21-2, 56, 61, 81, 93, 103-4, 105-6, 119, 124, 128, 152
    battles/campaigns of, 30-1, 41, 53, 57, 101-2, 118-9, 139, 152-3, 165, 167, 185 n.12
    Diocletian's reforms of, 160-2
    expectations and pay of, 6-7, 9, 10-1, 48, 123, 151, 160
    lack of discipline, 55-6, 58-9, 113, 168, 169
    role in picking own emperors, 49, 52-3, 59, 65, 91, 94, 95, 147-8, 156, 166, 169-70
    punishments of, 44, 45-6
    role in 3rd Century Crisis, 156, 157, 159-60
Augustus, Emperor, 1, 2-17, 20-1, 26, 35, 69, 73, 77, 129, 164, 183 n.27
    account of own life (Res Gestate), 8-13, 17
    achievements of, 8-11, 12-3, 54
    as model emperor, 23, 41, 70, 73, 92, 108, 152, 156,
    family of, 7, 21-2, 67,
    legacy of, 85-6, 101, 159-60, 188 n.10
    morality laws of, 29, 55, 183 n.24
    powers of, 4-7, 14, 17, 42, 61, 75
    route to power, 3-4
    and the Senate, 4-5, 6-7, 8, 12, 14-5, 75
    succession, 17, 19, 164
Augustus, as a title, 67, 73, 144, 160, 187 n.17
Aurelian, Emperor 270-275 CE, 157-8

Brutus, Lucius, 1, 2, 183 n.21
Brutus, Marcus, 4, 31-2, 180 n.2

Caecina, Alienus, 52-3, 57, 60
Caesar, Julius, 2, 3, 9, 14, 31, 50-1, 73, 111, 170, 180 n2 &5, 181 n.8, 183 n31
Caligula, Emperor 37-41 CE, 19- 42, 63, 76, 86, 97, 120, 122, 129, 132, 178, 179
    accuracy of accounts, 24, 33-6
    assassination, 31-2, 42, 44, 172
    cruelty, 25-6, 37, 83, 114, 134, 145
    campaigns of, 30-1, 41, 165
    expenditure, 54, 29-30, 70
    good acts as emperor, 22-3
    in popular culture, 19, 32-4, 38, 111
    Insanity, 37-8, 41
    meaning of name, 121, 128
    relationship with Senate, 37-41
    reputation, 19, 72, 76, 83
    religion, 26, 35, 142
    sex life of, 24-5, 26-9, 34-5, 47
Caligula the Film (1979), 19, 26, 32-4
Capellanus, 152, 153
Caracalla, Emperor 211-217 CE, 121-7, 128, 132
Cassius Dio 68, 76, 91, 93, 119, 122, 147
    on Caligula, 23, 34, 39
    on Commodus, 99, 101, 102, 109, 110, 111, 113
    on Elagabalus, 129-30, 131-33, 135, 138, 139, 142
Christians/Christianity 80, 142, 163, 166, 167, 194 n.5

Index

Claudius, Emperor 41-54 CE, 10, 27, 42, 51, 64, 71-2, 135, 137, 182 n.51, 188 n.2
   executions under, 77
   invasion of Britain, 41, 64
   marriage to niece, Agrippina, 34-5, 63
Claudius Gothicus, Emperor 268-270 CE, 156-7
Cleander, Marcus Aurelius, 104-6, 108
Clodius, Publius 5, 180 n.6, 181 n.10
Commodus, Emperor 180-192 CE, 62, 85, 86, 99-113, 116, 118, 122, 129, 178, 191 n.4
   assassination and attempted assassinations of, 108-9, 111, 115, 119
   consequences of death, 112-113
   clothes of, 132
   devotion to Hercules, 110, 114, 148
   grandiose behaviour, 99, 100, 110-1, 190 n.53
   jokes, 107, 133
   military policy of, 101-2
   paternity of (see also Faustina), 99-100
   performances in the arena, 99, 107-8, 109-10
   relationship with Praetorian Prefects, 102-6
   see also Cleander and Perennis
   Senate, 100, 104-5, 108-10, 111
   sex life of, 106
Constantine the Great, Emperor 306-337 CE, 129, 162, 163
Crassus, Marcus 2, 7, 181 n.17, 185 n.10

Damnatio Memoraie, 76, 121, 127, 191 n.6
Decimation, 45-6, 55, 185 n.10
Diadumenian, Emperor 218 CE, 130, 135
Didius Julianus, Emperor 193 CE, 60, 112-18, 176, 178
Diocletian, Emperor 284-305 CE, 129, 158, 159-62, 194 n.4
Domitia Longina, Empress, 67, 72, 83
Domitian, Emperor 81-96 CE, 61-83, 85, 90, 104, 131, 144, 157, 172, 179, 188 n.2
   alban villa of, 67, 75, 161
   assassination of and aftermath of, 78-9, 82, 87-8, 91-3, 95, 112
   building programme of, 70-1, 72-3
   campaigns of, 73
   growing paranoia, 79-82, 83, 114, 176, 178
   in 69 CE, 64-7, 74
   in court poetry, 39, 182 n.48
   see also Martial
   marriage to Domitia, 62, 67, 72
   morality laws of, 55, 186 n.4
   personality, 73-4, 81, 97
   relationship with brother Titus, 64, 68-9, 73, 74, 81
   relationship with Senate, 62-3, 63-4, 74-8, 79, 83, 108
   religion 73, 75, 80, 142, 157
Drusilla, sister to Caligula, 22, 38, 39, 40

Elagabalus, Emperor 218-22 CE, 128-46, 148, 172, 178, 191 n.4
   appearance of, 131
   and cult of Elagabul, 128, 138-40, 142
   death by rose petals, 133-4, 192 n.22
   end of, 143-5
   foreignness of, 137-8
   humour, 133-4
   origin of name, 128
   promotion of women, 140-1
   sexual excesses of, 134-6
   sources for reign, 129-30, 135, 140, 141-3
Emperors
   assassinations of, 31-2, 82, 85, 87, 108, 111, 114, 126, 128, 145, 147, 158, 174
   backgrounds of, 43-4, 69, 148, 156, 159, 161-2
   generosity to the people, 9-10, 14, 23, 46, 70, 92, 145
   importance of character, 11-3, 36
   powers of, 5-7, 17, 61-2, 159-63
   what makes a good emperor, 8-15
Eunuchs, 53, 58, 68, 70, 133, 138, 140, 145, 163, 173, 174

Faustina, Empress, 97, 99-101
The Five Good Emperors, 85-6, 101, 121, 164

Gaiseric, Vandal king, 175-6
Galba, Emperor 68-9 CE, 32, 43-9, 51, 52, 88, 95, 112, 144, 157, 178, 188 n.1

comparison with Nerva, 88, 90-1
harshness of, 43, 55, 44-6
   see also decimation
health, 46, 131
pre-emperor career, 43-4
relationship with the praetorian guard, 48-9, 116
Galen, 12, 182 n.39
Games, 10, 11, 15, 16, 88
   emperors role in staging 10, 22-3, 24
Germania, 7, 11, 32, 43, 64, 69, 73, 79, 88, 112, 127, 137, 164-5
   defeat of Quintus Varus by Arminius, 26, 185 n.6
   Caligula's campaigns, 30-1
   legions of in 69 CE, 49, 51-3
Germanicus, father of Caligula, 21-2, 183 n.6
Germanicus used as a title, 61, 73, 99, 164
Gibbon, Edmund 85-6. 95, 96, 101
Geta, Emperor 211 CE, 120-27, 128, 172, 178
   assassination of, 126
   personality of, 120, 122
   rivalry with Caracalla, 121-3, 124-7
Gordian I, Emperor 238 CE, 151-8, 177, 179
Gratian, Emperor 375-383 CE, 164-6, 167

Hadrian, Emperor, 117-38 CE, 36, 86, 129, 137
Heraclius, 173-4

Infames, 28
   see also actors and the theatre

Jews/Judaism, 7, 26, 34, 64, 68, 142
Josephus, Flavius, 34, 37
Julia Domna, Empress, 124, 126, 128, 132, 191 n.6
Julia Flavia, niece of Domitian, 63, 73
Julia Maesa, 128, 131, 132, 140, 143
Justina, 167-8
Juvenal, Decimus Junius, 27, 28

Laetus, Quintus Aemilius, 111, 113, 114-5, 119
Lamia, Aelius, 67, 76, 80, 82

Livia, Empress, 22, 188 n.2
Lucius Verus, Emperor 161-9 CE, 96-8
   and Marcus Aurelius, 97-8
   social life of, 96-7, 122

Marcia, 111, 119
Marcus Aurelius, Emperor 161-80 CE, 11, 62, 86, 99-100, 114, 118
   campaigns of, 101-2
   in comparison with Lucius Verus, 97-8
   paternity of Commodus, 100
Mark Antony, 3, 4, 28, 46, 77, 125, 181 n.8, 185 n.10
Macrinus, Emperor 217-8 CE, 128-9
Martial, poet, 39, 71, 78, 79, 137
Maximus, Magnus, 167-8, 169
Maximus Thrax, Emperor 235-8 CE, 148-9, 151-4
   background of, 148
   death of, 153-4
Messalina, Empress, 27, 35

Nero, Emperor 54-68 CE, 27, 44, 45, 48, 76, 96, 130-1
   death, 42, 47, 81, 87, 112, 188 n.2
   Piso plot, 89-90
   popularity, 46, 51
Nerva, Emperor 96-98 CE, 87-95, 144, 178, 179, 182 n.5
   acts as emperor, 91-2
   becomes emperor, 87, 112
   connection with the Piso plot, 89-90
   praetorian plot against, 93-5
   pre emperor career, 88-91

Otho, Emperor 69 CE, 49, 60, 74, 76, 80, 90, 188 n.2
   dandy past of, 96
   fights Vitellius, 52-3, 56-7, 65, 185 n.12

Perennis, Sextus Tigidiús, 102-4, 105, 106, 108
Pertinax, Emperor 193 CE, 112-3, 114, 115, 117, 118, 119, 121, 144, 157
Petronius Maximus, Emperor 455 CE, 171-77, 179
   acts as emperor, 175-7

conspiracy to murder Valentinian III, 174-5
involvement in the murder of Flavius Aetius, 172-4
pre-emperor career, 171
Philo of Alexandria, 34, 36, 38
Pliny the Younger, 80
on how Trajan became emperor, 94-5
relationship with Domitian, 62-3, 76, 77, 79, 83
Pompey the Great, 2-3, 12, 23, 31, 180 n.5-6, 181 n.10, 181 n.17
Praetorian Guard, 42, 47-8, 57, 91, 111, 119, 126, 152, 156, 185 n.12
plot against Nerva, 92-5
rewarded and expectation of reward, 23, 46, 116-7, 118, 146, 152
role in removing emperors, 31-2, 47-9, 112-3, 128, 144-5, 153, 159
sale of the Imperial throne, 115-6

Quintillus, Emperor 270 CE, 156-8, 178

Religion, 26, 34, 110, 75, 136, 140, 141-2, 163, 167, 194 n.5,
Imperial cult, 15, 35, 37, 63-4, 73, 74, 77, 110, 157, 181 n.8
introduction of Goddess Cybele, 138-9
Secular Games, 71-2
Vestal Virgins, 8, 30, 80, 136, 141, 143
Roman Republic, 1-4, 13, 17, 31, 42, 71, 104
Augustus claims to have restored, 4-5
failure and collapse of, 2-3, 7, 180 n.6
founding of, 1

Sabinus, Flavius (brother to Vespasian), 58, 59, 65, 76
Sabinus, Nymphidius, 47-8, 103, 116
Sejanus, Lucius, 21, 22, 40, 47, 103, 120, 144, 182 n.5
Senate/Senators, 23, 26, 42, 47, 61-2, 66-7, 73, 87, 89, 90, 99, 103, 125, 128, 137, 139
during the Republic, 2-3, 5-6
forming of, 1-2
importance of pleasing, 13-5, 49, 63

involvement in plots against the emperor, 39-40, 82, 108-9
overlooked, 56, 61, 74-6, 104-5, 115-16
persecution of by emperors, 29, 31, 37, 40-1, 76-8, 79, 81, 85, 100, 109-10, 111
relationship with Augustus, 3-5, 7, 8, 12, 14-5, 17
relationship with other emperors, 63-4, 88, 91-2, 95, 117-8, 129, 131, 135, 140-1
role in treason trials, 20, 21, 40
Septimius Severus, Emperor 193-211 CE, 120, 121, 128, 132, 137, 176
addresses sons behaviour, 122-3, 125
becomes emperor, 118, 119
Sex, 23, 31, 55, 81, 100, 135, 140
see also Caligula the film
homosexuality, 26-7, 28-9, 50-1, 106, 135
incest, 29, 33, 34-5, 38, 140, 186 n.4
sex lives of emperors, 24-5, 26-9, 30, 63, 106, 134-6
Silbannacus, Emperor 253 CE, 154, 155
Suetonius, Gaius Tranquillus, 9, 20, 43, 48, 51, 54, 131, 140, 182 n.3
account of Caligula's reign, 21, 22, 23, 24, 26, 29, 30, 33-7, 41
dismissed from court, 184 n.60
on Domitian, 63, 64, 67, 68, 69, 70, 71, 72, 73, 76, 77, 79, 80, 81
reliability of, 24, 33-6, 41, 64, 68, 76, 80
Sulla, Lucius Cornelius, 2, 3

Tacitus, Publius Cornelius, 6, 7, 21, 36, 37, 44, 47, 88, 89, 148
lost account of Caligula, 34-5
on Domitian, 66-7, 75, 77, 79, 93
on Year of the Four Emperors, 49, 53, 55, 56, 57, 59, 65
Tarquinius Superbus, 1
Theodosius the Great, Emperor 347-395 CE, 168-69
Third century crisis, 48, 146, 147-9, 154, 159-60, 161, 162, 164, 167
See also Gordian I, Silbannacus, Quintillus
Tiberius, Emperor 14-37 CE, 19, 23, 29, 35, 36, 50, 61, 70, 76, 131, 179, 182 n.5, 183 n.6

persecution of Imperial family, 21
personality of, 20, 22, 182 n.3,
training to be emperor, 7, 17, 21, 69, 70, 181 n.17
treason trials under, 20, 25, 39-40
Titus, Emperor 79-81 CE, 62, 65, 75, 80, 90, 129, 182 n.51,
rivalry with brother Domitian 63-4, 68-9, 70, 74, 81
Trajan, Emperor 98-117 CE, 85, 86, 94, 95, 137, 156
Tribune of the Plebs, 5-6, 62, 95, 180 n.5, 181 n.10

Valens, Fabius, 52-3, 55-6, 57, 60, 148
Valentinian I, Emperor 364-375 CE, 164-6
becomes emperor, 166
power threatened by Arbogast, 168-70
Valentinian II, Emperor 375-392 CE, 164-70
Valentinian III, Emperor 425-455 CE, 172-4, 175

assassination of, 174-5
murder of Aetius Flavius, 173-4
Vespasian, Emperor 69-79 CE, 63, 68, 73, 76, 85, 90, 129, 135, 182 n.51
battle with Vitellius, 56-9, 60, 64-5
propaganda of, 50
rule of, 61-2, 67, 69, 70
Vitellius, Emperor 69 CE, 50-60, 63, 66, 74, 86, 95, 129, 144, 145, 178, 179, 188 n.2
abdication, 58-9, 60, 65
declared emperor, 49, 51-3, 148
gluttony of, 53-5, 120
loses of control over army, 55-6, 58-9, 60
pre-emperor career of, 50-1
response to Vespasian's advance, 57

Year of the Four Emperors, 69 CE, 49, 50, 61, 87, 90, 112, 149
see also Domitian, in 69 CE
Year of the Five Emperors, 193 CE, 112, 149